THE RAILWAY PAINTINGS OF

Wrenford J. Thatcher

Caught on Canvas

THE RAILWAY PAINTINGS OF
Wrenford J. Thatcher
Caught on Canvas

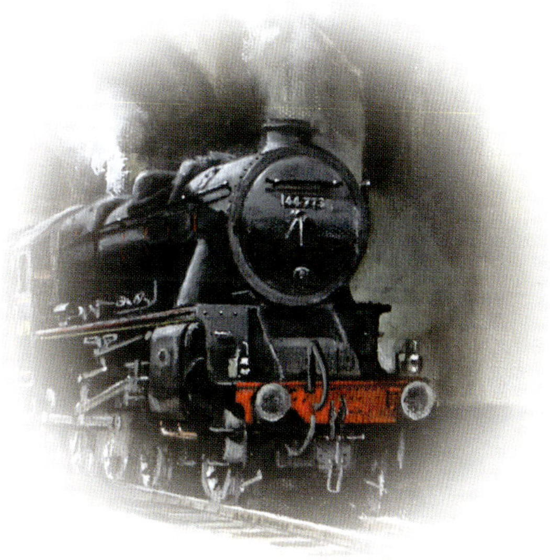

HALSTAR

First published in Great Britain in 2015

British Library Cataloguing-in-Publication Data
A CIP record for this title is available from the British Library

ISBN 978 1 906690 60 1

HALSTAR
Halsgrove House,
Ryelands Business Park, Bagley Road,
Wellington, Somerset TA21 9PZ
Tel: 01823 653777 Fax: 01823 216796
email: sales@halsgrove.com

Part of the Halsgrove group of companies
Information on all Halsgrove titles is
available at: www.halsgrove.com

Printed in China by Everbest Printing Co Ltd

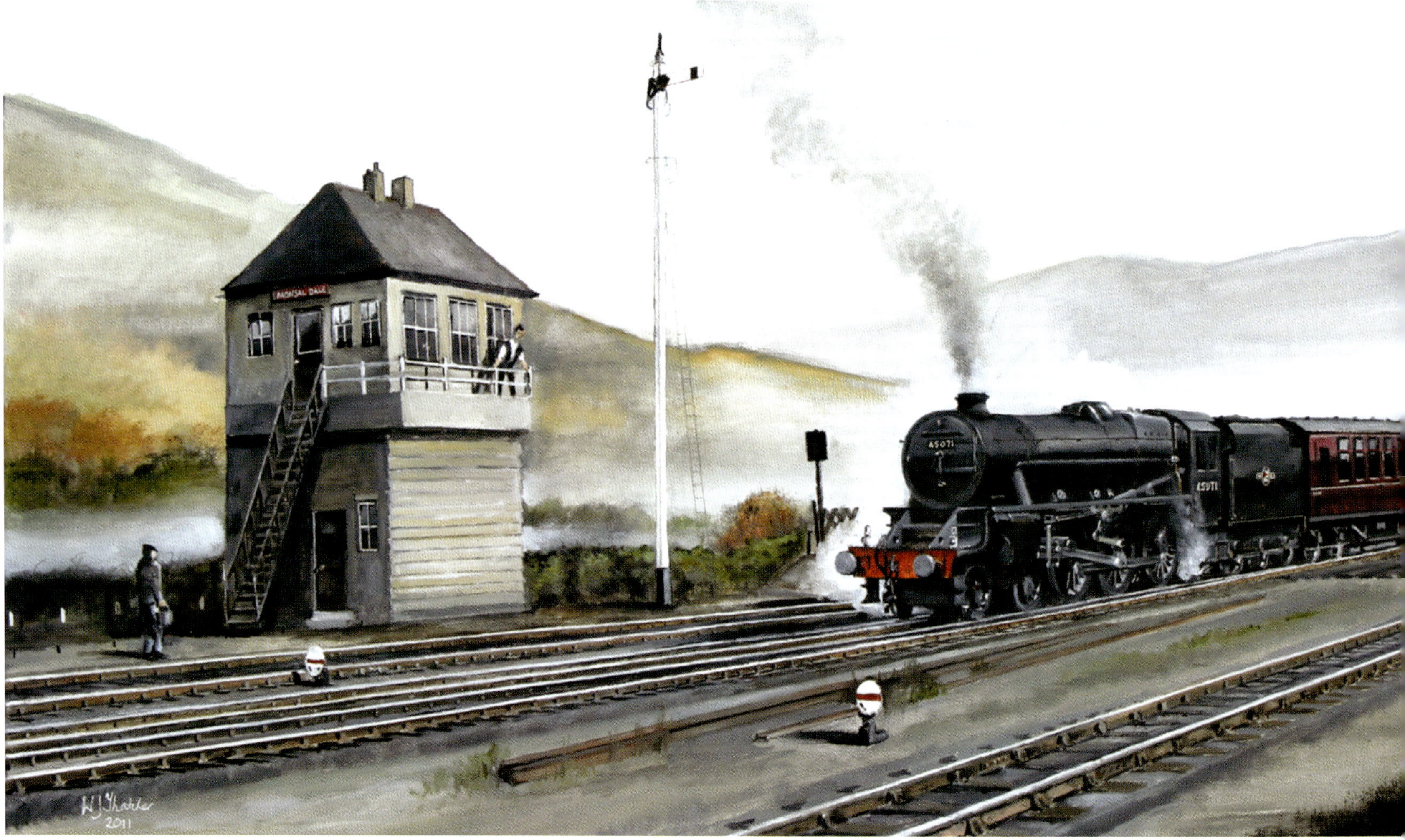

Contents

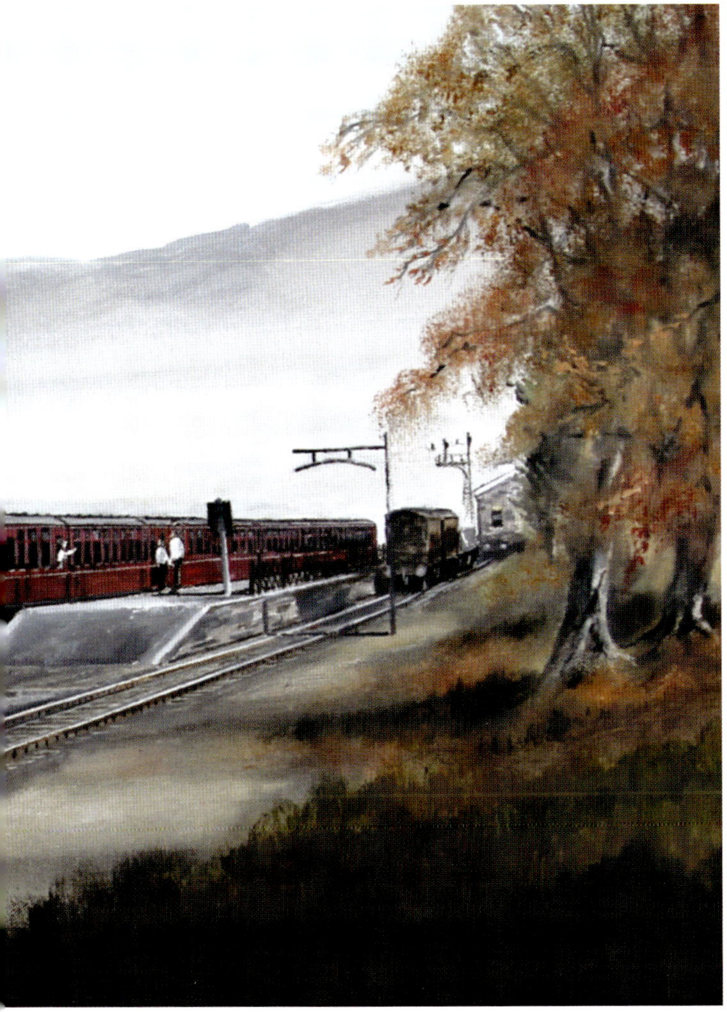

Acknowledgements 8

Foreword 9

Introduction 11

All Our Yesterdays 13

THE PAINTINGS

Early Paintings 21

New Beginnings 27

Paintings of the Big Four 38

Images of the War Years 56

The Birth of British Railways 60

Index 144

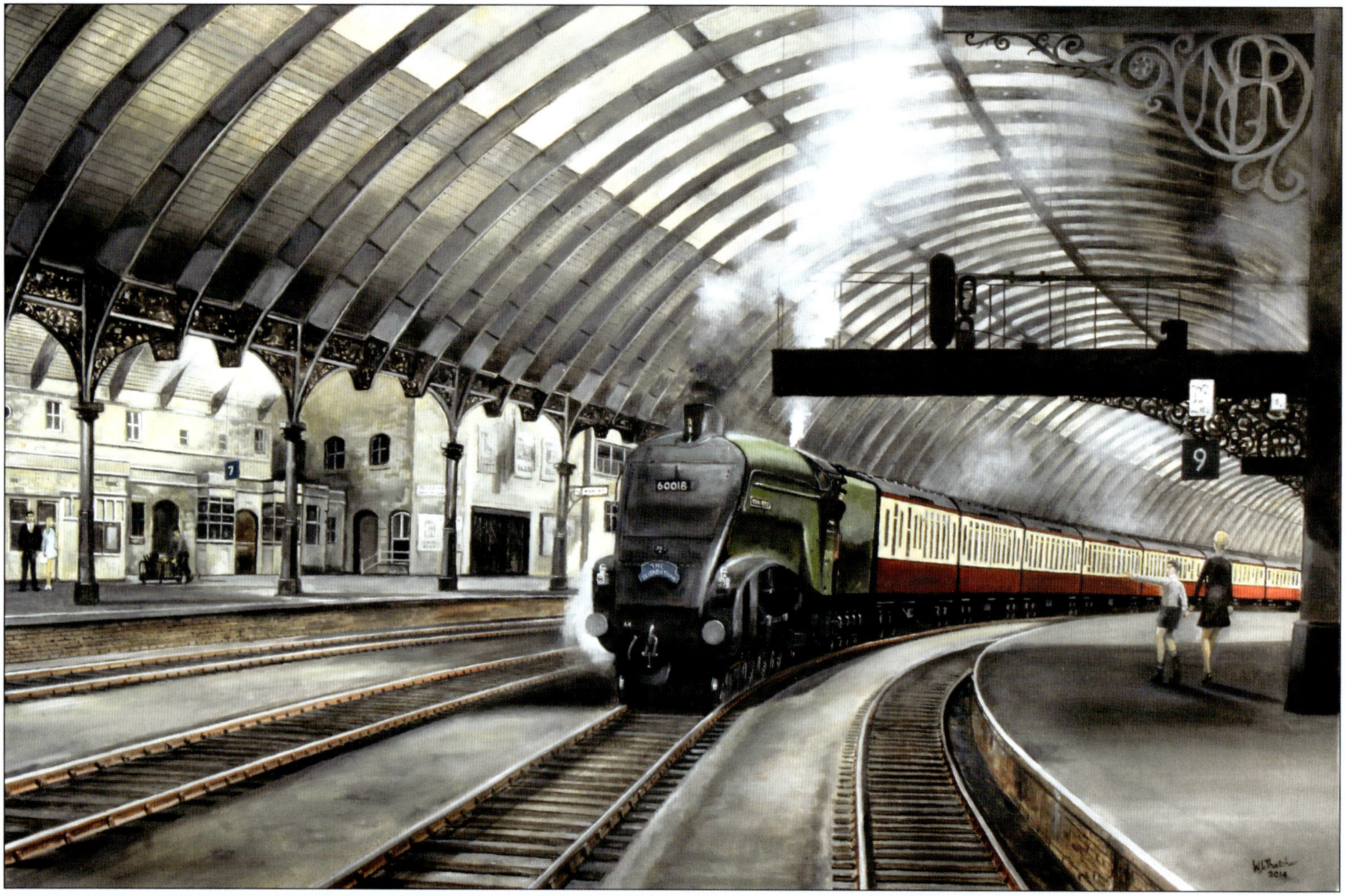

Sparrow Hawk, a streamlined A4 Pacific on the Elizabethan Express, non-stop from Kings Cross to Edinburgh Waverley.

The Non-Stop

...1953 – Fog in London
thick, yellow, it hangs over the station.
Even the steam and smoke
are lost in the gloom and darkness.

Slowly, with infinite weariness,
the great train grumbles its way over the points
and rattles its way over the joints
of rails laid in the form of a maze.
from a terminus which has known better days.
From the Thames to the Forth – leaving at last,
through gasworks tunnel, not too fast,
up the bank so slow to Wood Green,
with power to spare, she blows off steam,
and gathers her stride as we pass Hatfield South,
the whistle now blows like foam at the mouth
of a galloping horse, as the wheels beat a tune
and we start to emerge from the dark and the grime.
'cross the Cambridgeshire levels we racket along
with the click of the wheels a joyful song.
Past Huntingdon's Spires, to the plain of York
she lives up to her name – she's called 'Sparrow Hawk';
for this is her calling, this her trade
built for speed, that's why she was made.
The last of the line, the best of them all,
tho' neglected-run down, still answers the call.
Her coat, once green, is now sooty black
but the headboard she wears is the pride of the track.
There's rust on her now, and her piston glands leak,
small boys at the trackside still yell 'it's a streak!'
The smell of hot steam, cinders and coal
to drive one of THOSE still is their goal;
as we thunder along and the coupling rods fly
the wheels just a blur as the smoke streams by;
the windows of carriages covered in grime,
unloved and uncared thro' the ages of time;
but the passengers know from the buck and the sway
and a glanced station clock as we speed on our way'
this train still means business, this train is still quick
just listen how those rail joints click;
only slowing for York as we take the great bend
through the station and out, a message to send.
Just watch us fly now – now that we're free,
covered in filth and grime, maybe,
but Darlington's next at a mile a minute
a task so easy, no need for the limit
imposed on the train, the track and the crew,
with a white hot fire, see what they can do
as we flash through the station at 90 again
and leave behind in the wind and the rain
the glorious smell of smoke and hot oil,
a just reward for the engineman's toil.
As we sweep round the coast and over the border
the exhaust still beating in rhythmic order
until at last we ease down and drift into Auld Reekie
as Edinburgh was once known.
But not today, as we snuffle gently under the cavernous roof of
Waverley station.
Windows are pulled down.
Hands struggle with door handles,
Doors slam, people meet and hug;
Suitcases are thrown on trolleys,
and the great locomotive sighs gently as her fires cool,
and she basks in the admiring glances
of those who have come to see this hero –
who got them in 3 minutes early...

W.J.Thatcher
March 2007.

Acknowledgements

I HAVE BEEN ENCOURAGED by so many people I can only hope that I do not omit people who have inspired me either in my painting, photography or writing. My earliest encouragement, naturally, came from both of my parents who submitted my work into competitions at the early age of 4. Success is usually motivating to a child, and a succession of teachers, notably Mr Brown of Green Lanes School and Mr Cannell, art master of St Albans County Grammar School, gave me unstinting help, guidance and opportunity. The famous war artist Adrian Hill also gave me both encouragement and self confidence in my early teens. In later years I received help from so many, including Hazel Thatcher, our daughter Lorna, and her husband Francois; also Dr David Williams, Margaret Dalton, John and Joan Dewhurst, Mary and Bob Tout, Karen Bethell of the North Norfolk News, Adrian Hill (senior) and Adrian Hill (junior), and all the staff of Picturecraft, Simon Butler of Halsgrove, Dr Karl Heinz Ognibeni, Richard Philips, Mary and Jeffery Springham, Nigel and Juliet Sayers, Tony Cornell, Dennis Glew, Amy Rigg of The History Press, Laurie Carmalt, Derek and Joan Sidaway, John and Janet Brown, Julian Crutch and Tricia Horry, Graham Elliot, Graham Kenworthy and all the members of the Norfolk Railway Society, John Blake and all the staff of the North Norfolk Railway, Brian and Barbara Merry, along with the former chairman of Goodyear Chemicals UK, Norman Wood, and last and most importantly Patricia Elstow, together with John and Irene Nockel without whom I may never have started exhibiting my paintings at Picturecraft, much less written this book.

Foreword

I CAN VIVIDLY RECALL Wrenford Thatcher's opening introduction… *"I've met THE Adrian Hill … are you by some way related?"*

Bearing the same name as a highly respected artist has inevitably prompted many similar conversations over the years, particularly as my life revolves around working within the fine art industry. However, Wrenford Thatcher's conversation led me to discover that we both shared a great interest in *THE* Adrian Hill.

In the very earliest days of television Adrian Keith Graham Hill (1895–1977) became a household name presenting a BBC Children's programme called 'Sketch Club'. Wrenford Thatcher was amongst thousands of children greatly influenced by this long-running television series and eventually found himself featuring on the programme where his own artwork was showcased and personally appraised by Adrian Hill. To this day Wrenford Thatcher attributes the encouragement that he received from meeting Adrian Hill as a significant factor in furthering his interest to paint.

My personal interest in Adrian Hill developed from a curiosity which eventually started my investing in and eventually becoming an avid collector of his original works. Research into my namesake revealed that he had been a past President of the Royal Institute of Oil Painters (PPROI) and a member of the Royal British Artists (RBA). An official War Artist on the Western Front from 1917–1919, many of Adrian Hill's paintings and sketches are now held at the Imperial War Museum in London. My collection contains many of Adrian Hill's inspirational books that were published as instructional guides on painting and drawing techniques. Like Wrenford Thatcher, I now find myself also following in Adrian Hill's footsteps, not as a painter but as an author of several titles published by Halsgrove.

I was delighted when Wrenford Thatcher asked me to prepare the Foreword for this wonderful book that features so many of his superb paintings. I have been privileged to represent Wrenford's original works in my gallery for a number of years and his exhibitions have always been met with tremendous enthusiasm, particularly on the occasions when he decides to paint on site. His knowledge and fascination for British railways, especially his love of the era of steam, is deep rooted and derives from early years spending time in the company of his grandfather visiting railway stations and travelling on trains.

Wrenford Thatcher has perfected a style of painting that encompasses precision and great attention to detail. He readily accepts any challenge demanding of complex perspective and is a master in the subtlety of light in his work. Each painting faithfully represents an accuracy within its own historical timeframe reflecting Wrenford's unquestionable passion for railway engineering – both on and off the track.

I confess to having been cautious when originally showcasing Wrenford Thatcher's paintings, a subject that we openly and honestly discussed from the outset. Initially unsure of its appeal and commerciality we agreed for a trial exhibition where a modest collection of six original oil paintings were shown. Wrenford chose to exhibit landscapes, just one depicting a steam train. This single exhibit proved to be the highlight of the collection and the interest expressed by the public signalled a positive way forward for Wrenford to concentrate solely on railway paintings.

Working tirelessly over many months for a one-man exhibition in his home town of Sheringham, Wrenford was devastated to discover at the 11th hour that the venue was unable to stage his show. How fortuitous that I was in a position to come to his rescue. Not only was the exhibition in my gallery tremendously successful, it achieved exceptionally high levels of attendance and virtually every painting was sold. More importantly for me it paved the way to furthering our personal friendship and close business association.

As the pages turn, 'smell the steam' and immerse yourself in Wrenford Thatcher's extraordinary ability to take you on a nostalgic journey through each of his remarkable paintings.

ADRIAN HILL
The Picturecraft Gallery,
HOLT, Norfolk

JANUARY 2015

Introduction

IT ALL BEGAN BY ACCIDENT. As a child I had won several prizes by having paintings exhibited on 'Sketch Club', a BBC television programme run by the celebrated war artist Adrian Hill – of whom more later. By chance I was loaned a book about the paintings of Felix Berlusconi and on the inside of the jacket was a reference to Adrian Hill of Picturecraft, an art gallery in Holt, Norfolk, and only 6 miles from my home. Thinking that this must be a relative of *the* Adrian Hill I promptly visited the gallery with some of my book prizes from the great man only to discover that neither Michael Hill nor his son Adrian was related to him, but that Adrian was writing a biography about his namesake! And so it was that I started exhibiting there, and eventually contacted Simon Butler and Halsgrove publishing through their gallery.

So here it is. A book containing most of my railway paintings accomplished over a period of nearly 70 years. Not all, because in the folly of my youth I did not keep photographic records of my paintings and it was not until Kodak launched Kodachrome 64 slide film that I was able to make adequate copies of my work anyway. I estimate that some 30 or so paintings have never been recorded but subsequently sold, so if you are in possession of one of these early masterpieces, I hope you will do the decent thing and dispose of it quietly!

Introductions are traditionally used to outline the contents of a book. This book is all about the paintings, information about the subject of the paintings, and anything related to composition and execution. However, the section entitled 'All Our Yesterdays' is included to set the tone of the paintings and the era in which they were done. Very soon there will no longer be anyone alive who actually grew up in the time when steam engines were the norm, an era when diesels were unheard of or at least invisible to the British public. We have already reached the time when the Heritage railways run diesel galas; the lifetime of these machines were so brief that they are already history. Steam had lasted 150 years; diesel locomotives were to last about 30.

Of course, when young, we thought that steam would go on for ever. With our ABC spotters' books we would see a frequently viewed locomotive and shout 'Scrap it!'.

Well... they did.

The paintings in this book represent my attempt to relive the years before that fateful day in 1968 which saw the end of working steam on our British railways. In creating these paintings I have had to make use of my own extensive library of over 1000 books and journals, and my own photographs;

about 2000 negatives but most of poor quality or composition. I have also been fortunate enough to be painting in an age when the internet can be used as a wonderful source of reference. Railway enthusiasts are renowned for their attention to detail when it comes to their favourite locomotive; how often have I heard statements such as 'there wasn't a rivet there!'

Well I have done my best to appease the rivet counters, but with a difference. The vast majority of contemporary railway photographs – and paintings – are ¾ front views of locomotive and train. Some of my paintings are too, but a large number are not. I am looking for memories – what I remember of the stations, signals, tracks, buildings, even the weather. Often this has entailed a journey to the location of my chosen subject so that I can feel the atmosphere of the area, even if the original buildings are long gone. The photograph below is an illustration of this approach.

This photograph of Hatfield yard in 1959 illustrates the grime and dereliction of the place still recovering from the war. The old style lights and station canopy were in place; indeed the goods yard was there. Today the platform is almost bare save for a bus shelter in the middle. The coal, steam, dirt, lights, signals, engine shed, tank engine and yard have all gone. A housing estate stands in its place. Three tracks sweep through the station on the opposite side of the platform. Modern electric units speed past at over 100mph... as once did A4 streamline Pacific 'Silver Link' in the 1930s! Fortunately this latter event can be recreated on canvas as the reader will see.

Another of the advantages the paintbrush has over a camera lens is that pictures can be created that would have been very difficult to obtain at any time photographically, such as an aerial view of a station or a head-on view of a locomotive at speed. An example of this is the painting of north London in 1952, seen on page 61. The details of this painting were obtained by using an Ordnance Survey map of the entire area for that year together with all the information which I could glean from various sources such as local libraries, and the internet. Altogether the research took about six months and the painting about the same length of time.

With each picture in this book there are accompanying notes such as the foregoing, which outline facts about the subject matter and other points of interest. The railway enthusiast will know most of the facts about the locomotives but may not know all the details about the location and its history, so I have tried to include a little of both.

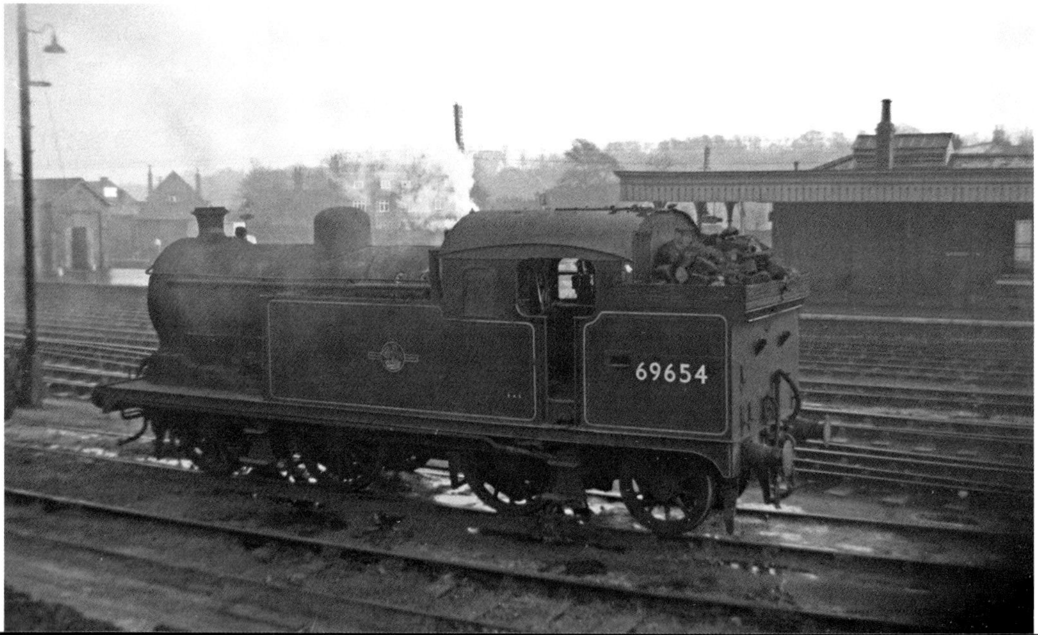

All Our Yesterdays

RECENTLY I HAVE TAKEN an interest in my family tree (as people tend to do as they get older!) and I observed how close to the place of their birth all my relatives lived. Often they moved no further than the nearest village, say two or three miles away. My paternal grandfather, Ernest Henry Thatcher (ET) was an exception. Born one of eight children, in the East End of London opposite the Blackwall tunnel which had not long been engineered by Marc and Isambard Brunel, he ran away to sea. When he returned some time in the 1890s he joined the Great Eastern Railway as a cleaner, and worked his way up through the ranks to the job all small boys wanted – an engine driver.

By the time I was born in 1944, together with my twin sister Penelope, one world war and the intervening years of depression had passed and another world war was in progress. We were moved frequently to avoid the V1 and V2 bombs which were by then falling on London and the home counties. Food was scarce and in the years of rationing which followed, there was not a lot of improvement. My parents left us with my grandparents at such times, as Grandad Ern had an orchard, a large vegetable garden, which he and my father cultivated, and a chicken run. He was also rearing pigs. Poor health meant I was spending long periods in the newly administered NHS hospitals which were still the dingy old buildings which had existed before the war but were now bomb damaged as well. However, as far as ET was concerned his grandson was not going to go short of food, and so it was that I learnt (when my mother was not watching us both) to scrape my plate clean with my knife and use it for pudding! It did not take long for this process to transfer itself to the footplate of grandad Ern's locomotive where his pigs provided the bacon and his hens the eggs of many a breakfast. ET was organised and took a special long-handled skillet into the cab which he hung beneath the driver's aspect glass. I dare say it was cleaner than a shovel. For all his care of his grandson, he was not an easy man to please on the footplate and could be very grumpy if he did not get his usual 'mate' firing for him. I remember him drawing a chalk line down the centre of the footplate and telling a new man to stay his side of the line and keep away from me while he was swinging the shovel. Ern and his mate seem to have been together since GER days, as he was still with the same man in the early BR days after the war. In his latter years as a driver ET suffered severe shock and subsequent ill health after a fatal accident in Bishop's Stortford yard in which a shunter was crushed between his engine and a rake of coal wagons.

It was during one of my rare spells at home between hospitals that I started my drawing and painting career! At the age of 4 I did a drawing of a battleship in huge seas, colouring it bright yellow with a crayon, and my mother (a state registered nurse) put it into a competition in the

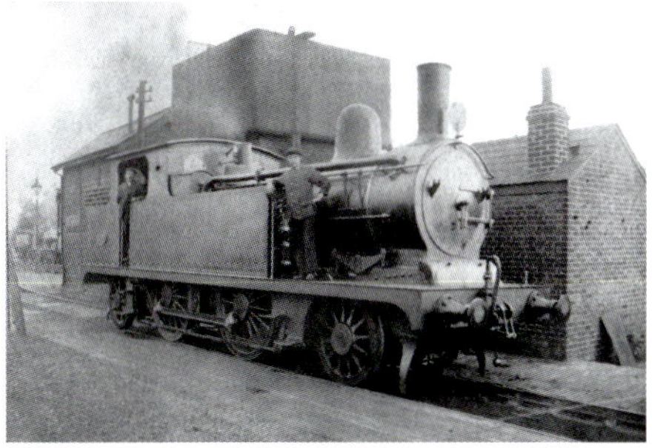

Ernest Thatcher (ET), fireman, leaning on the Westinghouse pump of 'his' engine c.1900. Taken with a plate film camera.

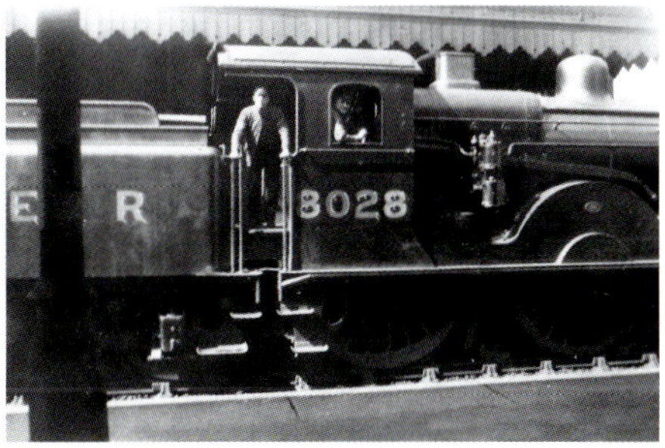

ET and mate in GER days at Bishops Stortford station. Photograph taken with a 'new' Kodak roll film camera.

Nursing Mirror. The judges must have been desperate because it won and was published too!

In those straightened days my parents would often take us for a walk on a Sunday afternoon – it was the sort of thing families did in the early 50s, and I am sure they thought it was good for my health, and that this was more than a contributory reason. Even during a walk in nearby Sherrards Wood (it is a housing estate now) we would inevitably head towards the wire fence which edged a very rural single line from Welwyn. There were only three trains a day on this branch, but I would wait for hours there in the hope of seeing one. My parents were very patient. I would go home and draw engines running between massive trees.

And so the seeds had been sown for my future hobby of railway art. Alas, my father had no interest in the railways, being a design draughtsman at the time for Welwyn Electrical, but he did his best by drawing steam engines with a ruler and compasses and sending them to me while I was in hospital. As my health deteriorated, so my parents became more desperate. We were living in a flat – built between the wars and which would be classed a slum by today's standards – at 17 Rodney Court in Hatfield, directly opposite the De Havilland aerodrome. It was cramped and although my mother kept it clean everywhere smelt mostly of boiled cabbages and urine. The aircraft factory was developing the new jet engines at the time for the Comet airliner, a world first, and the wind tunnel used for testing was run night and day. There was no noise abatement act in those early post war years. Eventually Dad was given a council house and the Rodney Court, together with Cumberland Court and Haddon Court were raised to the ground.

There was a bonus! The new council house was only a quarter of a mile from the railway, and Hatfield was on the East Coast main line! I had missed a lot of my early childhood involving gangs of trainspotters on the platform, and in any case the early Ian Allan ABCs were not easily available until the mid 1950s. Money was very tight to start with I could only afford an Eastern Region spotters ABC for the exorbitant sum of 2/6d (12p) but in those days a semi detached house cost £300; so the equivalent value of that ABC was £50!! I still have my first combined 1957–1958 volume ABC which cost 10/6d. It took me two years to save up for it. Armed with these priceless volumes I now started collecting numbers with a vengeance. My health had improved dramatically, thanks to a new drug called Terramycin, an antibiotic which was to have most unwanted consequences although it was a life saver at the time. I was now at a grammar school in nearby St Albans, a 25 minute bus ride away, where I soon met kindred spirits mad keen on the railways. A particular friend, Michael Bew (I wonder if he is still alive?), would visit me occasionally and I remember staying with him in his house in Harpenden overlooking the Midland line out of St Pancras. From there at about 7am and before school we would watch the sleeper trains from the north creeping past towards London; then catch a local train to St Albans, usually hauled by a Fowler 2-6-4t or occasionally a Fairburn tank. Of course we were strictly partisan. To me, nothing surpassed the Gresley Pacifics of the east coast, especially the A4s. To Michael, the Royal Scots and Jubilees were the zenith of railway design, although he did concede that he had visited Watford, that far flung suburb to the west, and seen Duchesses and Princess Royals which just might be a bit better!

At the age of around twelve I was able to venture as far as London. Although my first visit was with Michael I preferred doing this on my own, because my interests in the steam engine had already stopped being merely the 'copping' of numbers but the incredible aura of power these machines exuded. The memories of my first sight of Liverpool Street Station, a smoke-filled people-infested cathedral of steam, full of the noise of panting Westinghouse brakes, and announcements about trains to Gidea Park, wherever that was! Those huge new Britannia locomotives. You could actually get to *touch* them! Occasionally the driver would even let you on to the footplate, especially if I mentioned Ernest Henry Thatcher! (My other step Grandfather, Jimmy Dennis, was also a driver, on the MGNR now absorbed into the Eastern region).

Kings Cross was busier, but somehow more remote, and the staff decidedly less friendly, but St Pancras – what a magnificent station; but where were the trains? Compared with their eastern neighbours there was virtually nothing coming in or out of the station.

The Doric arch still bestrode Euston but the station did not live up to the grandeur of its entrance; it was tatty, seemingly an assemblage of large half-built sheds and although plenty of trains came and went it was quite difficult to see the arrivals if you were on the departure platform, and vice versa. Waterloo and Victoria similarly failed to impress. But if Liverpool Street was the king, Paddington was the queen of them all. The excitement of seeing the first copper-capped chimney of a 'Castle' as the stairs from the circle line gave access to the forecourt of that magnificent building will never be forgotten. The London stations became a heaven of sorts for me and hundreds of other small boys.

Rationing continued until the mid 50s, and so even these trips to London were done with the minimum of food. At home we would make up a day's milk supply from a blue and white tin labelled National Dried Milk, and at night both my sister and I were given a tablespoon of cod liver oil and malt, a sticky brown substance which looked like black treacle. To supplement the shortage of food, my father would dig three full-sized allotments and, with our neighbours, trade some of the vegetables for sugar or other rationed items. I would help him dig and weed those allotments – I still grow vegetables today, no doubt a result of those years. Gradually however, the rationing ended and food became more readily available. When sweets came off ration there was such a rush in the shops everything was sold out, and the government had to re-introduce rationing until the sugar supplies could keep up. Milk was now delivered in bottles, at first with a cardboard top then later with the aluminium foil caps which made wonderful flying saucers at school. And I wonder how many people remember those glass bottles of Corona with their wire clipped lids?

Still, I digress. While my interest in railways blossomed so did two other hobbies, photography and painting. At school I was considered to be naturally gifted by the art teacher, Mr Cannell, who I remember so well. He was a very short man with a ginger moustache and a fiery temper. I came top in art throughout my school life and I have never ever seen a man so angry as he, when I announced to him that I was going to London University to read maths and physics. I had by this time won eleven prizes from the BBC television programme 'Sketch Club', and naturally my interest was primarily in drawing and painting steam engines I also had a fascination in old buildings and in doing sky and seascapes; but photography was a quicker way of recording the images I wanted to treasure, and all my pocket money went on film, first for a dreadful little Kodak Brownie 127 plastic camera with an equally dreadful plastic lens. This horror had a single shutter speed of 1/25 second and a fixed-focus lens which gave gross prismatic aberration in the corners of every print. With it I tried to 'freeze' trains travelling at 70mph speeding through Hatfield. The camera had been a present from my parents so I persisted longer than I should, but eventually bought a Ferrania 44 which gave decent images and a shutter speed of 1/250, so at least the image quality started to improve if not the composition. I don't suppose the image quality was enhanced by the fact that I did my own developing of the negatives, without a developing tank, to save money. This was accomplished in a cupboard under the stairs after sunset but many a film got 'fogged' when someone went upstairs and put the hall light on!

Eventually I accepted the folly of taking such risks and purchased a Johnson's 'Universal' developing tank. Universal meant it could suddenly come apart in your hands in the dark leaving you searching for the end of the film for the next 10 minutes or so! Still it was a great improvement on trays of developing solution and fixer, and enabled results such as the one shown below.

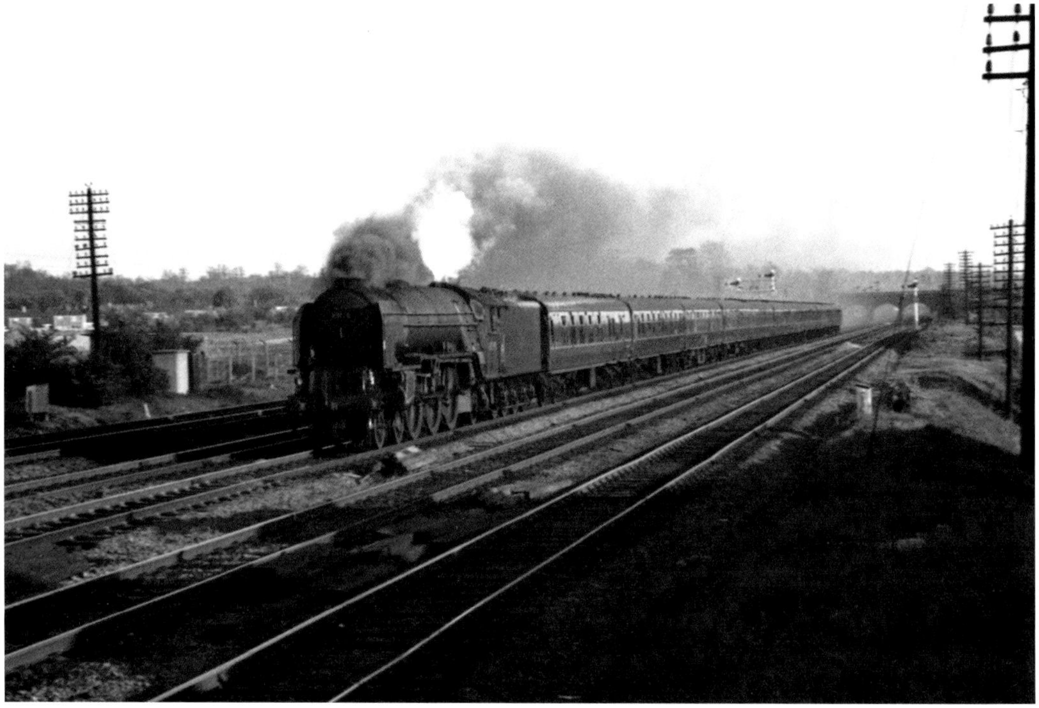

60120 Kestrel on the ECML at Hatfield

Like so many, I had no idea that the life of these wonderful locomotives was to be so short. Even the advent of the first diesels did not sound the warning bells it should have. Steam had *always* been there – it always would.

But then normal life in the shape of, youth clubs, girlfriends, then university intervened, and my time for railways became greatly diminished. It was not until I was married and living in St Andrews in Scotland that it resumed to any extent. I had by then completed a first degree in London then an

MSC and a PhD in Aston Birmingham, followed by a post-doctoral fellowship in Liverpool University. In St Andrews my interest in railways resumed in the company of Dr David Williams. It was immediately apparent that David was a lot better photographer than I. Our attendance of the St Andrews Railway society was occasionally graced by WJV Anderson, one of the all time great railway photographers. How I wish he had photographed more of the infrastructure, because he, like so many others, concentrated on the locomotive and train. When he composed pictures of steam in the landscape the results are outstanding.

During this time David arranged passes from Ian Allan and *Trains Illustrated* for the two of us to photograph the end of steam in West Germany. The line from Rheine to Emden was a Mecca for all steam enthusiasts as steam had been banned in the UK since 1970, the last public steam train having run in 1968. Unlike the UK the Germans had sensibly kept theirs running until electrification had been completed, thus largely avoiding the expensive interim phase of dieselisation.

I realised that I needed some much better kit than I had hitherto carried and invested in a Ricoh XR7 and a Minolta SLR, one with black and white film of far better quality than my post-war material, and the other with Kodachrome 64, probably the best slide film produced. Thus equipped we were able to get some good shots of the last days of steam there, and the article was duly published. David in the meantime had seen some of my railway paintings, which had started to emerge again, and commissioned a painting to celebrate the trip.

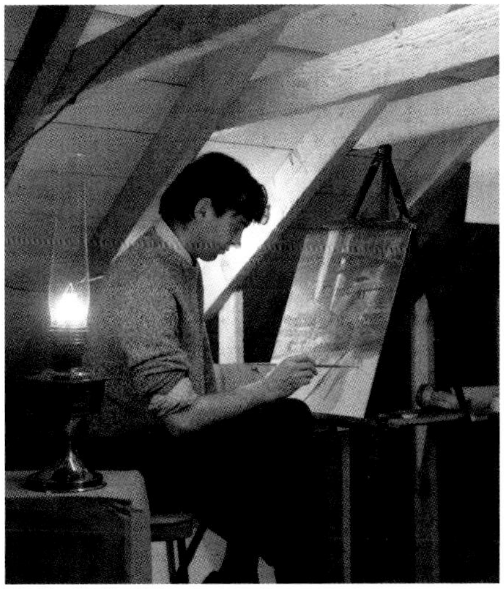

Artist at work in Cupar, Fife...

The loft of our house in Cupar was a good place for a studio, as it kept me, and the smell of turpentine, out of the main living area. There was no natural light so I painted using special blue 'daylight' bulbs. I now notice that these early paintings have a faint, not unpleasant, warm cast to them. I received a number of commissions after exhibiting in a local art club show, and to my surprise some of these came from overseas.

At the weekends my wife Hazel and I used to go walking in the hills to the north of Dundee, and spent a lot of our holidays on the west coast of Scotland exploring the Hebridean islands. On one occasion a gentleman by the name of Conan, an American, saw me sketching and asked if I would do a painting of his car. It was a 1900s steam car, and he had shipped it over on a Cunard liner! I agreed to do a painting at what I thought was an exorbitant price, only to learn later that Mr Conan was one of America's wealthiest civil engineers! When I had completed it, I sent a slide of the finished article to him for approval. Back came the reply, the fisherman in the river is holding the wrong sort of fishing rod! – and the arc of the bridge is one degree out!! I corrected both, but to this day do not know if I was being wound up! I was invited to the hanging in New York but because of work regrettably I was unable to go.

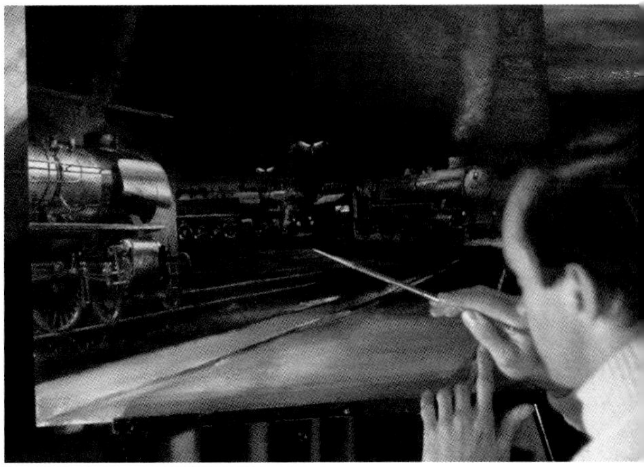

...and painting German steam

It was about this time I started experimenting with the new acrylic paints which, I was promised, would have the same permanence as oil paints but dry much quicker. And how! As a medium, in my view, they are for the professional who gets it right first time. I also found it difficult to obtain the same subtlety of tone which I could achieve with oils, but acrylics had the distinct advantage that a painting could be completed 'on site' and dry enough to carry home. Thus it was that I started doing seascapes, inspired by the glorious sunsets which are a regular feature of the Western Isles.

I also discovered that, no matter how remote the location, as soon as I put an easel up and started work, there would be someone looking over my shoulder! It was uncanny. While being watched

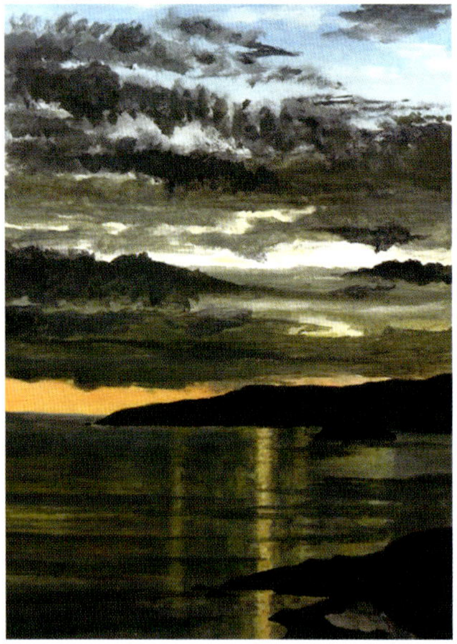

Lochinver sunset

whilst I paint does not worry me, it can be very distracting, and I found that I needed to work very quickly indeed with the rapidly diminishing light and ever-changing sky.

But our time in Cupar was not destined to be very long. Two events changed everything. My father died suddenly from a heart attack at the age of 56, leaving my mother a widow in Cromer, Norfolk, over 400 miles away. The other factor was my employment in the Department of Astronomy, St Andrews, where I discovered that the head of the department was not following normal University protocol, and this was affecting all the observatory staff. As Hazel's father was also unwell, and also 400 miles away, we decided with great regret to move south with our daughter Lorna who had been born a year earlier. I left the academic world behind for employment in industry.

The years from the mid 1970s to the mid 90s were as changing as those from the post-war years to the swinging sixties. Inevitably, with a new career, there is not much time for hobbies, and with the total demise of steam on the main lines, my interest in railway photography all but disappeared. Travel had a lot to do with it too, as my new employer, Xerox, sent me from one place to another, and it was with this company that I made my first journey to the USA, not realising that I was destined to make many such journeys in the future. My railway knowledge was of assistance in the business of house hunting. We bought a house in Hitchin, Hertfordshire, which was due to become the end of the electrified section of the ECML into London Kings Cross. Sure enough two years later it was, and we were able to sell the house and pay off most of our mortgage as a result of the enormous inflation of the housing market in that time. It was at Xerox that I met John and Joan Dewhurst. John saw the financial (and tax!) possibilities of setting up a company to market fine art prints of my paintings: And I saw the advantage of selling prints rather than seeing six months' work disappear in five minutes at an exhibition! So we set up T&D Associates, and had some of my paintings printed as fine art prints which we sold at exhibitions and craft fairs all over the south of England. These fairs taught us both about public perception of art and of railway art in particular. They were totally unpredictable; sometimes frustrating, sometimes very successful but always interesting.

After a few years with Xerox it became obvious that the company was cutting back and likely to close in the UK, so I moved again, this time to Somerset where I joined Coates, a company with whom I was to be employed for the next 24 years. Regrettably, with the distance involved, it became increasingly difficult to keep T&D operating and we closed it down in the early 1990s.

During the years with Coates my railway paintings started to 'flow' again, but fairly slowly. I worked in the utility room behind the garage in our house in Frome, where I was able to leave paintings undisturbed during my frequent absences on business. In a way the paintings were a relaxation from the stress of work and sometimes took six to nine months to complete, but it was not a stress borne of necessity; more a desire to acquire a better lifestyle. Almost everything had changed since the early 1950s; from eating habits and availability of food to family life and travel which was now easy and cheap. The computer had arrived along with computer games. Youth clubs had gone and teenagers 'hung out' in the town centre of Frome. Street drinking became a problem and burglar alarms essential. Nobody left their back door unlocked anymore. In this new climate of growth, the railway preservation movement thrived, and I joined several of the preservation societies. The East Somerset railway was a mere six miles away, and I worked there as a guard at the weekends. During this time I was privileged to meet David Shepherd, the railway and wild life artist, on a couple of occasions. He was even kind enough to allow me to market some of my fine art prints alongside his in the station shop. David very much liked remembering the railways 'as they were', and to that end organised at least two 'dirty weekends' where all the locomotives, visitors included, were covered in BR style grot! David 'decorated' his 9F Black Prince using cocoa, flour, soot and almost any other material of a suitable hue. The result was incredibly realistic, and made me realize that painting steam locomotives needed to be done with the same skills. It was an education, and to this day I frequently adorn my locomotives with cocoa-coloured rust and streaks of lime in the appropriate places.

The turn of the century saw some major changes in my life. I was taken seriously ill and required major surgery, which entailed hospitalisation for a long period. This was rapidly followed by Coates, the company I was employed by, being taken over by a Japanese-owned American corporation, Sun Chemicals. That company, in its wisdom, started immediately cutting staff and reducing its area and range of businesses. At the age of 56 I was made redundant.

Redundancy at any age is stressful. Late in a career it can be a killer (my own father died of a heart attack after being made redundant). Determined not to follow his example, I looked for alternatives and went back to the education profession, this time teaching physics, and because of my artistic interests, media art. The local school of Somervale was underfunded and in special measures. I am pleased to say that during my time there it climbed to a 'good' rating and several students went to first class universities, some to read physics. I was also able to maintain some consultancy work as a result of my years in industry.

Sadly, while my career still progressed, my marriage did not, and I moved to Sheringham in Norfolk to look after my ageing mother, taking up a temporary teaching post in Swaffham. Five years later, at the age of 98, my mother died. She was one of the fiercest critics of my paintings. Nothing was ever right! If there were no people in the paintings it was 'where are the people?' If there were people they would be in the wrong place or the fashion would be wrong! She was an enormous source of encouragement.

This aside, the move had a profound effect on my painting hobby. Now, with a house of my own, I was able to use one room as a studio and another as a store. As a result of my fortuitous introduction to Adrian Hill at the Picturecraft gallery in Holt, I was encouraged to paint more than at any time before, and now I have the time to do so. I hope you enjoy the results in this book.

The Paintings

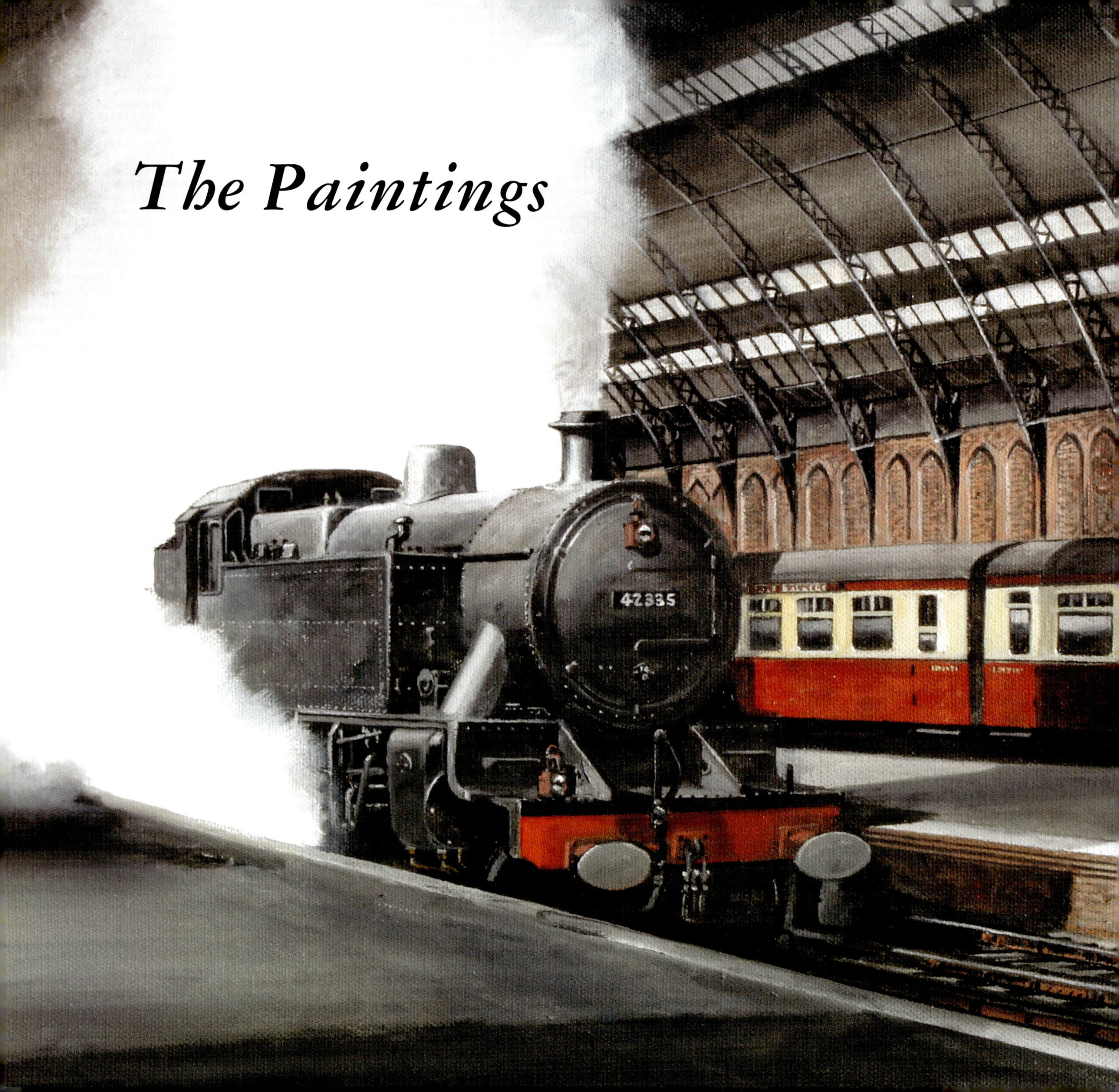

The Early Paintings

I HAVE DIVIDED THE PAINTINGS into three main categories: those which I completed prior to the turn of the century; the second section covering the pre-nationalisation period when the locomotives appeared in the liveries of the 'big four'; and the biggest section of all, the post-nationalisation period up to 1968 and the end of steam. I have also included a painting from the preservation years; a tribute to the many volunteers and employed railway staff on our heritage railways.

Looking back, my early paintings are clearly very different from those which evolved in the later years. For a start there is an almost complete concentration on the locomotive. Sometimes I even included a train, but not if I could help it! As a result these paintings lack the interest of the railway scene as a whole which I tried to capture in my later work. Evidence also exists of the experimental techniques used with the oil paints, a tendency to use a palette knife to cover large areas quickly or to paint smoke, sometimes successful others not. Many of these early works were also done on canvas board, which is much cheaper than stretched canvas and also much more rigid, making the paintings of fine lines somewhat easier. I was unaware of the tendency of these boards to curl with age, thus making the use of a strong frame essential. A finished painting can be enhanced or ruined by a frame. A good frame should ideally pick up the colours of the painting (or completely contrast them) and sit comfortably on the wall or final location in which the picture is to be hung. Frames are a very personal choice because of this, so I adopted a technique of painting round the edges of the canvas when I moved on to stretched canvases. This has several advantages. If desired, it does away with the need for a frame at all. It gives a three-dimensional aspect to the picture, and it 'opens up' the picture so that the subject does not seem to be restricted by the boundary of a frame. This latter characteristic seems essential to me with steam engines which may appear about to run into a solid wall when framed, or with cityscapes which should appear to spread far beyond the confines of the canvas.

Finally I abandoned the practice of varnishing the finished painting. This is normally done after about a year or two, i.e. when the painting is thoroughly dry. It has the property of brightening up the colours, essentially by dissolving the top layer of paint, and was carried out for many years as a means of protecting the pigments of the paint when those pigments were often hand ground, and the paints formulated by the artist.

Several things have happened since then; modern oil paints are very much high technology and utilise stable pigments wherever possible, together with binders, surfactants, fillers and solvent. A good knowledge of paint technology is important to any serious painter and my years spent employed by Coates Ltd were well spent in this context. In addition to this the varnish, even matt varnish, can reflect the light and make it very difficult to view the painting without it being spoilt by unwanted glare. And the wrong sort of varnish can have catastrophic results; it can remove the paint altogether.

Oil paints are still the medium of choice for me. Acrylics are too 'bright' and dry too quickly for my style of railway painting although ideal for landscapes. Oil paintings still have an enduring quality which acrylics have yet to demonstrate. After all my earliest paintings are now nearly 50 years old!

Rugby

Rugby lies east and south of Birmingham on the original route pioneered by Robert Stephenson for the London and Birmingham Railway. It is a very old railway town with a very long and proud railway tradition. The original station was opened in 1838, modified in 1840, and relocated to the present venue in 1885. In those early days of the railways, and long into the period of the London North Western Railway, Rugby was a location for changing locomotives, just as it had been for changing horses on the old coaching route. Rugby had railway connections to Stafford (the West Coast main line) Leicester, Birmingham, Peterborough and Northampton. It also had a second station serving the Great Central Railway. As locomotives became more powerful and capable of running longer distances with the aid of water troughs en route, the need to stop at Rugby gradually became less and less. Rugby is not large, compared with its neighbours of Birmingham or Leicester. So stopping train such as the one shown in the picture opposite became unusual in the latter days of steam, and by 2008 Rugby ceased to be the railway hub it once was.

The painting was one of my early essays into oils. I loved the sight of the railways at night, and steam added a wonderful dimension of excitement to it all. The sight of the dimly lit signal box with its row of levers I came to know well; today we have great 'power boxes' which cover vast areas of the railway network, though thanks to Mr Marples and Mr Beeching, none of it is as complex as it once was. I always marvelled at the complexity of the signalling system around Rugby. Coloured light signalling had long been adopted by the time this scene was portrayed. How drivers managed to unravel which signal was 'theirs' when semaphores were used will always remain a mystery. Coupled with the fact that the Midland division of British Railways was a very late adopter of automatic train control (ATC) this meant that misreading the signals could have disastrous consequences.

The locomotive shown is 'Princess Arthur of Connaught'. This name always appealed to me because I could not see how a Princess could have a male name! It was an unwise locomotive to choose because the number plate was twice as long as most of the other members of the class but at least it was a good performer – some members of this class of locomotive were definitely not. I did not do the necessary research to see if 46207 ever did actually stop in Rugby at night. I am sure someone will tell me it did not. The period of the painting is given away by the colour of the locomotive. From early BR days the engine had been painted Brunswick Green, but a very sharp PR department in the division decide in the late 50s to return some of the express locomotives to their LMS livery – a move very much approved by the public even if the standard of cleaning on the Midland did not allow it to be seen very often.

One thing which has not changed is the reflection of coloured light signals on shiny rails, although there are a lot fewer of them. But nothing will replace the glare of an open fire hole in the cab of a steam locomotive, the raw power of the machine visible for all to see, especially at night.

The painting was 'acquired' by my father who regrettably died very shortly after its completion, It has hung on my mother's wall for 42 years since, until her recent death at the age of 98. It still tells me the story I set out to capture.

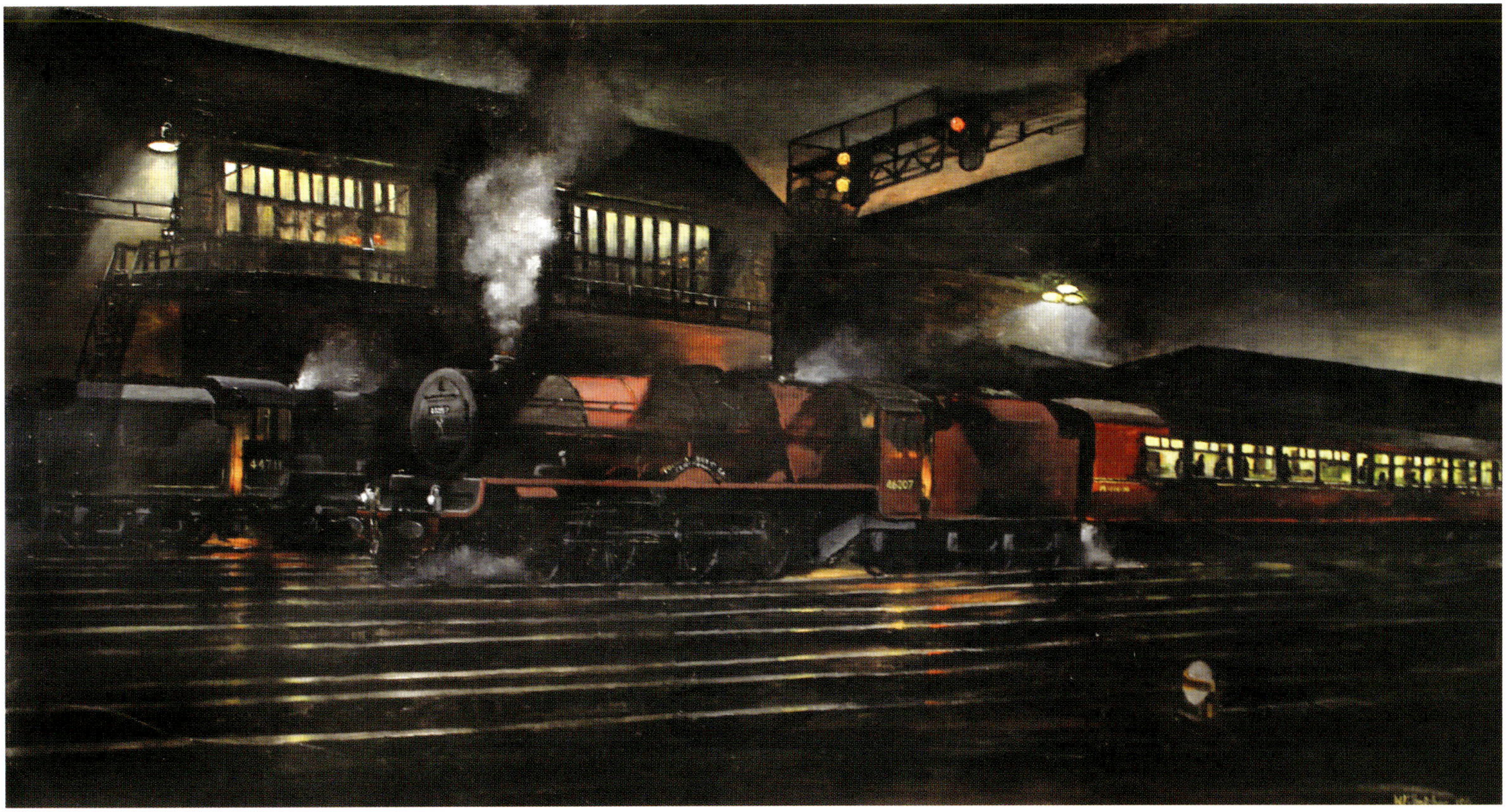

Princess Royal class locomotive 46207 'Princess Arthur of Connaught' departing Rugby at night. A Black 5 passes in the opposite direction, and although there are plenty of people in the train the signalman does not seem to be bothered whether his train has left as there is no one in sight.

Cromer Beach

Having both grandfathers as steam engine drivers had the tremendous advantage that whenever we travelled to see them, whether for holidays or for the day, I was bound to see a steam engine at some time or even get to go on the footplate. As my mother's parents lived in Cromer in Norfolk, this was always likely to be a holiday event, usually for two weeks, and a footplate ride was almost guaranteed due to the sheer proximity of the engine yard to their house at 60 Central Road, which incidentally was the house where my mother had been born.

This terraced property was once owned by the railway. It had been built by the Midland and Great Northern Joint Railway which I shall abbreviate to the MGNJR in future. My grandmother was a far-sighted woman and saved prudently all her life after her first husband was killed near Ypres in 1915. This and her war pension, together with the earnings of her second husband, James Dennis, enabled her to buy the house from which he set off to work every morning by walking twenty yards through the passageway between two mill-like buildings on the opposite side of the road to the engine yard of Cromer Beach station.

This is the view that he would have from this passageway, a view I had many times since I was given the job of taking Grandad Jim his morning tea still hot in a jug, and a bacon sandwich for his breakfast, to be delivered to him on the footplate of his engine, most often the elderly J15 seen in the picture. So this painting was done entirely from memory, and it was only much later that I was able to check whether I had got things in the right place with the help of the Norfolk Railway Society. Amazingly my memory was almost 100 per cent accurate. The space was a little more cramped than I have shown it, but to the eyes of a child of 6 or 7, spaces are always larger. The engine shed was also smaller and further to the left, and there was less space in the foreground, the turntable being right up against the bank; but apart from that it was just as I remembered it.

In the painting my grandfather can be seen leaning out of the cab, while his fireman does all the hard work pushing the engine around, a circumstance I have to say which was most likely true! Walking away with the bucket is uncle Fred, for many of my relatives seem to have been associated with or worked for the railways. Perhaps Uncle Fred is the reason why a man with a bucket appears so often in my paintings. In this case Fred's bucket would have contained the wood, oily rags, and paraffin that had been used to light up the fire, a ritual which I watched with great enjoyment when I got there early enough. The great lumps of wood were mixed with finer sticks and chopped up birch. These were thrown into the firehole and a few shovelfuls of coal lightly sprinkled over the top, with some paraffin poured over that. A paraffin-soaked rag was put on the shovel and lit with grandad's cigarette lighter (he always had a hand rolled cigarette dangling from his mouth), and this was thrown in on top of the coals. I never knew this technique to fail. The amount of filthy smoke from the chimney was incredible and the smell of all these things will forever remain in my nostrils, but it took no time to raise a big fire (well it seemed big to me) and about an hour later there was enough steam to move.

Today the yard has all gone, replaced by a supermarket car park. The station has all but gone, consisting now of a single platform and a bus-type shelter. The old station building is a public house and restaurant. The B1 and the water tower are no more but the cemetery is still there and so is 60 Central Road and the passageway.

What chance did I have of *not* wanting to become an engine driver?

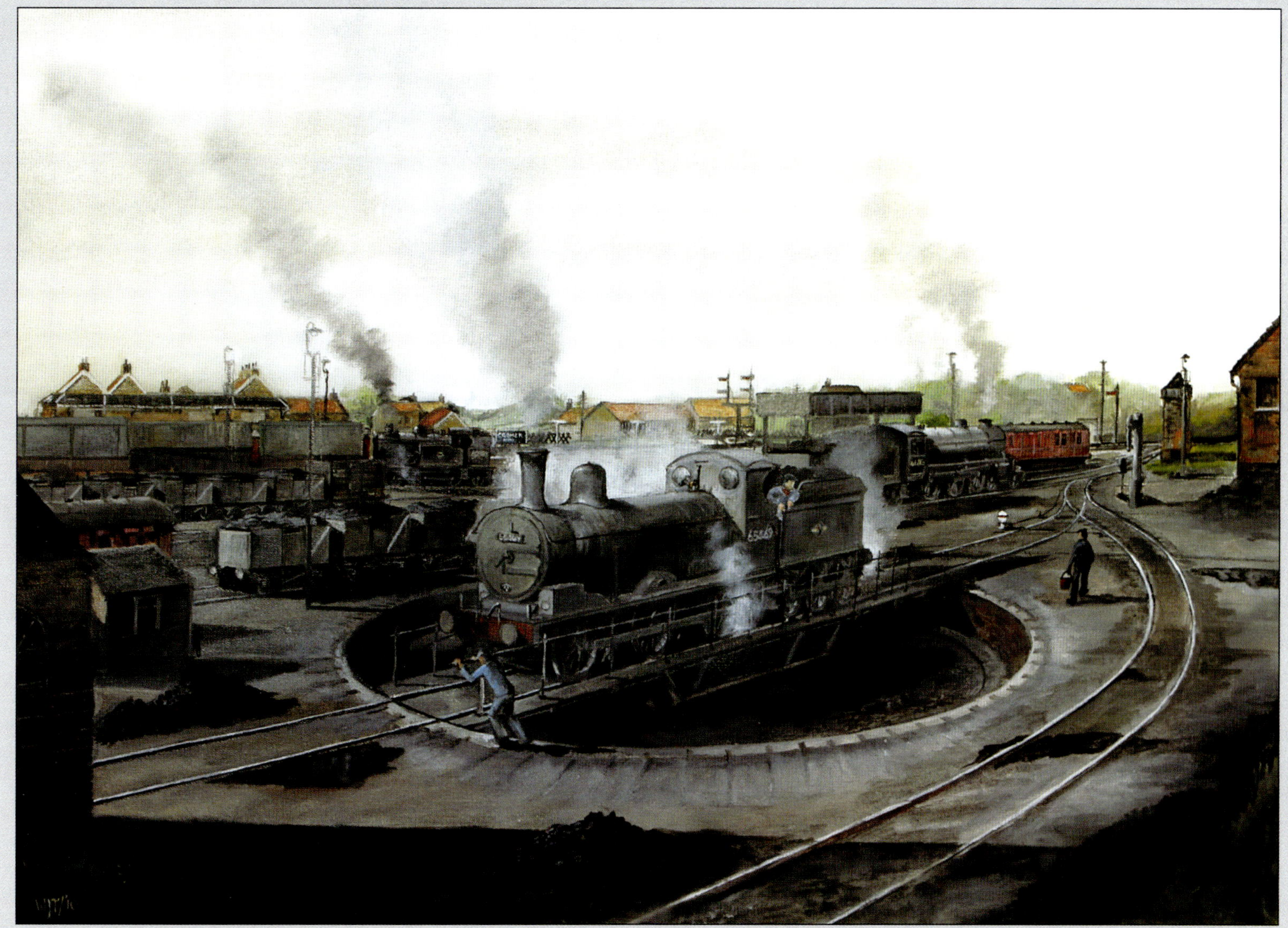

The engine yard and turntable at Cromer Beach

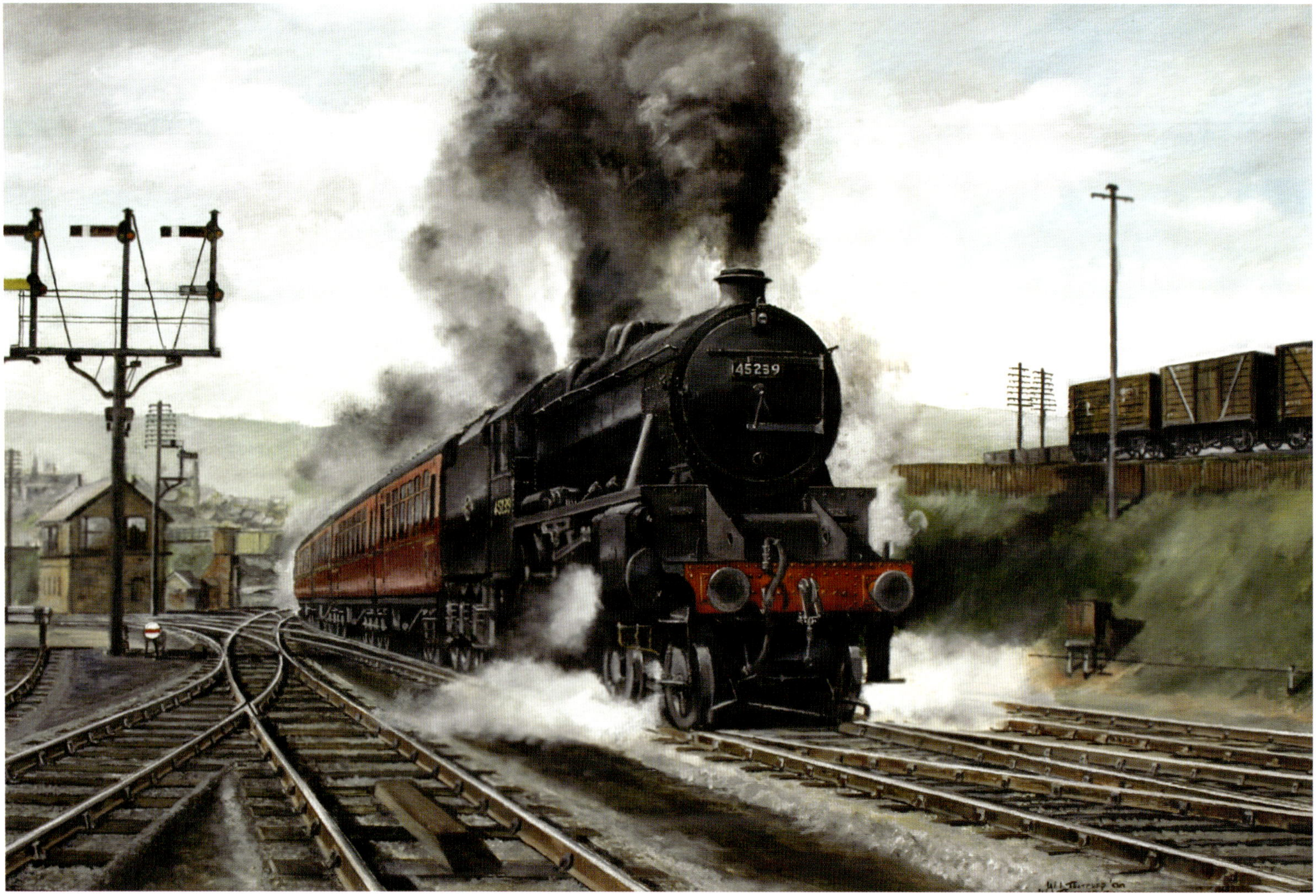

Black 5 at Buxton

Buxton was an important junction when the station opened in 1863, serving Manchester which was only 26 miles away, and via the Midland Railway, the route south to London St Pancras. Even in the 1950s there was a large amount of passenger and freight traffic through Buxton, much of which passed through Dovedale, Millers Dale and Chinley, all locations well known to the railway photographer. There seem to have been very few photographs taken of the station area itself. Alas the station was closed in the 1960s as part of the rationalisation plan, and the elegant frontage is all that remains. A road now runs through the site of this painting.

New Beginnings

IN THE EARLY 1980s my paintings took a significant new step. This was mainly due to Mr Norman Wood who was the Chairman of Goodyear UK at that time. I was working for Coates, a British company with a low profile but a very large market share in the manufacture and supply of printing inks, mainly for the newspaper industry. Goodyear UK was one of Coates' customers and during the course of business Mr Wood learnt of my painting hobby and interest in steam locomotives. His interest was mainly in collecting art, and this led directly to a viewing of my existing paintings followed by a commission. Like most non railway experts (!) he wanted a painting of the Flying Scotsman which must have been the best promoted and advertised train and locomotive of all time. This commission coincided with another development which had occurred while I was with my previous employer, Xerox UK. There my good friend and colleague John Dewhurst had suggested that my paintings could be marketed as fine art prints, enabling me to keep the originals which sometimes took over six months to complete, especially as my work frequently took me away from home for long periods of time. We had tentatively teamed up and formed a small concern, T&D Associates which we jointly financed and used to test the market, the first print actually being made in Midsomer Norton, the location of my new employer, Coates. More of this later.

Mr Wood's interest was twofold. He also saw potential in having a fine art print of his original painting, reasoning that the prints would enhance the value of the original; and so it was that he commissioned not only the original but a fine art print run of the same painting. Having learnt how expensive six-colour offset lithographic printing was, we looked for a printer with lower costs and found a small company local to my workplace who was printing cartons for a well known soap manufacturer using a six-colour offset Heidelberg press. Using a separate company to produce the artwork and printing two A3 sized images on one sheet enabled us to significantly reduce the manufacturing costs and produce Mr Wood's prints, half of which were kept by him as part of his commission agreement. The next time I approached the same printer to do another set of two prints he had learnt just how good his Heidelberg press was and the price doubled!

Looking back, I do not know how I managed to do this, while still painting in my spare time and working full time during the day. It was an exciting time, especially seeing one's own work being produced and emerging at great speed from an offset press. The speed is such that it takes the first 150 prints for the colours to settle down to their correct levels, so a print run of 1000 produces 850 useable prints, the first 150 being destroyed. And of course limited edition prints are numbered, for example 25/850.

Whatever the shortcomings of our enterprise on the Flying Scotsman, the new owner was so pleased with his painting, he took my wife and I out to dinner and insisted on having the painting propped up on a chair beside the dining table to be admired by the waiters. I think we all had rather too much wine that evening!

One feature worth mentioning is that about this time I started putting my bicycle in my paintings whenever it was realistically possible as a sort of trademark (in a similar way to Terence Cuneo's mouse, but a lot more practical – after all the bicycle often got me to the location of the paintings whereas the mouse... ?). It now occupies quite a lot of time for observers at my exhibitions who will spend hours looking for the bicycle, just as others did looking for Cuneo's mouse. There are a number of paintings in this book for you to practise on!

W1 Class Tank at Stewarts Lane

This was the second commission from Mr Wood. He had wisely discovered that giving a painter as much freedom of choice as possible with a commission gave rise to a much less stereotyped result. In this case I was given complete freedom of choice in terms of subject matter! So I chose to paint one of the very hard working W class tank locomotives which regularly plied their trade transferring goods from the north of London to the south, usually via the North London line. They were real working engines, which greatly appealed to me. None of the glamour of the big Pacific locomotives, and rarely seen on the major routes, except in the London area, these powerful machines went about their job with little fuss and less maintenance. They were developed by R.E.L. Maunsell from his successful N1 class, and entered service in 1931. Their high tractive effort of almost 30 000 pounds made them ideal for the heavy transfer freight trains.

The painting shows one of the members of this class, 31919, a Hither Green engine, standing outside Hampton's at shed 73A, Stewarts Lane. The painting very much relates to the history of the period and from the derelict appearance of the building, the date can be worked out at around 1953. Many photographs exist of this famous location, but always with a large Pacific locomotive outside (I have done a painting of one!), but the humble freight engines were ignored. It also gave me another opportunity to experiment with smoke-laden yellow skies so typical of the London area and most of the industrial cities of the Midlands and North of England. We have nearly forgotten how much yellow sulphur dioxide (along with carbon dioxide) was pushed into the atmosphere in those days – so much in fact that by the 1960s some environmentalists in Europe were complaining about destruction of their forests as a result of acid rain; the sulphur dioxide dissolving in the rain to form sulphuric acid. Considering that in the 1950s Britain had no option but to use coal – the country was nearly bankrupt as a result of the war – there was not a lot that could be done about it until the economy recovered.

The driver and fireman of 31919 seem to have had an argument from their body language! This was not intended but as the characters developed it seemed like a good idea. From the colour of the smoke coming out of the chimney perhaps the fireman has left the fire in a poor state. With the inferior condition of the track, as a result of wartime bombing in and around the southern part of London, it was the practice of most firemen to load the box, i.e. fill the fire box with coal every time the engine was at rest, as shovelling coal into the fire hole of a moving steam engine is not easy on a good track, and on a bad one the coal would often end up all over the footplate.

Stewarts Lane was no different to most engine sheds. Disposal of ash from the smokebox – the fireman's job – left heaps of ash in various places which had to be collected later and thrown up and into a wagon before being carted off for disposal. There were 120 locomotives and over 700 men employed at this shed in 1953, making it one of the largest railway depots in England. Stewarts Lane continued as a main line steam depot right to the end of steam. As steam declined it was converted into a diesel maintenance depot, a necessity for the Southern Region because third rail electrification had not been completed over the entire network, and British Railways were showing more interest in, first, dieselisation, then overhead electrification of the other routes out of London. Today, Stewarts Lane is operated by DB Schenker, a German company; which may be considered ironic considering the devastation of Battersea in the Blitz years.

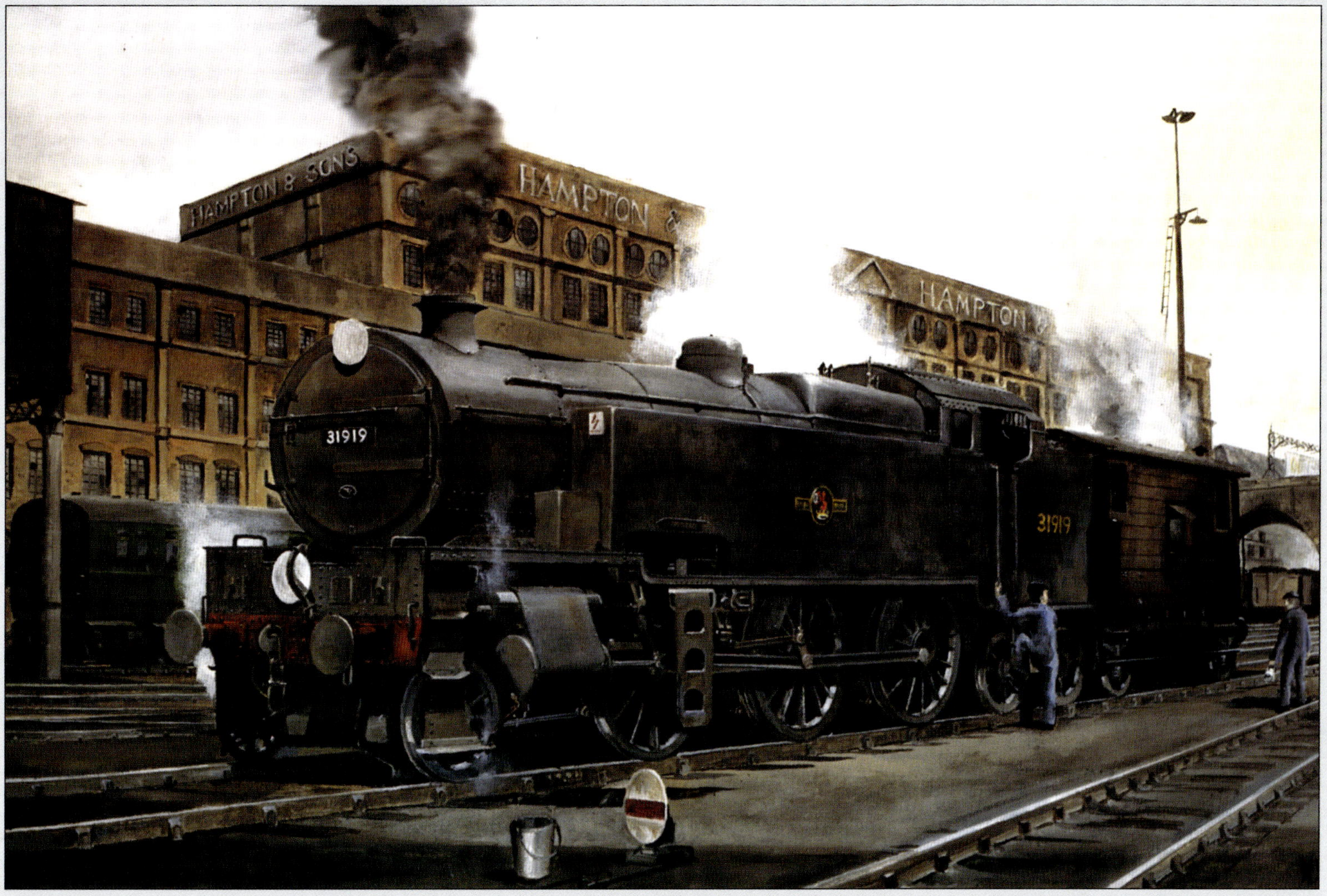

46200 W class tank at Stewarts Lane depot c.1953

'The Princess Royal' on Shap

Living in Scotland in the early 1970s gave me the opportunity of travelling and photographing locations in out of the way places. While my own particular favourite, the East Coast main line, had an easy passage into Edinburgh, it did not serve so many industrial towns as the West Coast main line. It did not have to climb Shap in the Lake District, or Beattock Bank in the southern Highlands either. Nor did it have to fight its way across the Pennine Hills as did the Midland railway. Whenever time permitted, I travelled to these places. My inspiration was undoubtedly the photographs of Bishop Eric Treacy. I tried to imagine what it had been like for him carrying just six precious glass plate negatives, a plate camera and a heavy wooden tripod over the narrow paths and over the stone walls of the Lake District. Like him, I found that even the sunniest day would have a heavy shower in it at best; at worst the rain was horizontal.

My other inspiration was WJV Anderson, whom I was privileged to meet at the St Andrews Railway Society. WJV was much younger than Eric Treacy and furthermore was an early adopter both of 35mm SLR camera technology and colour film These early colour films were mainly Kodachrome with an ASA rating of 12 or less, meaning photography of a moving train was difficult and without sunlight, impossible. This is probably why Eric Treacy stuck to the faster black and white film. Matters improved when Kodak launched Kodachrome 25, then 64, by which time it was almost too late for steam. So I have never seen a good colour photograph of a red 'Princess' Pacific, much less in the snow, climbing Shap Bank in British Railways days. Hopefully this will produce a spate of such photographs; enthusiasts have a wonderful hidden hoard of such treasures!

My solution was to paint the picture I would love to have seen. 'The Princess Royal' 46200 was the first of her class. I have had the dubious pleasure of travelling behind her twice since preservation; she broke down both times, the first with a catastrophic failure descending Shap! 'The Princess Royal' was the first large engine built for the LMS at a time when that group was desperately short of motive power for the Anglo-Scottish expresses. Much of the design was untried and untested, and the resistance to 'outsiders' by the Derby drawing office did not help either. Many of the earlier features of this locomotive showed the influence of Derby design practice, features which were modified from the third locomotive of this class onwards. In the course of time the modifications were also applied to this machine too. Apparently William Stanier was not impressed with her original build quality, but nothing can detract from the graceful lines and sense of power of this great machine, which I have tried to capture in the painting. It is very unlikely that the engine was ever as clean as this, especially after a hundred miles or so of travel! As is so often the case, with hindsight there are things I would have done differently. This painting was amongst my earliest, painted in the 1980s, and is still on canvas board. Since completing it I have studied probably thousands of images of smoke and noticed that there are characteristic smoke effects from different locomotives. The smoke in this picture is not quite right for a 'Princess Royal'. Furthermore the Midland red livery applied to these engines varied considerably in shade from one locomotive to another, and varied even further with the light and state of cleanliness, appearing more pink in dull light or under a coating of grime. This shade of Crimson Lake was seen only in bright overhead sunlight, and when freshly applied, as will be apparent from the colour of preserved specimens in the National Railway Museum! The tendency to see steam locomotives through rose-tinted spectacles diminished as the years passed.

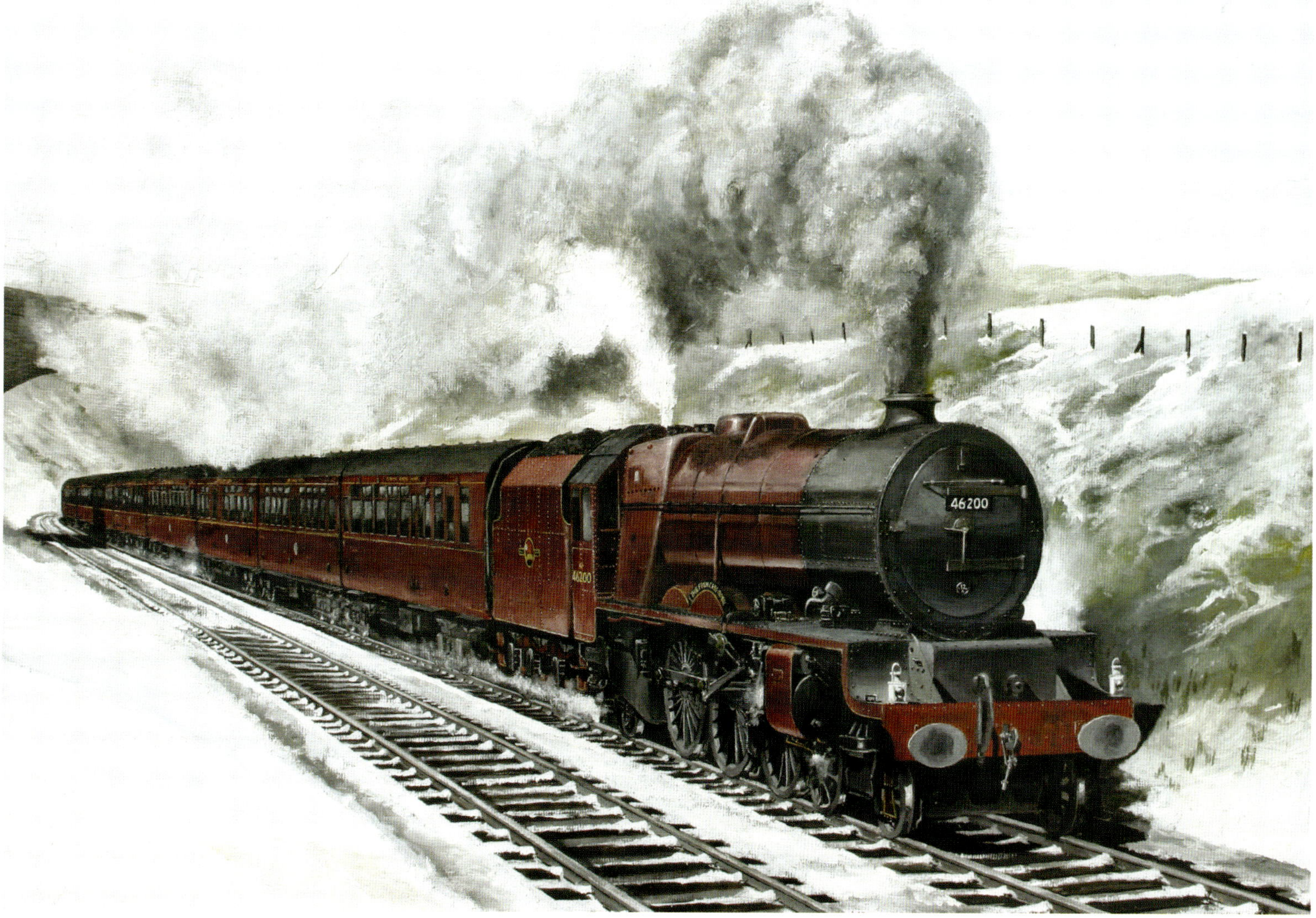

46200 'The Princess Royal' on Shap Bank

KGV at Old Oak Common

KGV was the abbreviation all trainspotters used for the first member of the King class locomotives, 'King George V'. The Western Region of British Railways was in most ways indistinguishable from its parent, the Great Western. The locomotive colour of Brunswick Green was little different from GWR green as applied at Swindon works. The Western continued to paint their carriages in chocolate and cream, instead of carmine and cream as used by all the other regions. In fact the Western carried on being exactly what it had always been, fiercely independent and absolutely confident that it was God's Wonderful Railway and better than any of its competitors!

And in so many ways it was! George Jackson Churchward, as chief engineer, had laid the foundations immediately after William Dean and the expiry of Brunel's broad gauge. Churchward realised the importance of maintenance as well as the need for modern efficient powerful steam locomotives, seemingly some 20 years or more ahead of his competitors. At some stage all the other major railway companies and their engineers (with the exception of the maverick of the Southern, Oliver Bulleid) turned to the Great Western for advice or guidance, or simply copied their products! Churchward introduced standardisation. He designed a range of boilers for each class of locomotives which were simply known as Swindon number 1, and so on. All the valve gears, wheel sizes and fire boxes were similarly standardised, and any new locomotive was designed around these standard parts. It was just as well that the original designs were so good, because the policy only gave a little room for improving on the performance of a locomotive, such as increasing the number of superheater tubes or altering the chimney dimensions. After Churchward's retirement, the job of CME went to CB Collett, a man of little tact with a great dislike of interference from anyone else, especially the ministry of transport. It is very easy to see why the Western Region continued to be the Great Western in all but name!

The King class locomotives were the ultimate in power on the GWR. Although a 4-6-0 wheel arrangement they matched the power output and performance of all their contemporary competitors, and were only ever surpassed by Sir William Stanier's Duchess class which was largely based on their design practices anyway! The Kings were heavy engines, and this did limit their range of usefulness to the GWR main lines principally from Paddington to Birmingham Snow Hill, Paddington to Bristol and Paddington to Plymouth.

This painting shows number 6000, KGV, at rest in Old Oak Common shed, just outside London. The Great Western was a very proud railway, and its locomotives were kept in immaculate condition, especially by Cardiff, Worcester and Old Oak Common sheds. KGV visited America from 24 September to 15 October 1927 as part of the 'Fair of the Iron horse', during which it was presented with a bell that remained on its front for the rest of its working life. It says much about the success of these fine machines that the only major change to it was the addition of a double chimney in December 1956, so this helps date the picture – it is just before 1956. A 9F freight engine stands to the right of KGV in a distinctly non GWR state of cleanliness (it was a foreigner after all). A Castle class locomotive is getting some attention on the left of the painting and a Manor class locomotive can be seen in the background. The cleaner is on his way with the bucket.

I have subconsciously made KGV lean away in a slightly supercilious sort of way! It seems quite appropriate in retrospect, as though it were aware that it was having its portrait done and was determined to show that it was, after all, King!

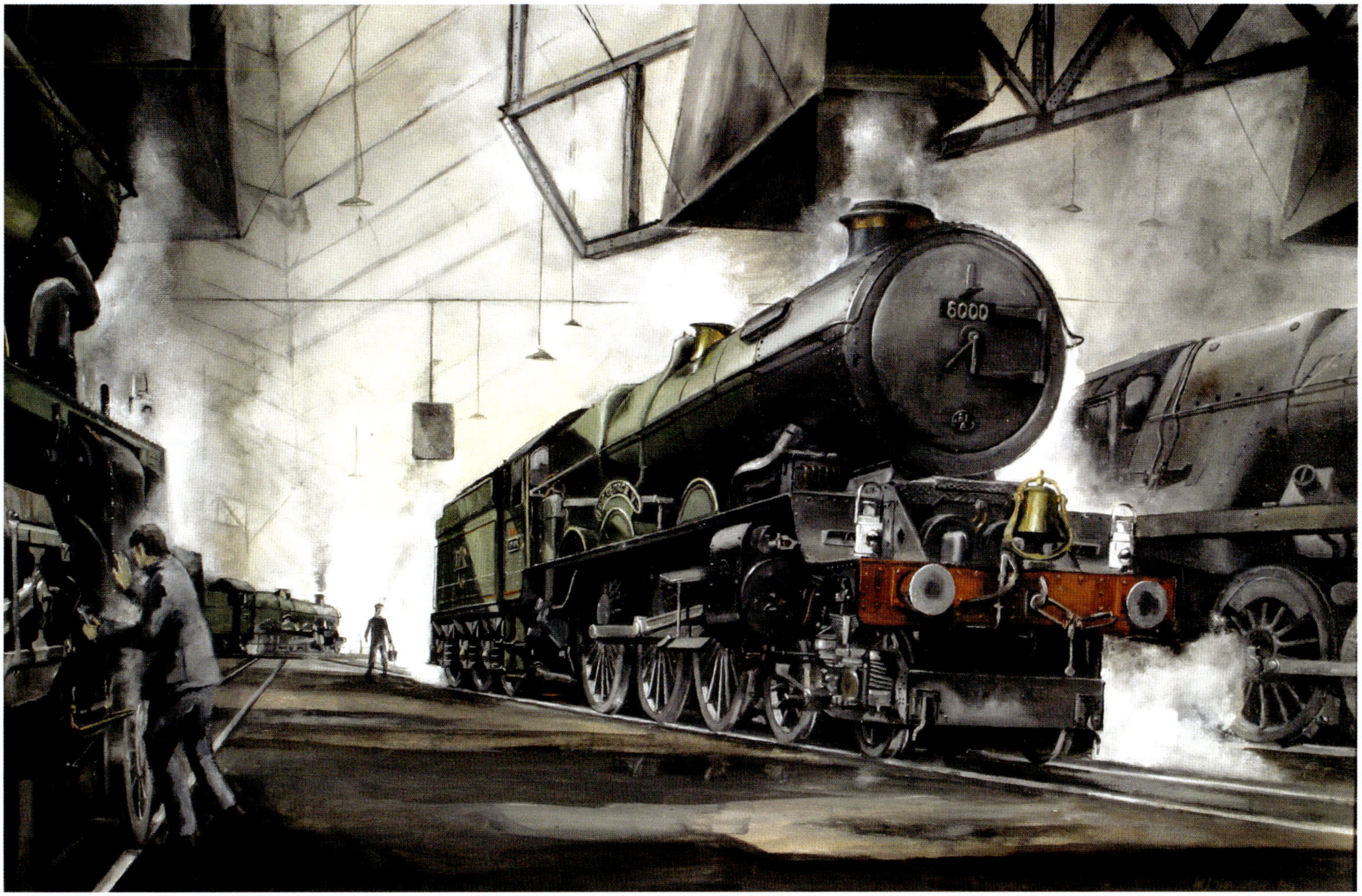

King George V at Old Oak Common

'City of London' on Camden Bank

The proximity of London to Hatfield meant that as a boy I was able, when pocket money allowed, to visit the London termini. Euston never impressed me much, apart from the view from the buffers at the arrivals side of the station. The rest of the place seemed rather tatty, with corrugated iron roofing in places and no roofing at all in others. So on one occasion I took a bus out to Camden to see the engine shed. Alas we were not allowed in and although it was possible to see the tops of the red and green Pacifics and Jubilees simmering in the very cramped confines of the yard below us, there was no good viewpoint immediately outside. This was rectified by crossing the road bridge to the North of the shed where a wonderful view opened up of the whole line with the huge carriage shed. Unfortunately it was still too distant to see the numbers on the locomotives in the yard. The frustration of the trainspotter with his Ian Allan ABCs!

Once again I resorted to imagination, that I could get down to line level just opposite the wall at the foot of the bank. And that is where this painting is located. Again, in hindsight which is a wonderful thing, I could have put this locomotive anywhere! Memories are hard to shake off though, and that day stayed in mine, so Camden bank it was. The choice of 'City of London' was easy – it was by far the cleanest engine on shed at the time, though 'Duchess of Hamilton', which I was to photograph at Euston later on the same day, ran it a good second. Both were painted red, while 'City of Chester', which I also photographed, was in Brunswick Green. Somehow the red suited the large Pacifics better. It distinguished them from their Eastern Region counterparts, the A1s, and made them look larger and more powerful. The Duchesses simply looked massive with their hunched up, somehow rather brooding appearance.

'City of London' was, surprisingly, built during the war and entered traffic in 1943. I was always under the impression that all the railway workshops were fully occupied with munitions at the time with the exception of Eastleigh which was constructing Bulleid's West Country Pacifics under the pretence that they were mixed-traffic locomotives and needed for the war effort. It now seems that Duchesses 6245-52 were introduced into traffic during the war which must have required some work on the part of Crewe, even if the construction had been completed in 1937 as most records indicate. It was thus quite a new machine, at least 10 years newer than its competing Gresley A4 streamlined locomotives on the LNER.

At the time it was built 'City of London' would have been streamlined too, but painted plain black for the war. Photographs of these fine machines in that livery makes them appear like upside down bath tubs. It is simple amazing what a coat of paint can do. Once restored to their original colours of crimson with gold stripes, or blue with white ones, these powerful monsters looked like the racing machines they actually were.

In the painting the streamlining has long been removed and also the sloping smokebox front which gave the machine an unfortunate appearance as though something heavy had been dropped on their nose! This was made worse by the fact that the Duchesses were built to the absolute limit of the loading gauge necessitating a very short squat chimney which looked as though it had been similarly flattened. The elegance of the GWR was definitely missing! The low lighting enabled the lovely spindly wheels to be seen to advantage and it will be noticed that the colour referred to in the painting of the Princess Royal (p.30) is a much brighter red than the Crimson Lake that it was supposed to be. It received this colour in December 1957 having previously been Brunswick Green. 'City of London' was destined to fame. It was used to haul an SLS special out of Kings Cross on the East Coast main line over Stoke Bank, a bank it ascended as easily as most of the Gresley A4s which came down the other way! Sadly it withdrawn in 1964, having done a mere 1 408 315 miles!

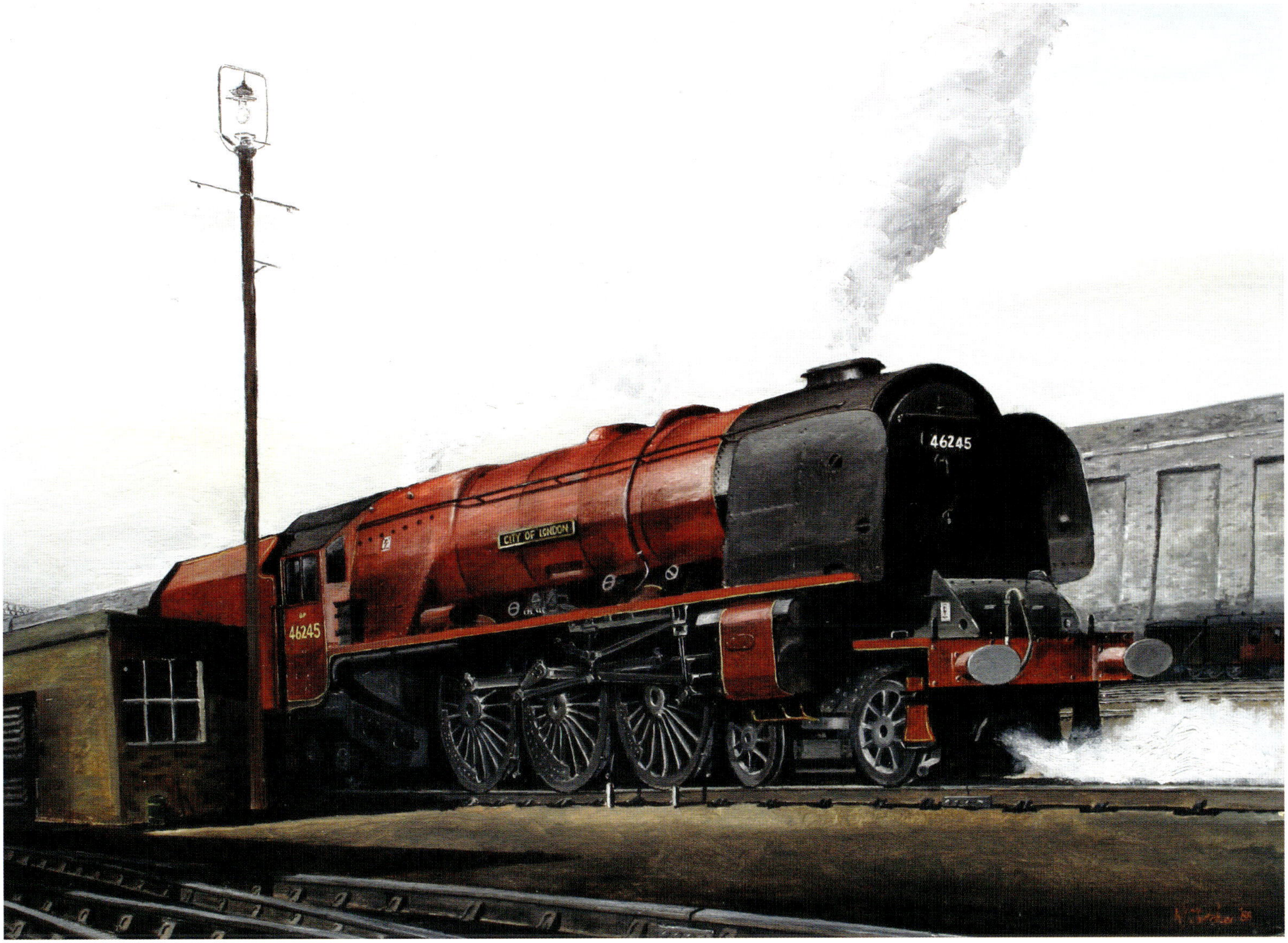

'City of London' on Camden Bank

'Geoffrey Chaucer' at Liverpool Street

The last painting in this section of my early work was also my largest. Liverpool Street Station is now unrecognisable from this scene which depicts the turntable at the end of the platforms in 1959. All of this has been swept away by 'progress' – in fact on a recent visit to the station I had to ask where the platforms were. In keeping with all the recent 'improvements' to the London stations, it looked more like a shopping mall than a station. The congestion caused by the narrow cutting immediately after leaving has not altered at all, it is merely darker, and more dismal than before and now covered in graffiti. Liverpool Street was my favourite of all the London stations. It resembled a cathedral and has been the subject of many of my paintings since, some of which appear in this book. The exterior of the station around the turntable was in no way cathedral like. It was busy, congested, with wrought ironwork and bridges which gave it that indefinable aura of a steam railway. The turntable was so close to the platform end that it was possible to sit on the battered railing that guarded the passengers from falling off the platform, not that they would have had much chance to do so with the number of us sitting there and sometimes being shooed back because we had encroached too far. The turntable was power operated being driven by the enormous cylinder alongside the turntable. It was fascinating seeing such heavy locomotives being turned so effortlessly. The locomotives came down from Stratford shed, now the site of the Olympic stadium. It seems that the Stratford drivers did not like travelling down the bank from the shed in reverse, so the engines had to be turned on the station turntable. Similarly the locomotives which had brought in the express trains from Norwich, Ipswich or Harwich were turned before sending them back up the hill.

'Geoffrey Chaucer' was one of the BR standard Britannia Class Pacifics of power class 7. Not as powerful as the A4s and A1s or Duchesses of the Eastern or Midland Regions but expected to do much of their work. I remember distinctly my first sight of these machines. My father was driving us to his parents' home in Bishops Stortford; en route we had to cross the Liverpool Street/Enfield to Stevenage line at Hertford and unusually a Britannia, 'Geoffrey Chaucer', had been diverted along this route which normally saw nothing larger than a B1. It was an inspiring sight, blocking the level crossing. All that was visible was the polished copper pipes beneath the cab, which seemed high in the air when you are sitting in a Morris 8 family saloon! The Britannia's were massive machines. Most of them were shedded either at Norwich or at Stratford.They were instantly liked on the Liverpool Street–Norwich turns as they were easily the most powerful engines the crews on this line had ever had.

'Geoffrey Chaucer' was chosen for the painting for obvious reasons, but also because I had a (very poor) photograph of this engine in the chosen location. Freshly coaled from Stratford engine shed, 70002 awaits turning ready to take the Hook Continental to Harwich, a short but high profile run connecting with the ferry. This engine was only built in March 1951 as part of the original plan for British Railways. Considering all that has been written before about the near bankruptcy of Britain at the time and our dependency on coal, the building of standardised steam locomotives (following the example of the GWR!) seemed a sensible thing to do. The subsequent abandonment of steam power for diesel had everything to do with the working conditions involving steam and nothing to do with economics. Both my Grandfathers were testimony to the dirty environment and the physically demanding nature of the work. The picture shows EHT in front of the engine on one of his final days on the railway before retirement. A Mark 1 coach in the new BR livery of maroon stands behind the engine and the sooty atmosphere of Liverpool Street pervades everywhere under the massive girder bridge over the station's mouth.

This was the first painting I had reproduced as a fine art print.

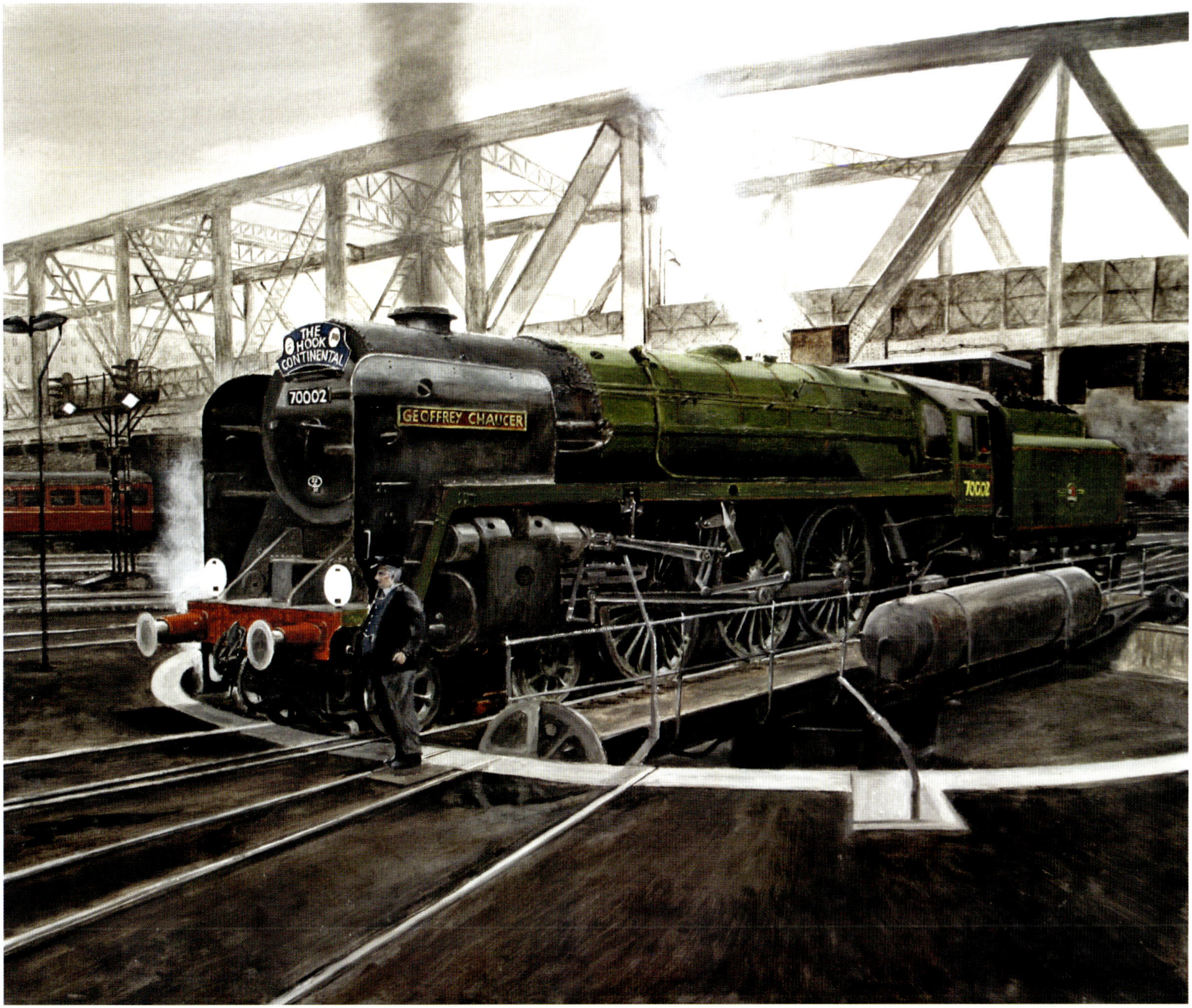

'Geoffrey Chaucer' at Liverpool Street

Paintings of the Big Four

IN 1923 THE SMALL RAILWAY companies which had been set up as private companies during the Victorian era were amalgamated to form four major railway companies. These were the London Midland & Scottish (LMS), the London & North Eastern (LNER), the Great Western (GWR) and the Southern Railway (SR). These large railway companies adopted their own liveries and operating practices – there was no standardisation apart from one thing, the gauge of the track which was four foot eight and a half inches wide, the width of the original coal tucks used on the Stockton & Darlington railway and adopted by George Stephenson as the 'standard gauge'. After the Second World War, in 1948, the Big Four were nationalised and formed into British Railways.

My railway paintings of this period are by necessity based on photographic records of the time, but are by no means just copies of those photographs. I have used location shots for accuracy only. And of course there are hardly any coloured photographs from this period.

'Silver Link' at Hatfield South – The Record Breaker.

Hatfield appears in many of my paintings. It was where I was brought up and where I have the most detailed memory. Alas, I was not alive when the streamlined expresses were introduced in 1935. On the 27 September of that year, newly built A4 Pacific 'Silver Link' set out from Platform 6, Kings Cross, with a special seven-coach streamlined and air conditioned set of coaches. It was the inaugural run of the 'Silver Jubilee', and it set long distance world speed records that have never been broken. The original intent was to show that steam power could match the speed of the German diesel railcar-powered 'Flying Hamburger' (competition between Britain and Germany was fierce); and 'Silver Link' did this in style. It set a new world speed record of 112 mph and averaged over 100mph for 43 miles.

My painting depicts 'Silver Link' in its original livery, and with its name painted on the side, speeding past Hatfield South where it was already doing 95mph, only 19 miles from London. The weather on that day was not ideal for record breaking . Records show it was overcast and raining for much of the journey, especially further north, so I have painted the sky with just a glimmer of brightness on the horizon. The weather that year had not been particularly good, and the trees lost their leaves early. Hatfield is protected from London by a so called green belt, and in the 1930s was quite a small suburban town, although very important as a staging depot for the coal traffic heading towards the capital. In all probability there would have been more trucks in the south yard sidings, opposite number one box, but this would have spoiled the painting! This run was supposed to have been restricted to the Press (who were on board in large numbers) but inevitably the information about an attempted record run leaked out, and the crowds gathered at every station. In fact no instructions were given to the engine crew to attempt a record. At the time 'Silver Link' was not equipped with a speedometer, and they did not know how fast they were going until the locomotive designer, Nigel Gresley, walked through the corridor tender into the cab, and told the driver to 'ease his arm, the passengers are getting nervous!'

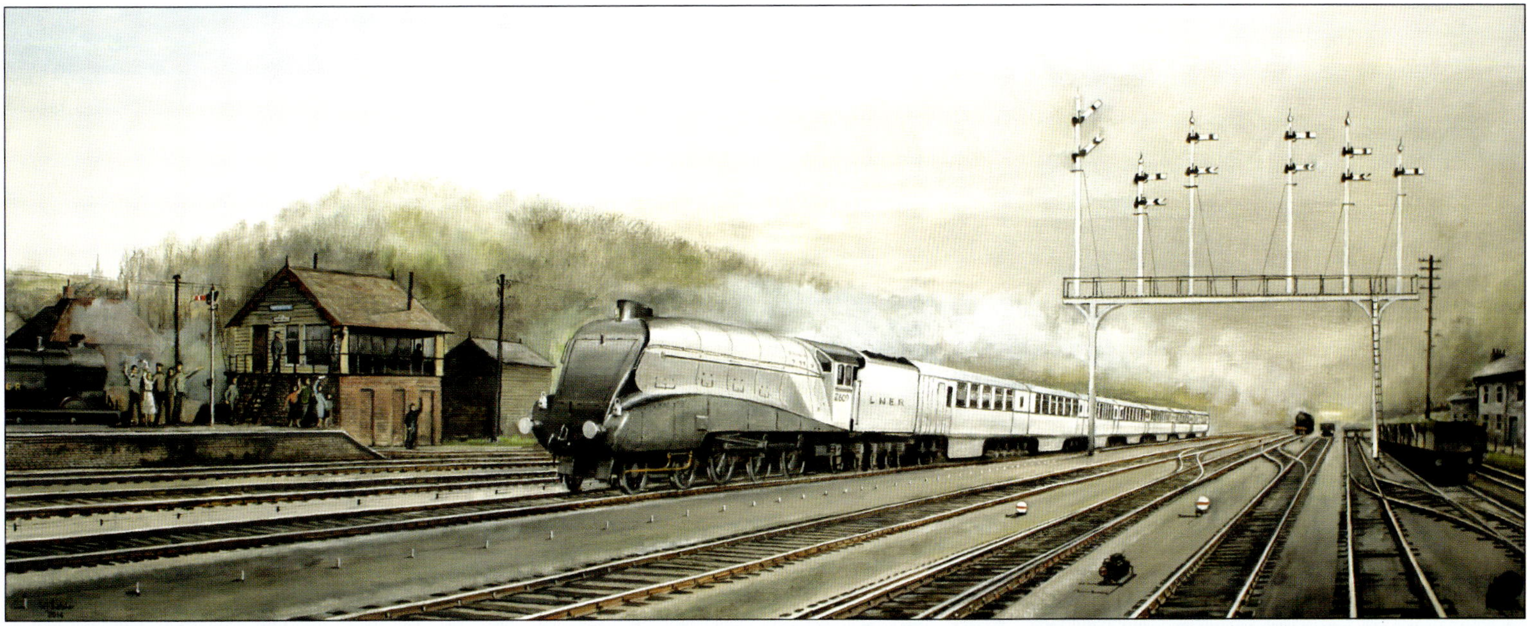

The Record Breaker

The original Gresley streamlined Pacifics were painted silver with grey fairings over the wheels. They had the name painted on the side of the locomotive. The 'Silver Jubilee' stock was luxurious in every way. Not only was it air conditioned, passengers had individual armchairs! Britain had suffered many years of depression from the mid 1920s, and the coming of the streamlined era was seen by many as the beginning of better times. Certainly the competition between the LMS and the LNER reached new levels as the companies sought the business custom between London and Scotland as well as the northern cities of England. It was a battle that the LNER won comprehensively, not because it had better locomotives (it didn't) but because it offered a better service and greater comfort.

Cannon Street Commuters

Just as Hatfield figures largely in my paintings, so do the London stations, as I had many opportunities to visit them. London has changed more than any other specific location, so doing historically accurate paintings of the city has depended more than ever on good photographic records. Fortunately there are a huge number of photographs of London and its stations, and the internet has proved invaluable as a research tool. Of course there is no substitute for seeing something live, even if there have been changes to the architecture, the layout of a city often remains much the same. Sadly this does not apply to London, and especially its stations. The view shown in my painting is now unrecognisable. From old maps of London I carefully worked out the angles and what would and would not be visible under the arches of the old London Bridge from the south bank. The twin towers of Cannon Street station can be seen, with St Paul's looming behind it surprisingly close to the station. In fact during all my paintings in and around the city, I have been amazed at how close the stations and all the other major buildings are. It is quite easy to walk round all the London mainline stations in a day, passing many famous landmarks en route. The section of the Thames known as Kings Reach lay behind the railway bridge out of Cannon Street, and beyond this Southwark Bridge.

The Southern railway had a very chequered history, serving the commuters who made their way daily into the city. London Bridge was the first London railway terminus, but this was located on the south bank; the Victorian gentry did not fancy the walk across the bridge to the City so other Southern London termini, Victoria, Blackfriars and Charing Cross as well as Cannon Street were forced to build their termini on the north shore of the Thames. This restricted the amount of traffic the stations could handle, both because the space for the terminal buildings was restricted, and because the bridges could only be built with a limited number of tracks on them for weight reasons. Thus it was that only Waterloo had a sizeable maze of tracks entering a large number of platforms – in fact the largest in London – but it was the wrong side of the river. More of Waterloo later! In the meantime the unfortunate commuters were treated more like cattle than human beings by the railway companies. Comfort was definitely not a major consideration, volume of traffic and numbers were all that mattered. This being the case the Southern were early adopters of electric trains. They had better acceleration, better utilisation, did not need turning and required minimal maintenance, and large numbers of people could be crammed into frequently arriving and departing trains. The passengers being taken home in real carriages hauled by a Maunsell King Arthur class locomotive were luckier than most; it may have been slower, but in the painting at least the carriages in use are fairly modern (the Southern had a huge range of carriage variations thanks to the numerous pre-grouping companies it absorbed).

As for London Bridge – well that now spans a lake in Arizona in the USA, and has been replaced by a modern concrete construction with none of the elegance of its predecessor. I have tried to reproduce the block work in a clean state, as it was mostly black in the Victorian era and only cleaned up in the 1930s. The homeward-bound rush hour can be seen crossing this bridge on foot. In today's London this exodus is just as great. The electric trains of the 1930s have improved slightly but are still overcrowded and cramped, although south London is now a much more desirable place to live and work, resulting in some reduction of the pressure, and is better served by the underground which has reached further out into the suburbs.

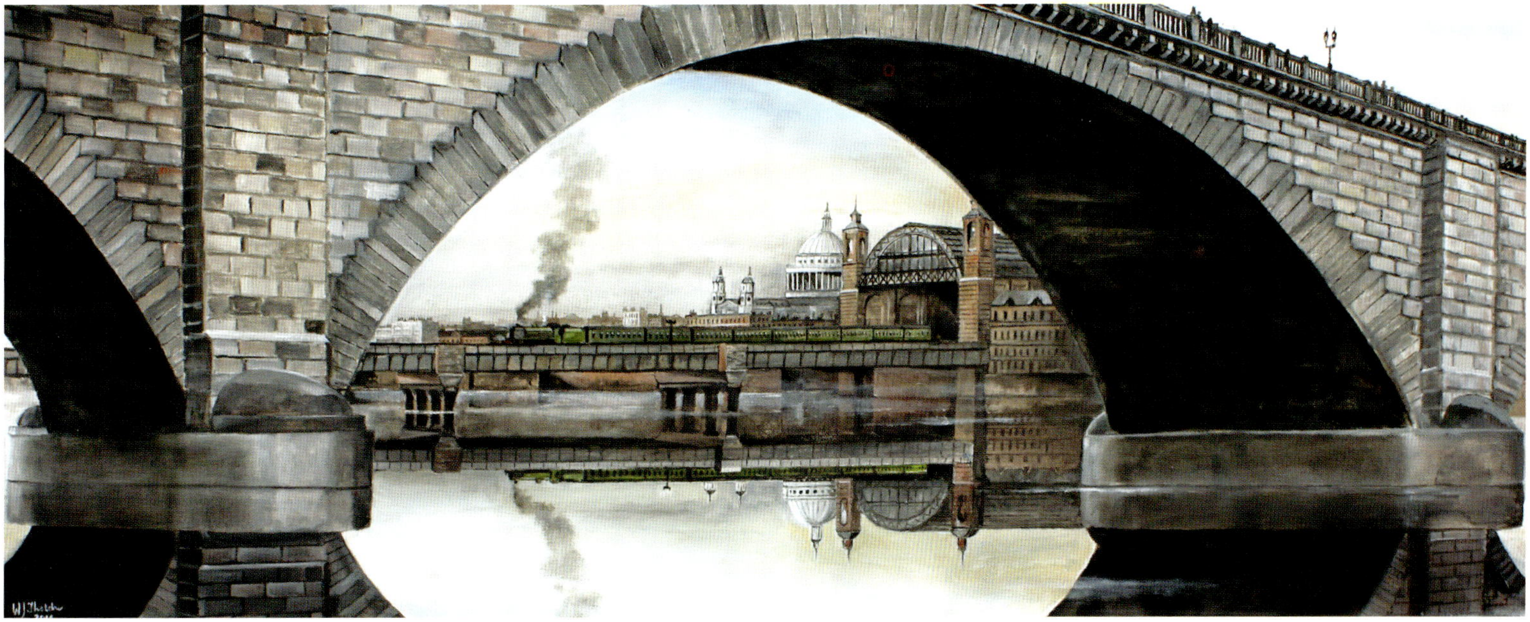

Cannon Street Commuters

The very low bridges built across the Thames by the railway companies in the Victorian era ensured that sailing vessels were not able to get up to Kings Reach and beyond. The river was extensively used for transporting goods, even in the 1930s, and this would have been accomplished using lighters or barges on the water, sometimes attached together convoy-fashion. Early photographs show that the water level of the Thames was considerably lower then than it is today, with beaches being visible below the embankment close to Charing Cross station. The piers of the old London Bridge would now be close to immersion.

Brunel's Temple Meads

Isambard Kingdom Brunel was the son of a French émigré, Marc Brunel, who, as a Royalist, had fled France in the face of the Revolution. Like his father before him, the young Brunel was an outstanding engineer; he was also an outstanding architect , and civil engineer. Almost single handily he surveyed and oversaw the construction of the Great Western Railway from London Paddington to Bristol, where his inventive genius became diverted into shipbuilding in the form of the SS *Great Britain* and other steamships which were to set records and change the world as it was then known.

It is therefore a pity that the magnificent interior of Paddington Station in London was not mirrored by the interior of his terminus in Bristol. Not that it lacked grandeur from the outside. The original Temple Meads station still stands today, surrounded by mean streets, tatty shops and the cacophony of the motoring age. When it was built, the church-like exterior was a grand entrance to God's Wonderful Railway. Here there was room for one's carriage to be drawn up right outside the station entrance while the ladies and gentlemen stepped down and straight into the sun-dappled interior seen in the painting. After their luggage had been collected by the porters and taken through to the platform, the horse and carriage could continue on the same arc of paved road and back out on the main Bath to Bristol road.

The station changed little for nearly 100 years. The trains got longer, the broad gauge came and went, along with two world wars through which the station saw little damage. Even the signalling remained substantially the same, controlled from the little box high up on the right hand side of the picture. Eventually though things had to change, not least because Bristol had become a through route to Exeter, Truro and Penzance as well as to Gloucester and Worcester. Bristol really was the cross roads of the West Country, while still being under three hours from London! Even today it is hard to realise that this is not even the halfway point between London and Penzance, and that the journey from Birmingham Snow Hill in the Midlands pre-empted the M5 motorway by over 100 years.

It was mainly the traffic to these northern towns (well northern to the GWR!) that continued to use the old Brunel terminus, right into the 1950s, after which it was closed and laid derelict for a while before part of it was reopened as a station car park serving the grand sweeping new Temple Meads seen elsewhere in this book.

My painting shows the old terminus towards the end of its working life. The choice of locomotive for that period is deliberately bizarre, as the more usual motive power seen under the train shed roof was a mixture of standard classes, especially class 3 tank engines and class 4 or 5 4-6-0s, together with the occasional Stanier Black 5. This was Great Western territory so I have shown one of Collett's Hall class locomotives waiting with a Gloucester stopping train comprising chocolate and cream stock. I particularly wanted to capture the light and shade of this fine old building and that, together with the proximity of my home in Frome, was the main reason for selecting this location

Fortunately part of this terminus has been preserved in its original state. The very end of the terminus as seen in the shaft of sunlight behind the signals on the left hand platform has been sealed off behind closed doors. The rest of the building remains an indoor car park, with the original cobbled platforms still plainly visible together with the intricate geodetic structure of the roof which gave strength without the need for the massive supporting girders one can see in Paddington or York.

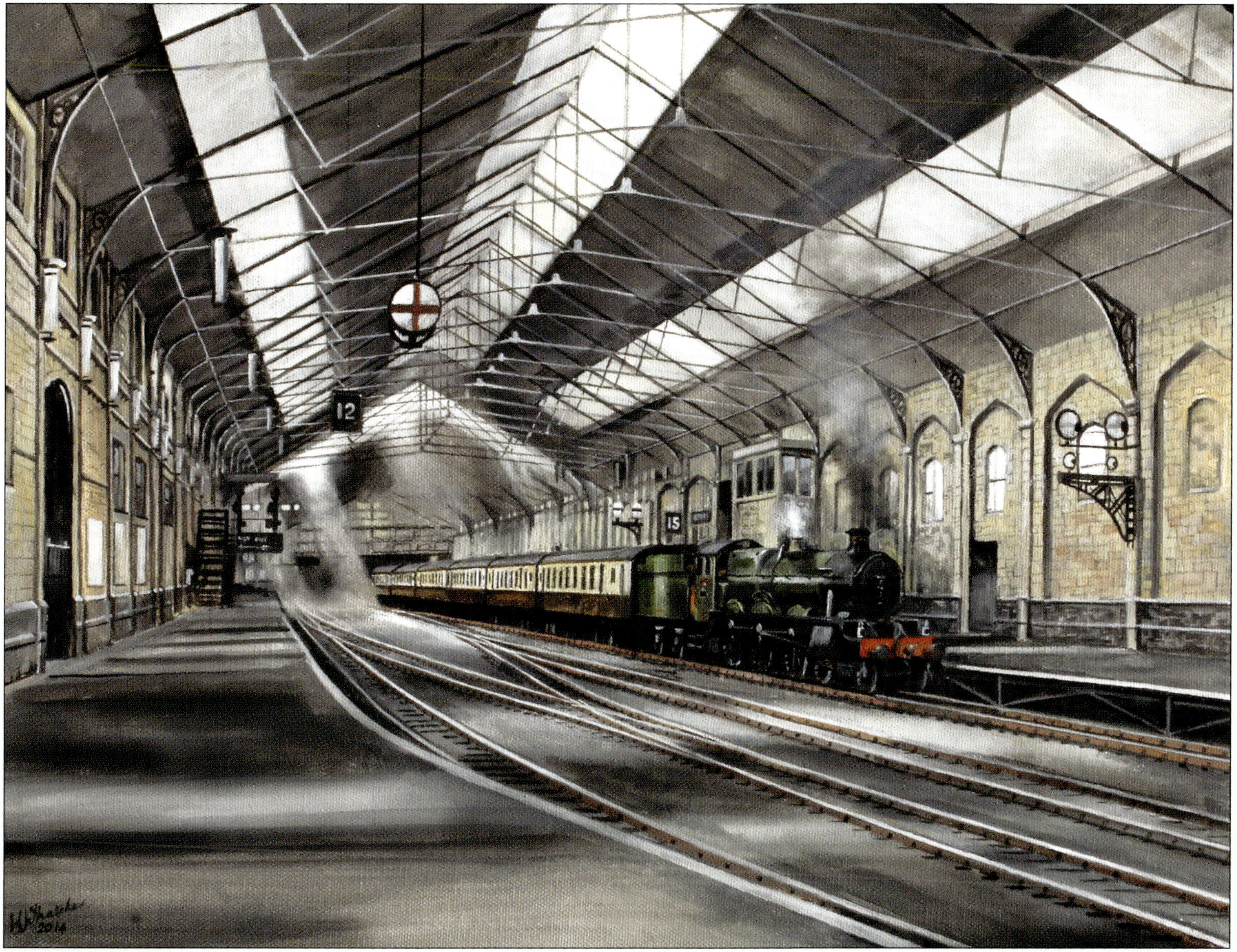

Sun-dappled Temple Meads

Fenland Morning

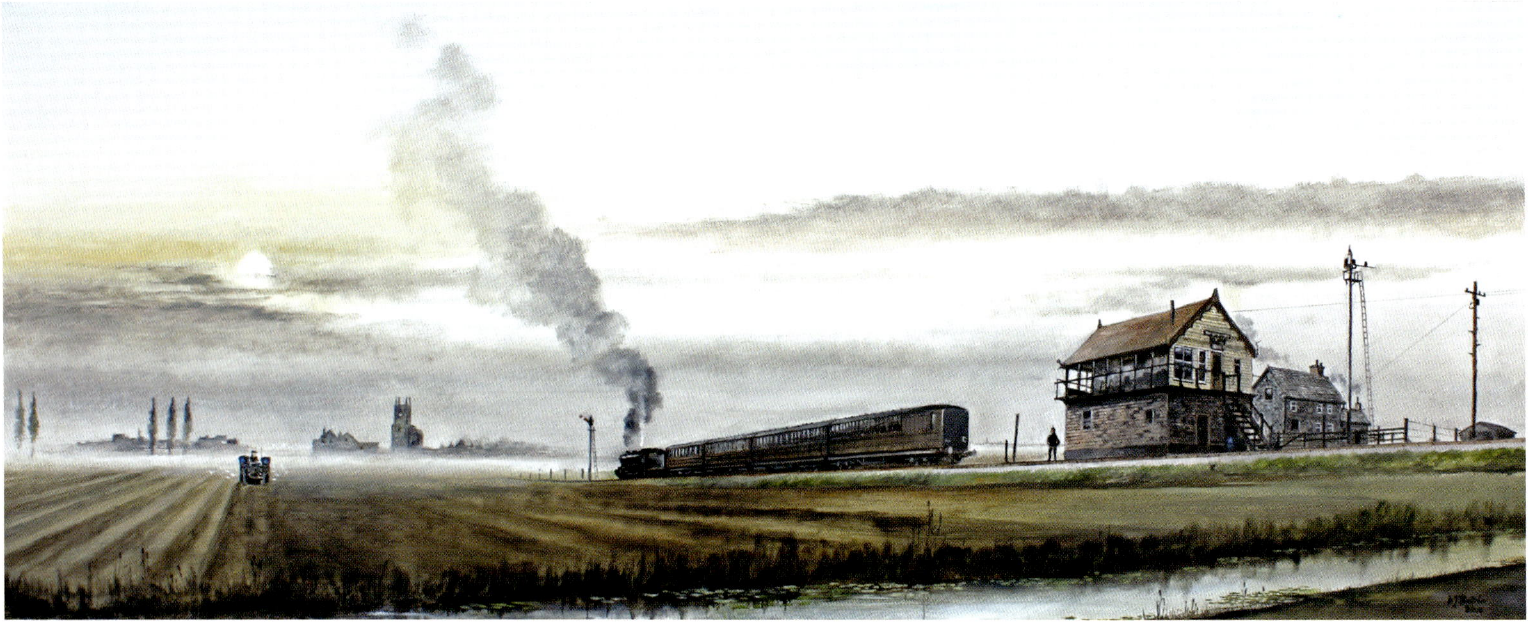

In contrast to earlier paintings, this one was came to mind as I was driving across the Cambridgeshire fens near Wisbech, very early one autumn morning on my way to Oxford. The sun was making a hazy, and late, appearance and mist still hung over the fields. The presence of the railway was identified by the mess of the electric catenary and the coloured light signals. Electricity pylons disfigured the view whichever way I looked. A multiple unit scurried its way southbound and I longed for the day when the signalbox had stood at the crossing instead of the half barrier that was about to let me pass, and the modern trappings of conducting electricity were yet to be constructed. The K3 with its diminutive train composed entirely of Gresley stock came to mind. A little research soon dug up the location of buildings although I have moved the signalbox further south so as to be in the picture and still keep the dyke in the foreground.

All red and gold

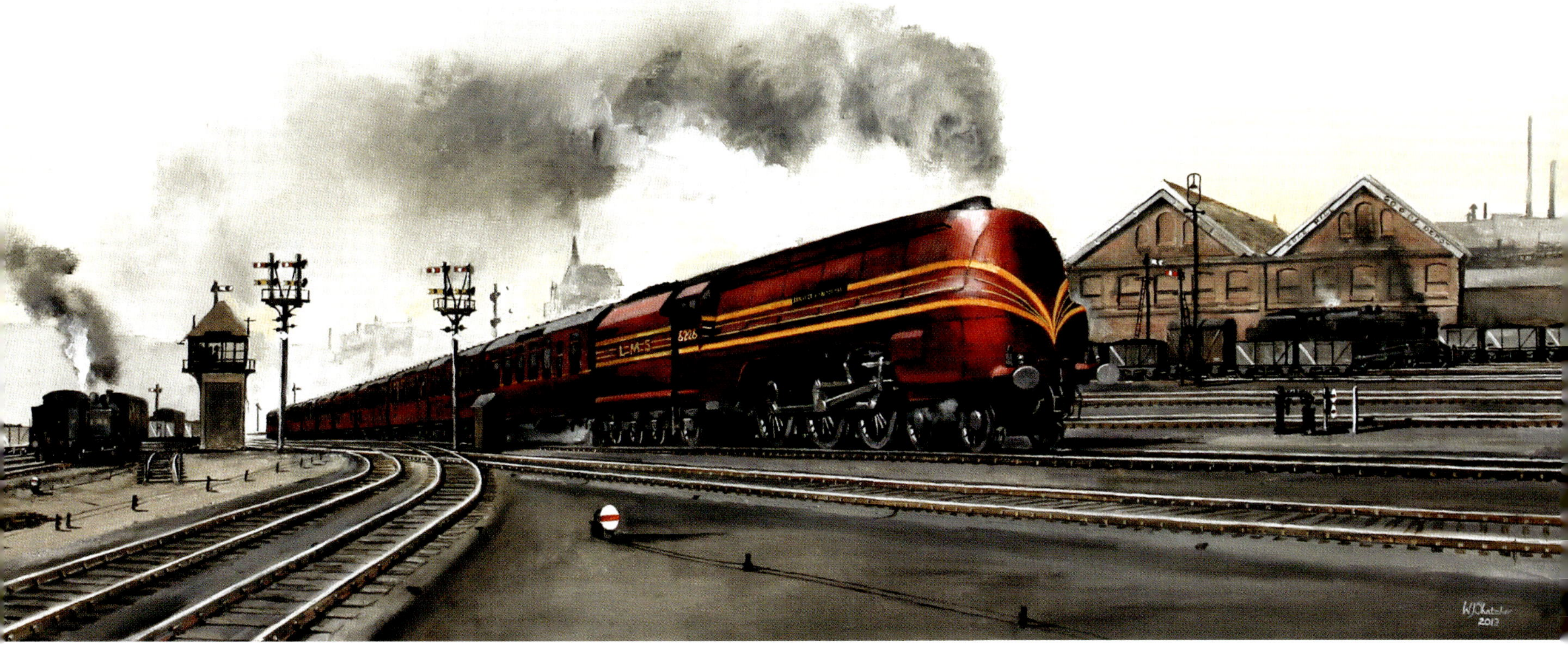

The streamlined Pacific locomotives of William Stanier, in my view, looked absolutely splendid in their alternative livery of red and gold. Although I only saw Edge Hill after steam had ended in 1970 much of the infrastructure was still there and I was able to stand at the end of Edge Hill station and look down into the tunnel of Edge Hill cutting. This location was strictly out of range!

Charing Cross and Trafalgar Square

In 2012 I decided to walk round each of the stations in London to see how much they had changed and how much, or how little, I remembered of them. Whilst I had often travelled to and from Paddington, Liverpool Street and Kings Cross, the other stations were unknown since childhood, the southern stations especially so. I suppose like a lot of trainspotters of my generation I viewed the Southern as a minority railway, with no big hills to climb and no great distances to travel. We happily ignored the LSW main line to Exeter and Plymouth, thus I spent less time collecting southern numbers than those of any other region. So it was that on my tour which encompassed Charing Cross I found a station which barely resembled a station. It was a shopping mall with polished floors and absolutely no railway atmosphere whatsoever. Worse, when I found the platforms and tried to take photographs of the establishment I was rapidly approached by some very unfriendly railway employees who demanded my camera (which I bluntly refused) and told me to leave the station premises immediately as photography was forbidden. Perhaps I had not missed much with the Southern after all, but I had no archive photographs of the station in steam days in my own collection at all. So I decided to research what the station had been like before electrification, before rebuilding and before world terrorism had made railway stations a no go area.

It seemed from the photographs I unearthed that Charing Cross was once a very attractive building, expressing the full grandeur of the railway company that built it, the South Eastern & Chatham. There is a wonderful description of the station by Sir John Betjeman in his book *London's Historic Railway Stations*. I was unaware until reading this masterpiece in prose, that Charing Cross, the monument just outside the station frontage, is regarded as the centre of London from which all mileages are recorded.

The reputation of the station was slightly unsavoury, but the hotel built into the station concourse was one of the finest Victorian Hotels in London, being equalled only by The Great Eastern Hotel in Liverpool Street station.

I decided to paint this station from the street side but wanted to include a view of the tracks and at least a glimpse of steam. The high buildings all around the station made this impossible, so the only thing to do was go up. And that is what I did. Using old maps from 1936, just prior to the war, I was able to work out where all the major buildings were around Charing Cross. Getting hold of a 1939 map was beyond me, I think the restrictions due to the war made sure that, if possible, none fell into German hands. However 1939 was a time when the recovery of the economy meant that all the buildings were at their best, so I have assumed that year for my painting.

The rest of the detail came from a trawl through the internet and libraries of all the buildings. Painting from this perspective is very difficult. There is no horizon to act as a focal plane. So it is not possible to have a specific focal point at which all the lines meet! Worse, the buildings at the bottom of the picture are almost vertically below the painter so only the rooftops are visible, whereas those at the top are getting towards the horizon, and only the sides of the buildings are visible. But I got the track and the steam engine in!

The line from Charing Cross used to leave over a flimsy wrought iron construction with narrow wooden-floored footpath running alongside it just below track level. This was Hungerford Bridge as I knew it and over which I had walked many times to the Royal Festival Hall on the south bank. It shook perilously every time a train passed.

The reader will be able to identify many of the buildings, but not the road system – it is pedestrian only now up to the National Gallery – and certainly not Charing Cross Station and Hungerford Bridge. My station has long gone and been replaced with a shopping arcade.

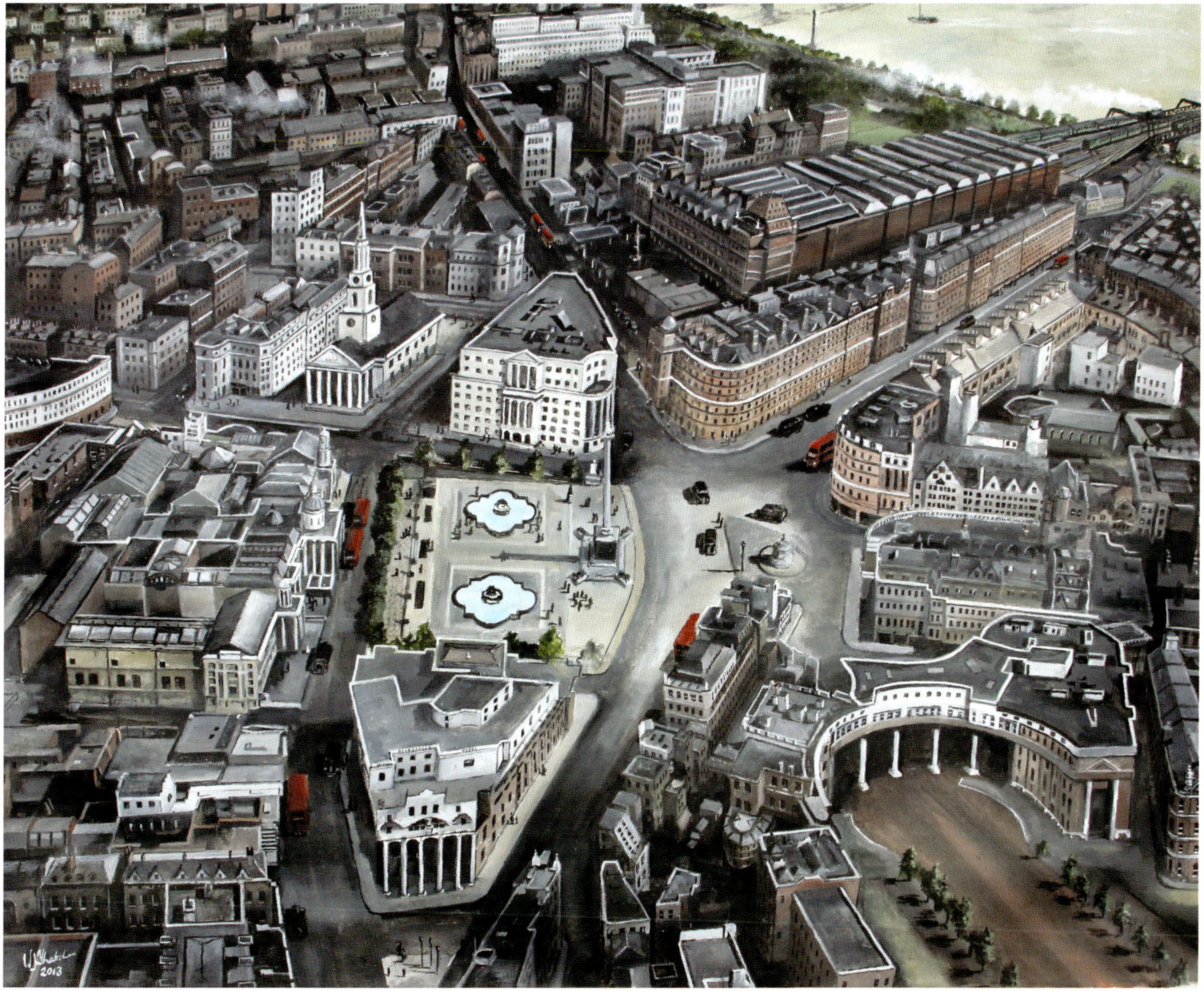

Charing Cross and Trafalgar Square

Castle at Wolverhampton

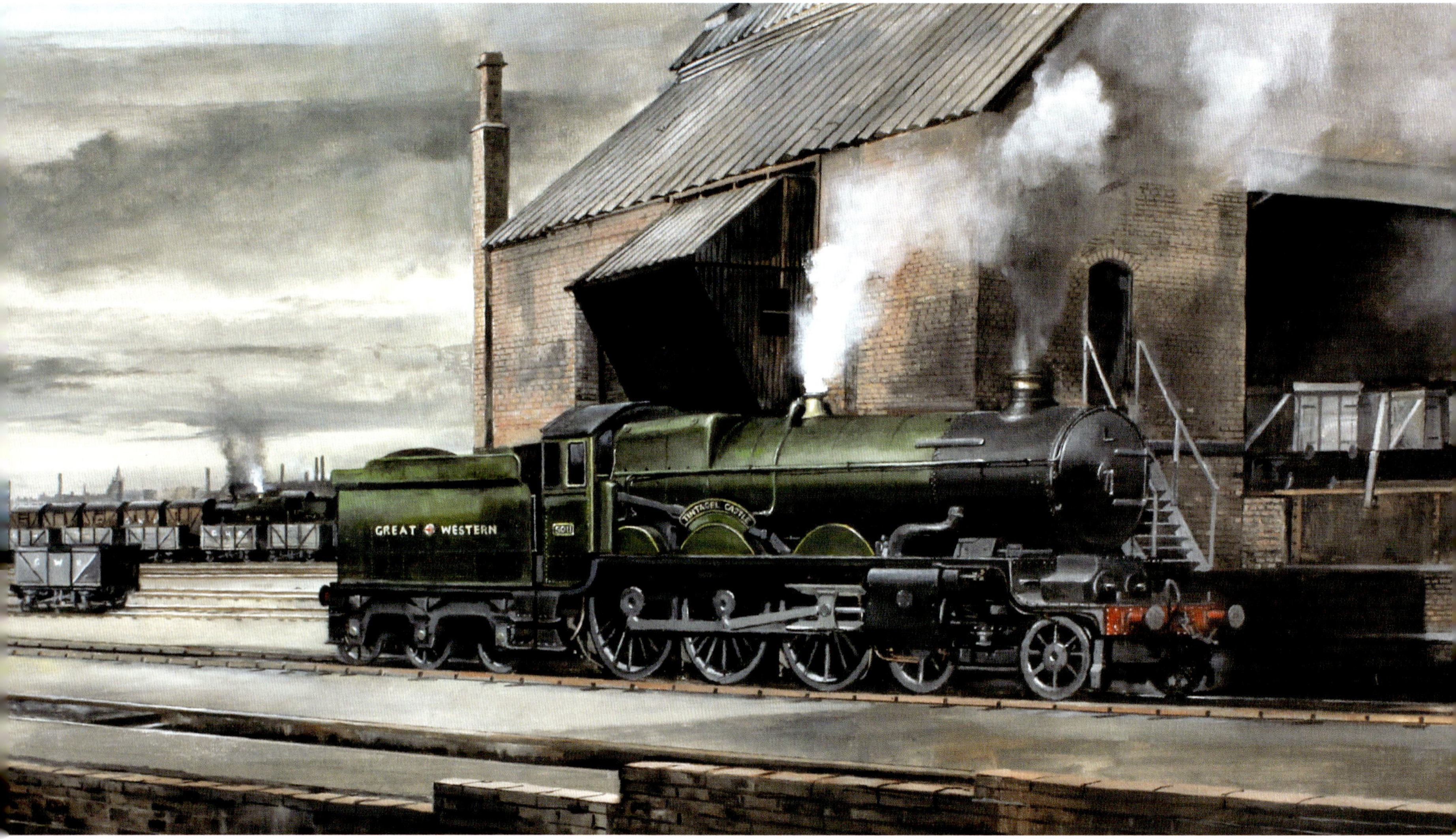

Wolverhampton Stafford Road Shed was probably the least glamorous location one might expect to find a Great Western engine. It was falling to pieces in the 1950s and was almost completely derelict by the time steam ended. This painting is one of contrasts, intended to highlight the graceful lines of 'Tintagel Castle' in its pre BR days with the scrappy environment of this Black Country depot.

Derby

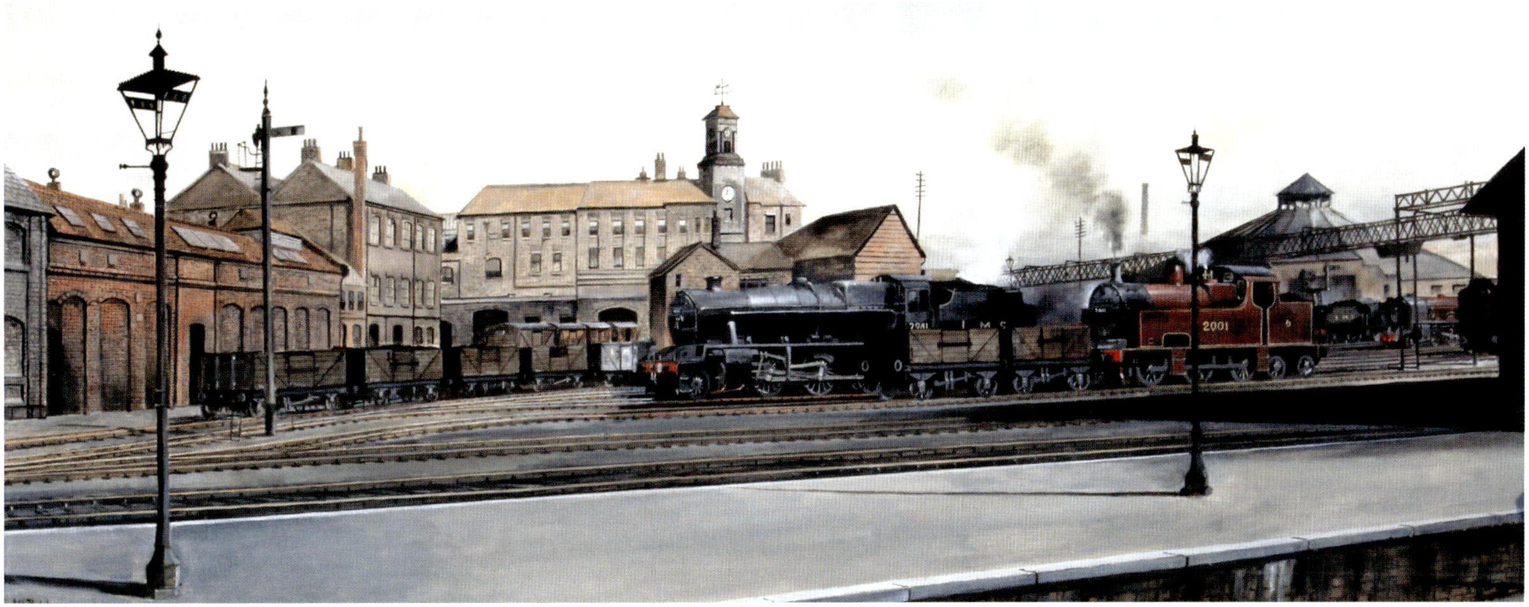

Another painting of contrasts, this time showing the changing order at the Midland Derby works in the mid 1930s. The buildings have not changed for half a century, and the station platform still has gas lighting. In the background can be seen a Royal Scot with its later form of smoke deflectors. Old Midland Railway wooden wagons litter the yard, but one steel wagon has made its first appearance. A 'flatiron' tank engine – one of Derby's least successful designs – shunts the yard resplendent in its Crimson Lake livery, but a brand new Stanier mogul has been pushed out of the works and awaits lighting up. The end is nigh for the 'flatiron'.

'Peregrine' at Retford

Although this was one of my earlier paintings it is included in this section because it is a curious anomaly. The A4 Pacifics were painted either silver and grey for working the Silver Jubilee, or Garter Blue for working the Coronation. Both express trains were the prestigious advertisements for the LNER, which had otherwise adopted a livery of Apple Green for all its most powerful express locomotives, and black for the remainder. It was easily the most colourful of the big four.

Inevitably there were times when the silver engines were not available for the Jubilee and so the presence of a blue locomotive on the front of this train was quite commonplace. I have seen no record of the reverse, though; a silver locomotive on the front of the blue Coronation stock. The silver locomotives were 'Silver Link', 'Silver King', 'Silver Fox' and 'Quicksilver', a total of four out of the thirty-five members of this class, so the chances must have been good.

During the war years from 1939 to 1945 the A4s were painted wartime black. At this time the valences or skirting which covered the wheels in order to improve the streamlining, was removed. This gave a considerable improvement to the accessibility of the valve gear, and also improved the problems of overheating of the middle cylinder and valve gear situated between the diving wheels. In the author's view it also improved very considerably the appearance of the locomotive which was otherwise too art deco! So that is the form in which I chose to paint the A4, dictated more by its history rather than place or location. The engines in wartime black were ugly. They did not look like the high speed machines they once were, especially as wartime maintenance had left them in a shockingly run down state. Hardly surprising since they had been used to haul trains up to 17 coaches in length, unassisted, from Kings Cross to York and Newcastle. In 1946 a slow start was made in returning the machines to their former glory, even though the Big Four were battling insolvency as a result of the lack of financial recompense from a government which had used them to the limit during hostilities. So it was that the blue livery appeared once more (but not the silver).

It had been recognised that some of the locomotives were faster and more economical than others. 'Mallard', which held the world speed record, was one of these. They were all equipped with Kylchap blast pipes and double chimneys, which dramatically improved their steam raising capability. It was not until 1956 that British Railways completed the same modification to the rest of the class. Again I felt that the double chimney improved the appearance, so the engine selected for my painting had to be blue, without valences and with a double chimney before 1948, the year the railways were nationalised! It was also desirable that it should have one of the original bird names, and not that of some unknown director of the LNER! The choice of No 34 'Peregrine' fitted all these requirements, and the painting shows her clattering over the points at Retford, with a fine array of LNER coaching stock. The location of this painting is very well known to the railway photography fraternity. I used a superb photograph taken by Frank Carter, of an A3 Pacific at this location in order to get the location details correct. I still regard the A3s as the most beautifully proportioned locomotives ever designed, whilst the A4s were the most striking.

Within two years from the date depicted by this painting, the locomotive was renamed 'Lord Faringdon' (who *was* he?) and painted British Railways Brunswick Green, a colour which also suited the A4s. Numbered 60034, this engine made her last visit to London in October 1963 and was cut up the following year. Fortunately six members of the A4 class have been preserved, but only one A3, the iconic 'Flying Scotsman'.

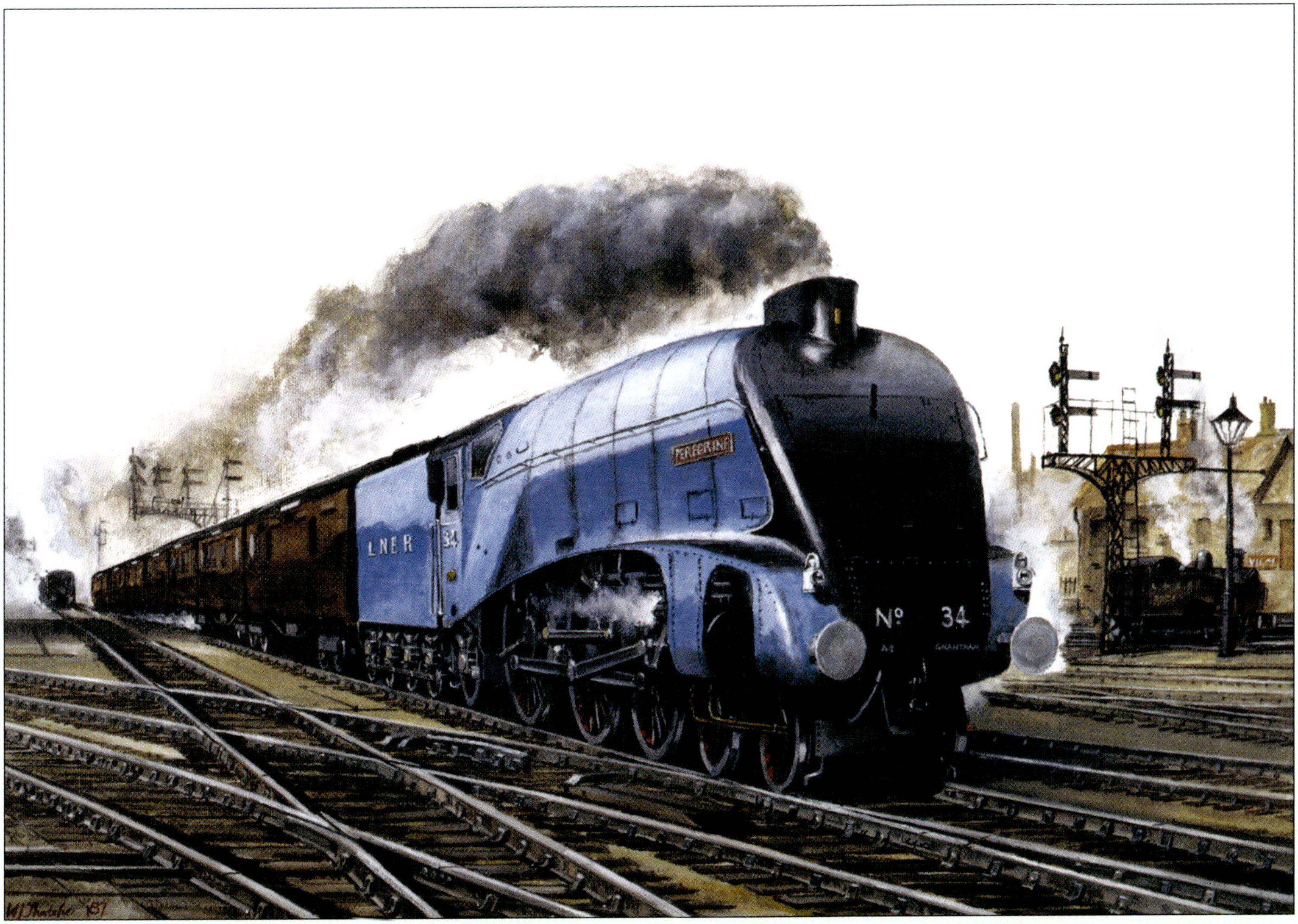

'Peregrine' at Retford

Melton Constable – The Final Years

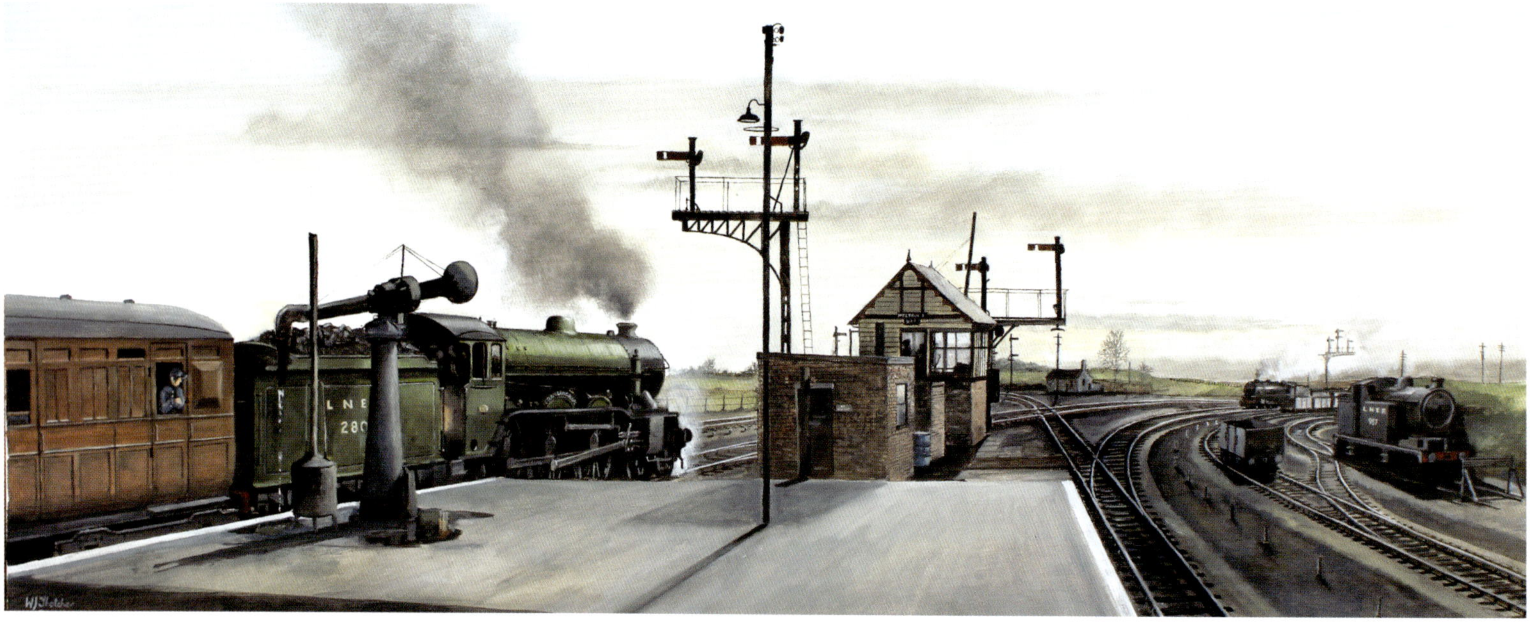

I suppose this painting has a rather wistful look about it, because that is how I felt about the location in particular. By the time I had moved to Norfolk to live, Melton Constable had long disappeared – not a trace remains today, just bare fields. My step Grandfather, Jimmy Dennis, drove from Melton every day so I wanted to capture the essence of the old Midland & Great Northern Joint. I was greatly assisted in getting the details of this location from the Norfolk and Norwich Railway Society, and especially local railway historian and author, Graham Kenworthy, who has provided me with much of my 'intelligence' concerning the rural railways of Norfolk. The approximate date of this painting can be worked out quite easily if one spots the WD approaching from the Cromer line. Since these machines were built during the war, yet the B17 has been returned to Apple Green, the date must be somewhere between 1946 and 1948 – probably nearer the latter as the repainting of secondary mixed traffic locomotives would have been a very low priority. Also note the building in the distance which was replaced with the signalbox in the last years of British Railways.

Out of Euston

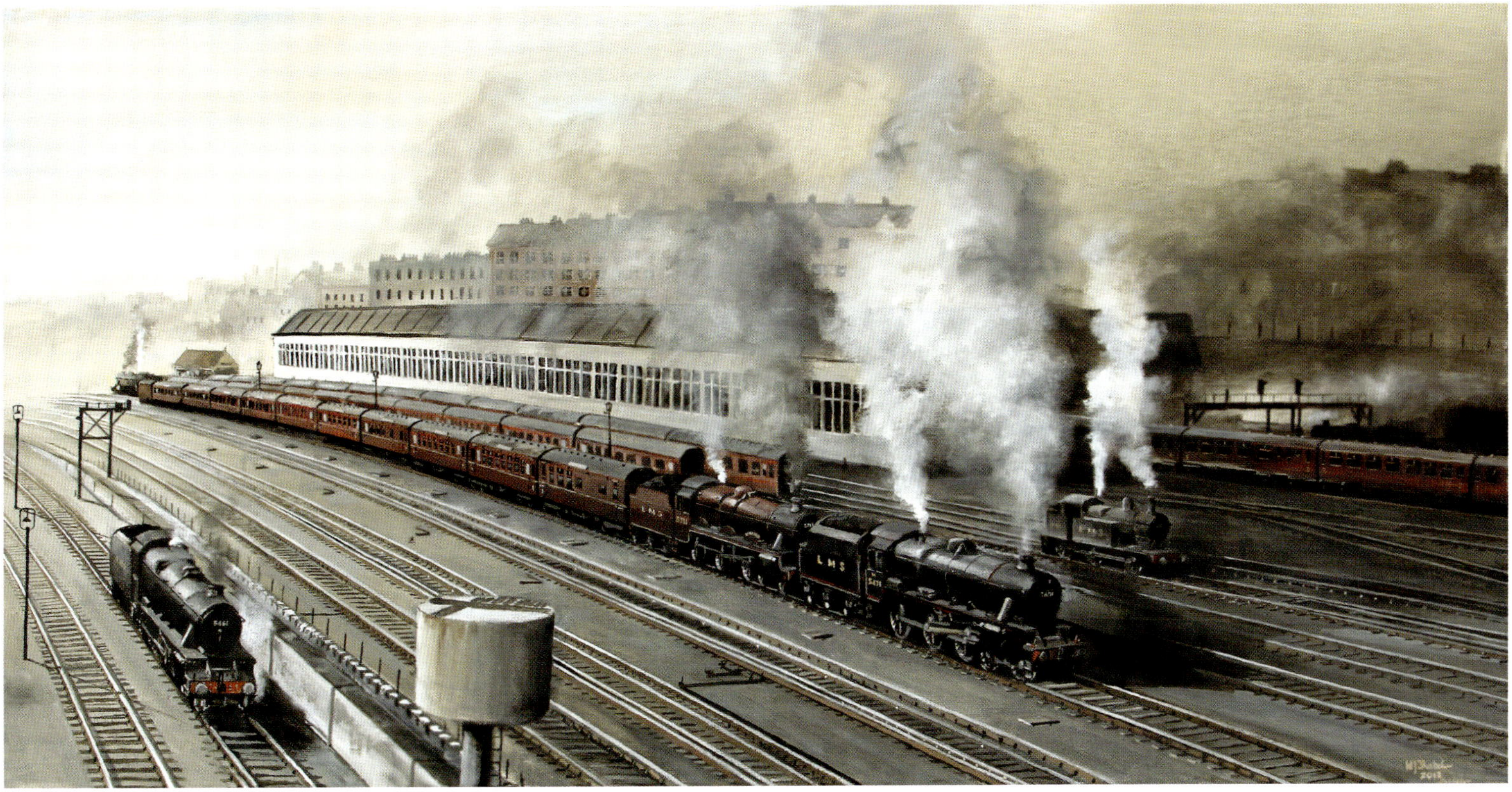

This is one of my favourite paintings. The location has been given earlier (see 'City of London' on Camden Bank, page 35). The red Jubilee still has its original Fowler tender which made these elegant machines look rather timid in comparison with the decidedly tough look of the pilot engine, a Black 5. Another of the same class waits to back down to Euston. I have deliberately left out an ungainly signal gantry which would have been located above the Jubilee, to improve the balance of the picture.

'Cock o' the North'

The ten years following the grouping from 1922 to 1932 were also the years of the Great Depression. This all started with the Wall Street Crash in the USA and affected the whole of Europe, not least Germany. In Britain anger and frustration led to some very dangerous acts such as when the Flying Scotsman was deliberately derailed during the General Strike. The emergence from the gloom of those years was a long time coming, and the building of 'Cock o' the North' was somehow symbolic of the early stages of recovery. It was an extravagant design. The brief that CME Nigel Gresley gave the drawing office was for a powerful locomotive capable of hauling the heaviest trains on the steeply graded and curved track between Edinburgh and Aberdeen. Gresley was assisted by a very young and very adventurous designer by the name of Oliver Bulleid. It seems that Gresley allowed the young Bulleid too much rope, although he must have been aware of all the novel facets of the design taking shape in the drawing office. 'Cock o' the North' was not only capable of replacing the ageing Scottish locomotives, it could probably tow two or three of them along as well!

When it was completed Gresley wisely sent 'Cock o' the North' to France for testing on the stationary testing plant there. The French were well ahead of the British in this respect and testing new designs had allowed them to produce some of the most efficient steam engines of the period. Bulleid was sent with the engine to oversee the results, but seems to have ignored the outcome, which showed that 'Cock o' the North' exhibited very high coal and water consumption, both on the test plant and on the open road. On its return to the UK it was duly sent to Scotland where it exhibited the same characteristics along with a tendency to spread the tracks on the sharp curves. It did also demonstrate a capability of hauling anything it was presented with! Bulleid complained that it was used in the wrong way and should have been used on the East Coast main line. He may well have been right, but he seems – not for the last time – to have forgotten his original brief!

Nigel Gresley announced to the Institute of Mechanical Engineers that the first 'Cock o' the North' would be the last 'Cock o' the North'. All his future P2s were a little more conventional in terms of valve gears, water heaters and so on, but the publicity this beautiful machine received was of enormous value to the LNER.

In my painting I have tried to capture the impact of the emergence from the gloom and despondency of the earlier years. What a startling sight it must have been as it backed out of Kings Cross station yard, into the gloom of the station itself. Nigel Gresley and Oliver Bulleid in the bowler hats – Gresley is the fatter of the two – look on! So does the driver leaning on the buffer beam of his very clean N2 tank engine. He must be thinking that the space age has arrived; more likely, given the conservative views of most engine drivers of that time, he is probably wondering if it will make it north of the border. I have taken some liberties with the position of the old signal box, and the platforms – also the spacing of the rails in the yard which was actually notoriously cramped. In fact the gasometers which surround this area would be roughly where the N2 is standing!

The dingy apartments bordering York road stand behind the signal box and York Road Station platform. A Quad Art set can be seen diving into the tunnel towards Moorgate. The ironwork of the bridge across the station mouth is yet to be demolished. Somehow these always made Kings Cross look desperately poor and tatty. I wish it was still there, along with 'Cock o' the North'. The engine lasted well into BR days, but as an ugly much rebuilt Pacific. It remained the coal miners' friend to the end. Perhaps Bulleid was right and it should (with different valve gear!) have been allowed to race on the East Coast main line.

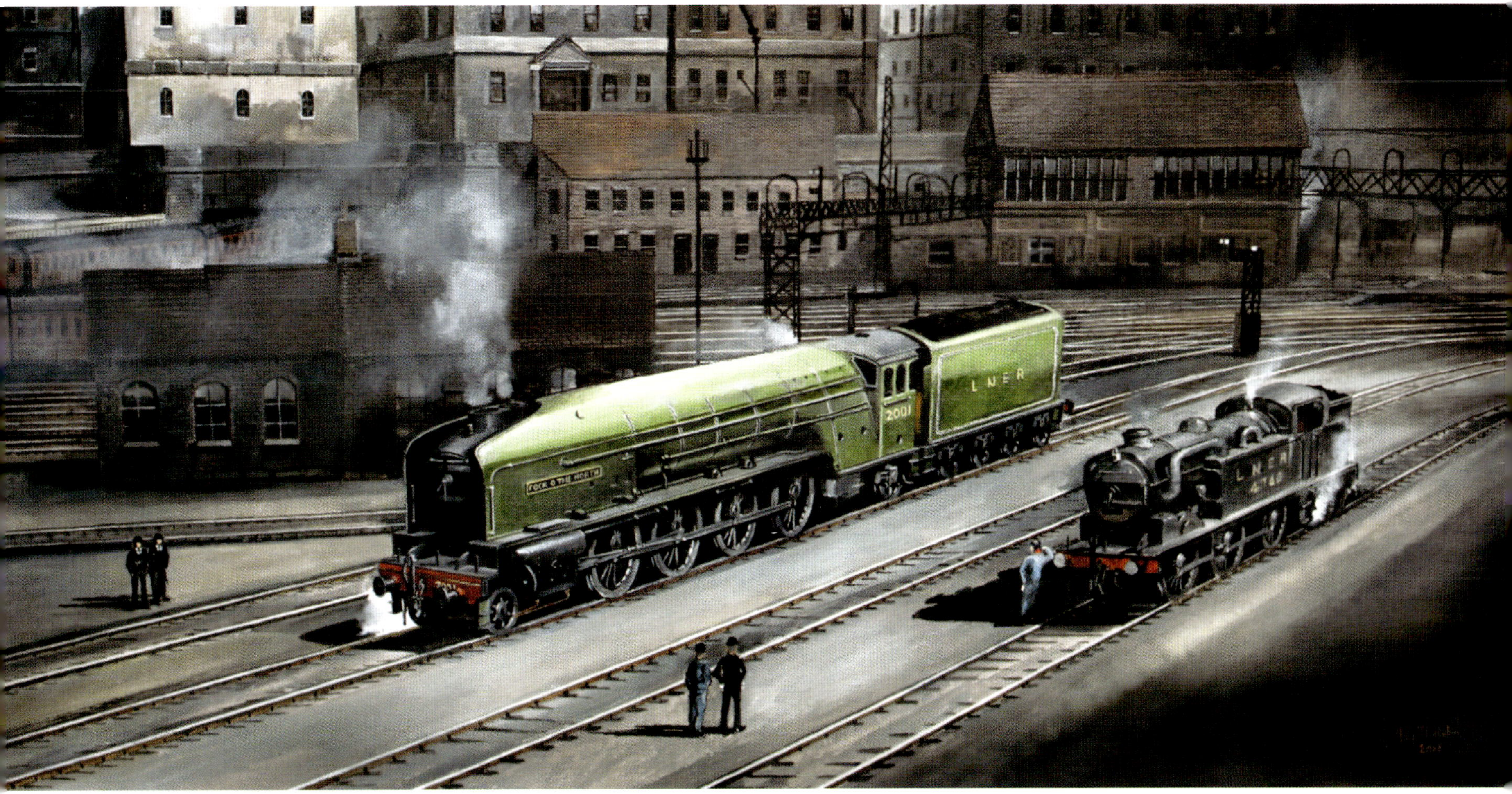

'Cock o' the North' in Kings Cross station yard.

Images of the War Years

The Lamp Store

Throughout the Second World War the railways were the main source of transport. The trains operated under dreadful conditions during the years of blackout. Even the fire from the locomotives had to be hidden from the sight of German bombers overhead. Photography of the railways was strictly forbidden, and there was precious little in the way of film anyway.

Both of my Grandfathers had to work in these conditions, and it took its toll. Grandfather Ern was particularly badly affected and his health never fully recovered. He suffered from gastric problems no doubt brought about in some measure by the stress, and died while I was still in my early childhood. The memories of him leaving his house in his overalls with a small canvas satchel containing his white enamel mug and some sandwiches still remain with me – that and the smell of paraffin and coal which never seemed to leave the house or his clothes! He often had to work night shifts, and the satchel would be accompanied by a hand lamp. It is the lamp I now own and which appears in this picture.

In this darkness, even in the war, the trains still had to be visible at rail level, and the signal lamps were made and maintained in various little huts usually next to the signal boxes. The painting is of a typical LNER hut with Grandfather Ern's three-colour aspect hand lamp being tested before returning to service. The inner part of the lamp rotated with a clear, amber or red window of celluloid in each. The inner part of the lamp was a paraffin tank and a wick which needed frequent trimming to prevent the acrid smoke from burning paraffin making life impossible. Another reason I remember these lamps and the smell so very well is because I spent many hours as a child in such huts and signal boxes and watching the railwaymen of my day attending to them thanks to my other Grandfather! It was so exciting seeing a signalman with his hand lamp walk out on to the staging of his box, hang his lamp on the post and pass the tablet (for single line working) to the fireman of a passing locomotive. I never ceased to marvel at the sureness and commonplace ease with which this was done.

I have two of these lamps in my possession now. The design changed hardly at all from LNER to British Railways. I suppose paraffin lamps still exist somewhere on our modern railways; it is unthinkable that this heritage has gone for ever.

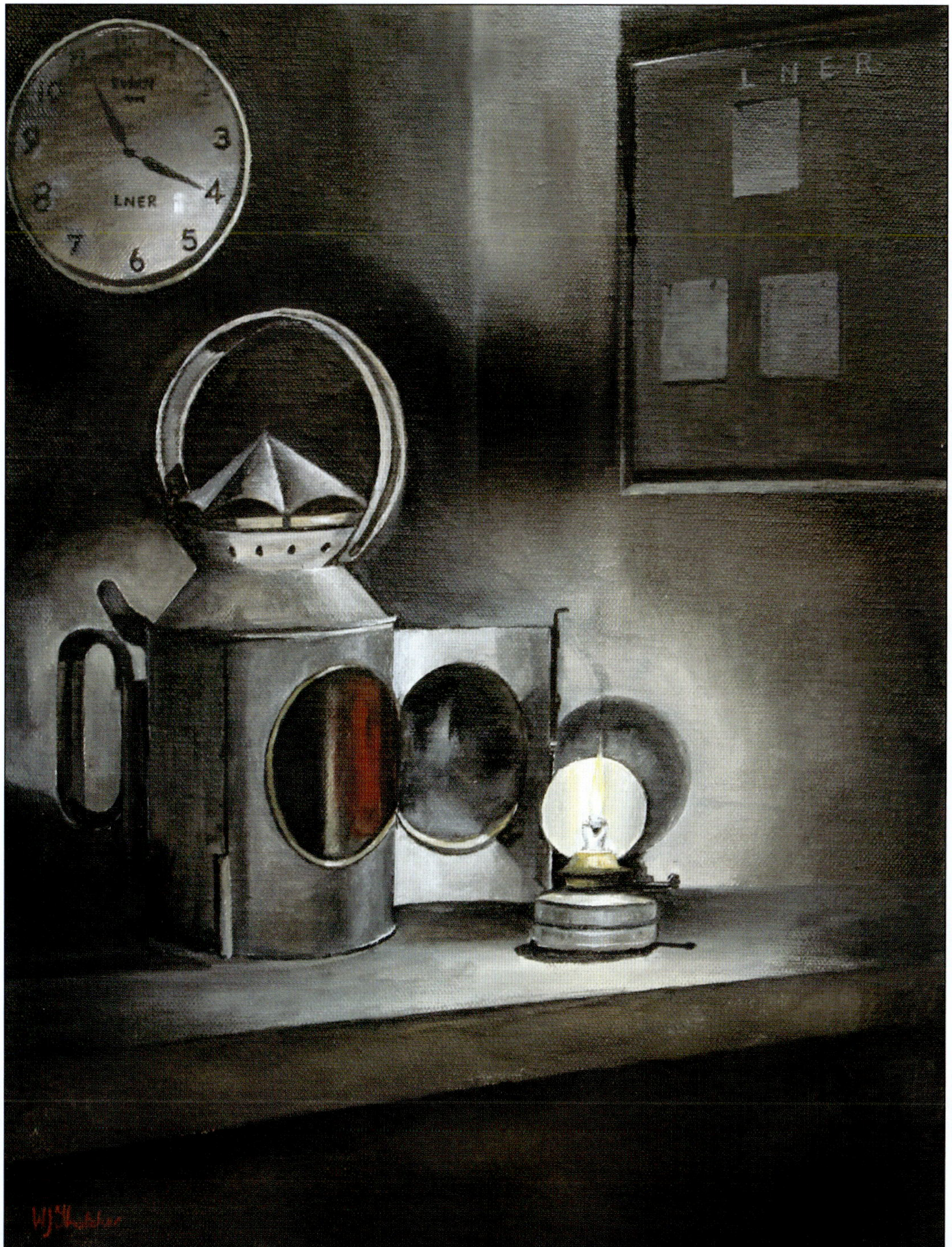
LNER
L N E R

Together Again

Liverpool Street station was bombed several times during the war. Fortunately the elegant Great Eastern Hotel was not hit and survived in original state until desecrated by the modernisation of the station complex in the 1990s. The painting shows a soldier from the airborne division (red beret) being greeted by his lady. The shafts of sunlight in Liverpool Street were even fewer during the blackout, and the couple are highlighted in one, with a K3 in a disgraceful state of cleanliness visible on the left having brought the soldier home on leave. The atmosphere of Liverpool Street Station remained the same until modernisation and continued as my favourite of all the London stations because of the wonderful display of light and shade, and the cathedral-like architecture.

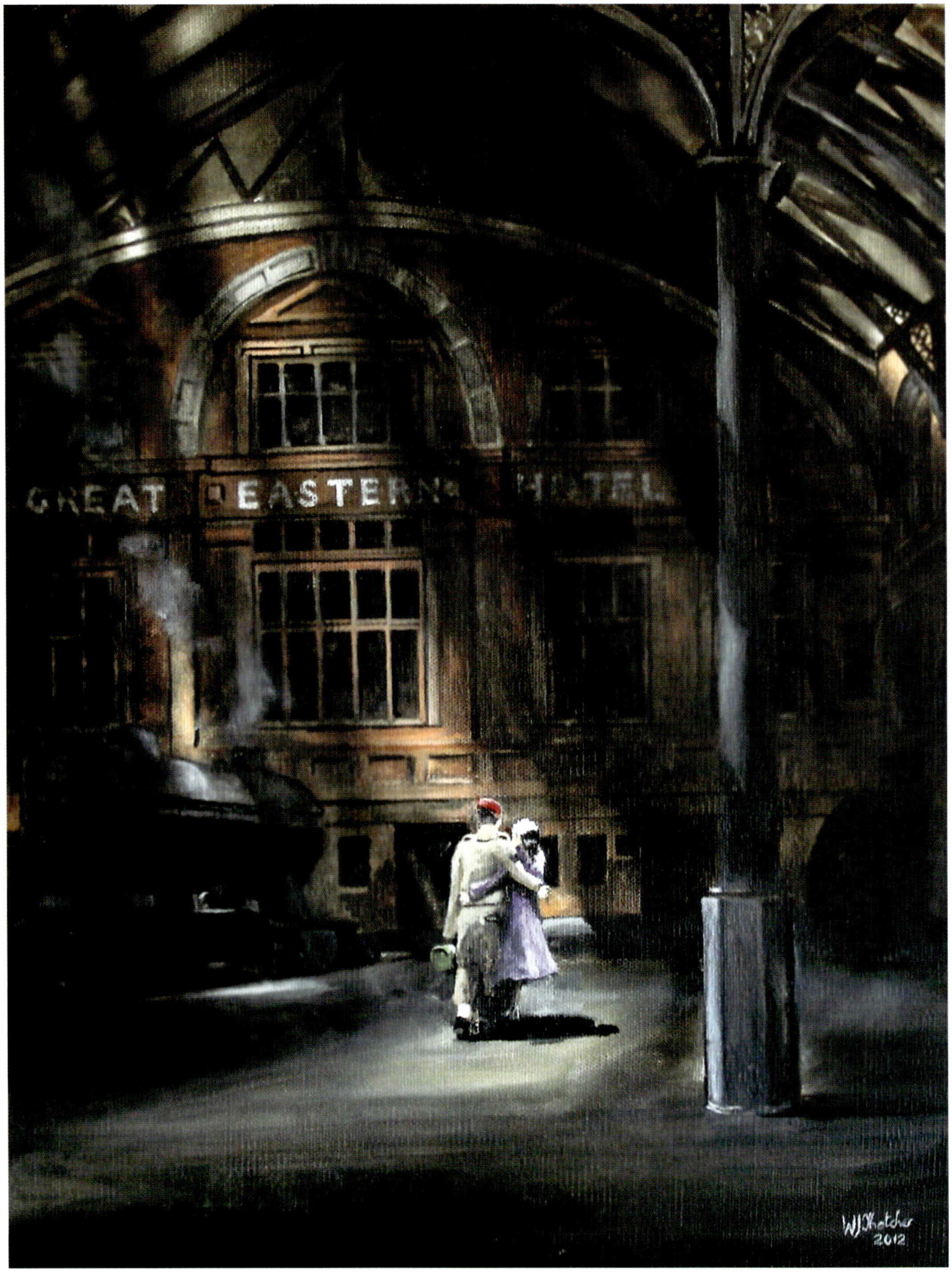

The Merseyside Express

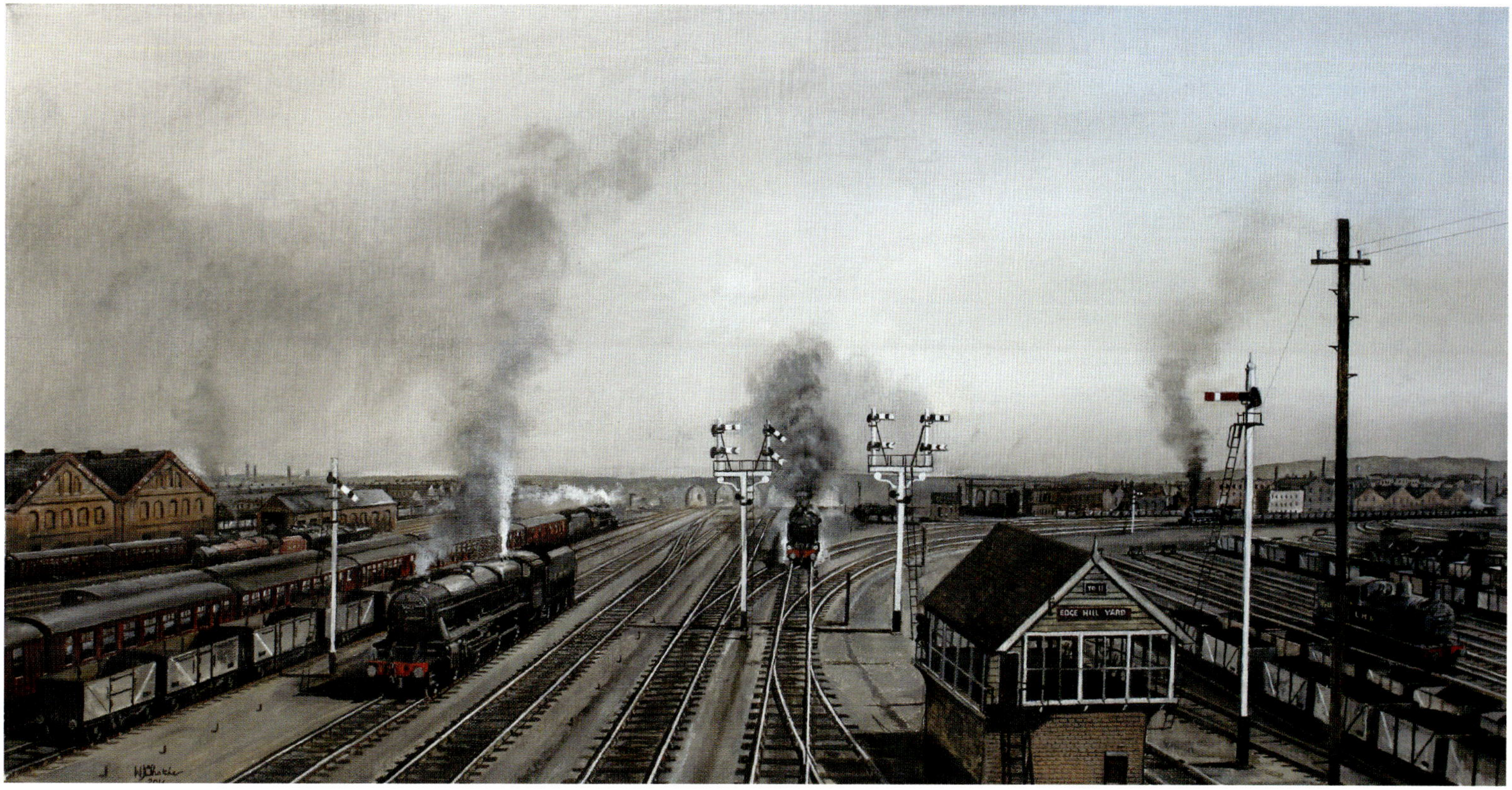

The view towards Manchester from Edge Hill station just before hostilities began in 1939. It is a view which would have been impossible to photograph without a modern cherrypicker or some similar device, but the painter always has freedom of choice when it comes to imagination! From this imaginary elevated vantage point we can see the Merseyside Express heading towards Liverpool. A Princess Pacific, in its original red livery can be seen in front of the sheds, and a Jinty sits cold and unmoving in the yard waiting for a fire and its next turn of duty. Hardly any of this remains today.

The Birth of British Railways

Having used, and abused, the resources of the big four railway companies throughout the war, a new government showed its gratitude by nationalisation. No doubt it was genuinely felt that by so doing the system could be rationalised and made more efficient, but the decision in the main was purely a vote-catching exercise. The railwaymen, most of them, wanted it; they hoped for better working conditions, better pay and shorter hours. Their frustration that none of these happened has been well documented. Furthermore the country was near to bankruptcy and, as early as 1948, it was decided that coal, which was the only source of energy not imported in the UK, had to be the source of power for the railways. The early hopes of the railwaymen for diesel and electric locomotives was still born, and instead a fleet of standard class locomotives was designed. Britain was to continue with steam for the foreseeable future.

Not all enginemen welcomed the change that nationalisation brought. The Great Western in particular always had considerable pride, not only in their engines but in their traditions. I think it is fair to say that where there was a tendency to look after their locomotives, such as sheds like Edinburgh and Kings Cross, the enthusiasm for nationalisation was muted. Many drivers who had worked their way up through the ranks of cleaner to fireman, fireman to driver, resented the fact that younger men might now attain their status in a shorter time with less hard work. Certainly my own Grandfather, Ern, felt this way, but my step Grandfather, Jimmy Dennis, felt the exact opposite! In the end both were disenchanted with nationalisation for different reasons.

The early years of the 1950s saw the catastrophic result of the dependence on coal as the only affordable energy source both in the home and on the railways. Exceptionally cold winters combined with an increase in the population (the baby boom) ensured a smoke-laden atmosphere. The low pressures associated with the cold weather also ensured that the smoke did not rise, and the resultant smog became a symbol of London for several decades. Indeed they are still regarded as such in the USA today. The newly formed National Health System struggled to cope with the increase in lung disease, a fact of life which affected your writer. It was a grim time.

London in 1952 was rarely as clear as is depicted in my painting. The fact that St Paul's Cathedral, was only a mile or two from Kings Cross was unknown to many. That great symbol of survival from the Blitz was no longer visible in the smog.

The North London line can be seen traversing the painting opposite where a W class tank engine is hauling a cross London transfer freight. The area in front of St Pancras and Kings Cross and bounded by this line was then a massive railway complex; a giant delivery yard for all of London's consumables. The docks in the East End point their finger like cranes into the sky to remind the railways that they too represent a source of both import and export. The back-to-back rows of housing, many of which had been built by the old railway companies, still grace the periphery of the railway complex – at least those which had not been flattened by bombs. But signs of the new are visible, the first stirring of recovery perhaps. Cars are beginning to appear on the streets. So too are red London buses of the half cab variety. Perhaps the warmth of the evening has encouraged the Londoners to walk about in their shirt sleeves. The advertisement board tells them it's 'Quicker by Rail', which was true when most people did not own a car.

The scene was painted from an imagined elevated position above Primrose Hill. Details were obtained mainly from old maps for there were few photographs at that time and none at all from this position. Almost nothing of this scene exists today. With the exception of St Paul's all the buildings have been spoilt, demolished, or hidden by tower blocks, interwoven with trees and graffiti-covered walls.

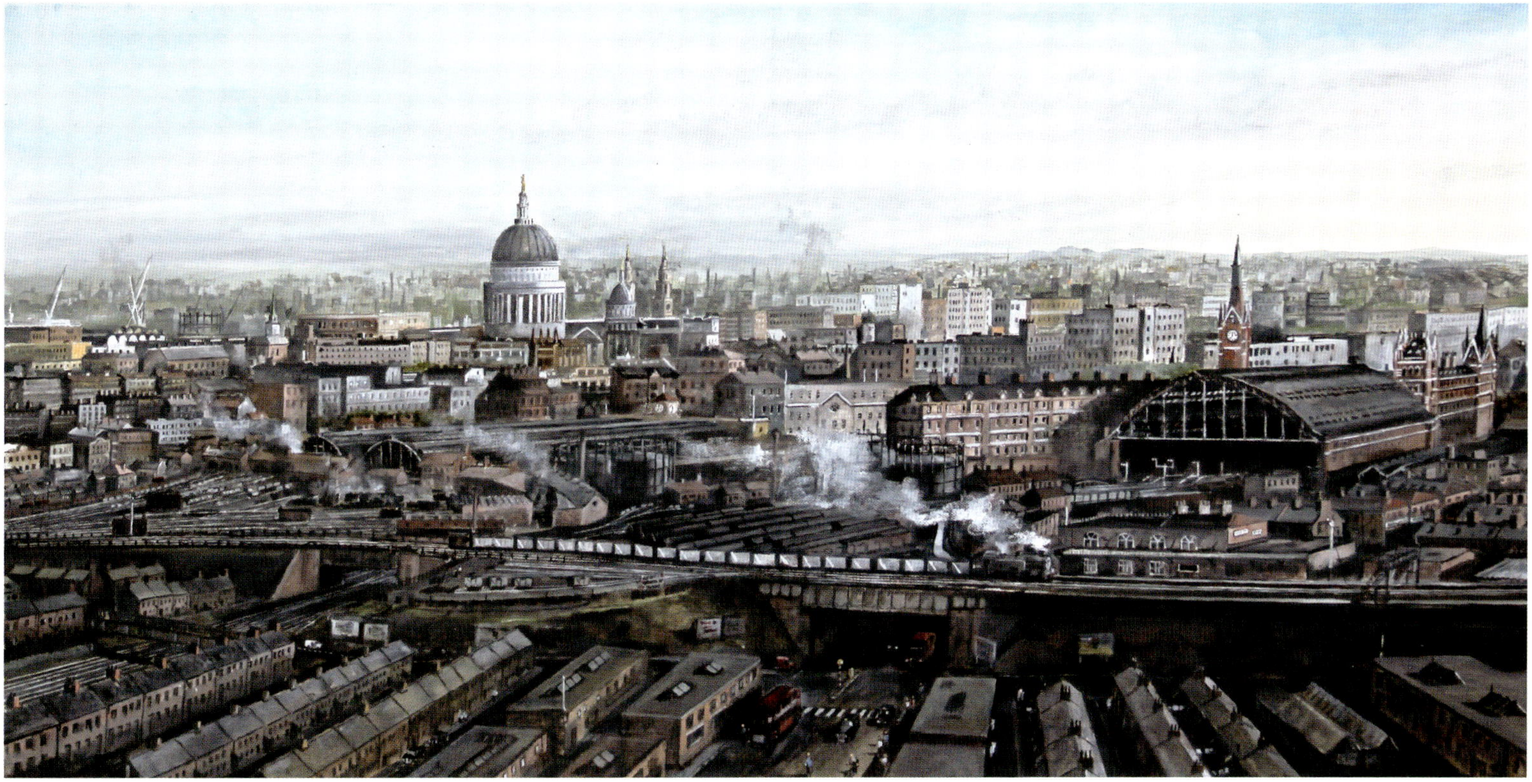

London 1952 from above Primrose Hill

Rannoch Moor

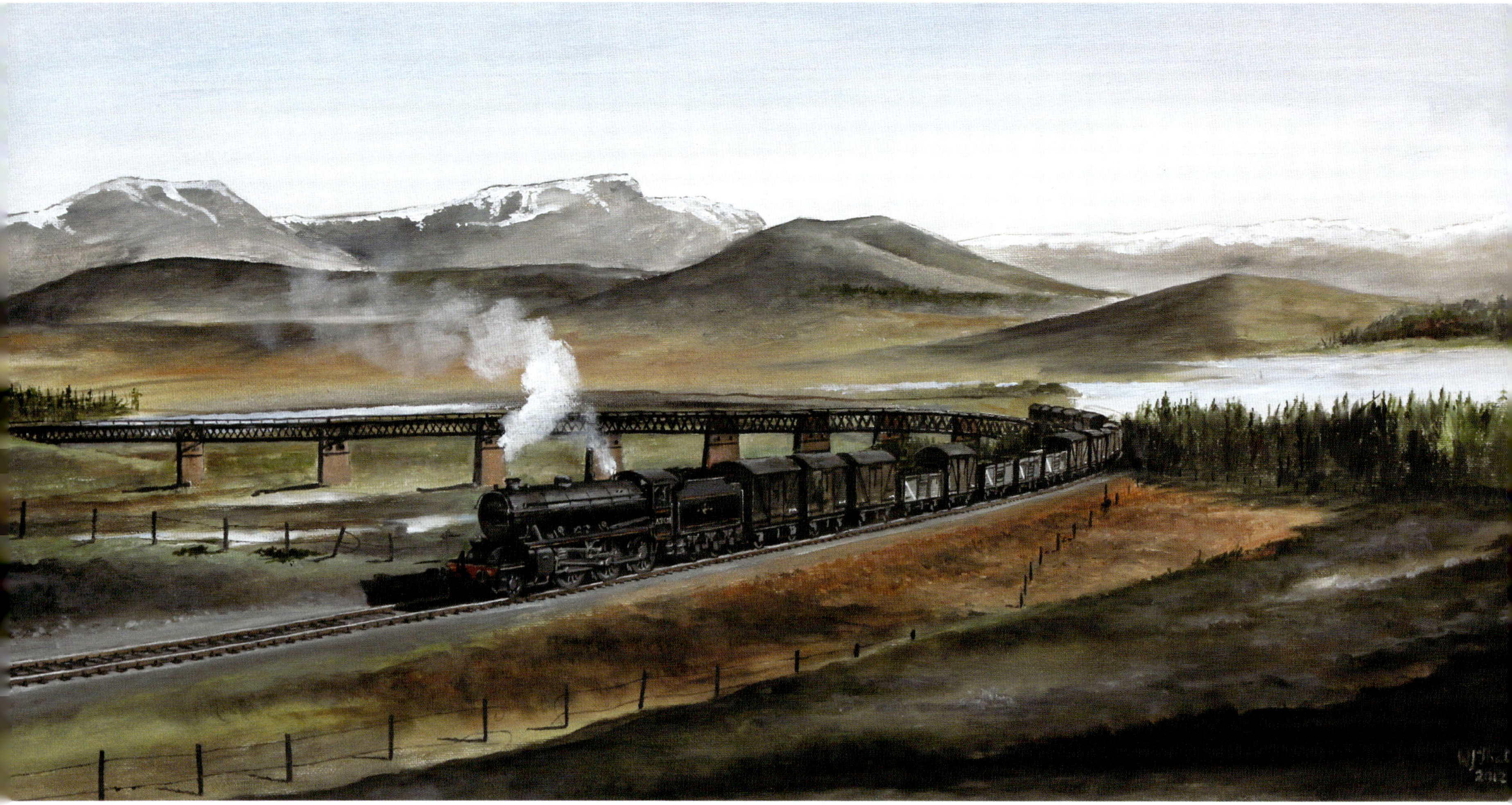

On the odd day that the sun breaks through, this is one of the most beautiful places one could hope to see. Once this area was covered by a forest of Scots pine and other trees. The reckless deforestation has left behind a peat bog of some magnitude, which the line from Glasgow to Fort William crosses with some difficulty. In the middle of it all is Rannoch Moor station, beyond which the line curves sharply over an iron and brick bridge. I was encouraged to do this painting as a change from engine sheds and lines, but also as a result of my interest photographing and painting in acrylics the seascapes and landscapes of the west coast of Scotland. This is the location I photographed one glorious day and used to imagine a K2 (once the mainstay of steam on this line) crossing it. The glorious colours of a spring day coincide with the remains of snow which still linger on the mountains above the moor.

‘King Henry VII’

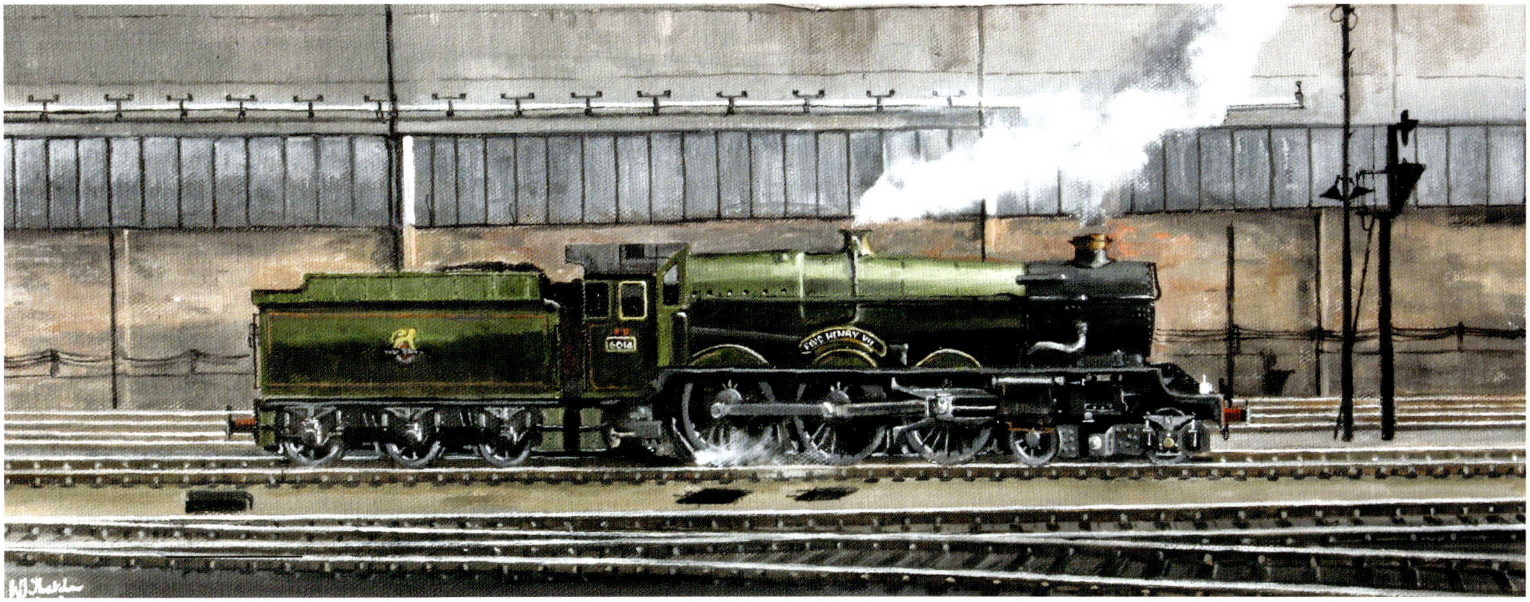

The London stations always had a fascination for me. Of course the sheer volume of traffic coming in and out of the metropolis had a lot to do with it. It is hard for us to realise that trains were leaving Euston or Paddington roughly every three minutes. Paddington was different from all the other stations. Its entrance was so *grand*, its steps leading up to a vast marble floored area, with a giant destination board proclaiming trains to Penzance, Swansea, Worcester, Birmingham and many other locations in between. Outside the station to the right was a long brick building, ideal as a backdrop. This painting depicts an unusual locomotive backing out of Paddington having brought in a West Country express. ‘King Henry VII’ was formerly streamlined by the GWR in an attempt to match the LNER and LMS publicity. The results were ugly in the extreme and were soon removed, but this locomotive retained its wedge-shaped cab to the end, which gave the firebox a slightly shortened appearance. Notice the elaborate frame arrangements around the front bogie!

Hitchin

Having moved home steadily northwards away from Hatfield, the home town of my childhood, I returned to Hitchin in Hertfordshire, a convenient location from which to commute to Old Welwyn. It was here that I was employed by Xerox UK. I had no idea that within a very short space of time I would be sent across to the USA to work. At the time of my arrival in Hitchin in 1975, steam had long gone and the steam ban was being strictly imposed. I stood on the northbound platform and photographed Deltics roaring through at 100mph, not realising that their day was numbered too, as the HST units which replaced them were making an ever more frequent appearance.

I had bought my house in Hitchin with the knowledge that the electrification of the ECML was soon to reach the station, and that would make Hitchin an easy commute to London, with its consequent effect on house prices. Sometimes an interest in railways has some benefits! However the station itself was little changed from steam days when I arrived, apart from the coloured aspect signals which replaced the old semaphores to the north of the yard.

Hitchin had been the outer limit of suburban working, even in steam days. Most of the services there had been hauled by L1 tank engines of Thomson design. They were powerful machines but their boilers were too small, and they had a tendency to run out of steam by Welwyn Garden City, and found Hitchin a distinct struggle. Thomson's more successful B1 locomotives took over in the latter days, especially as these machines were useful on the Royston and Cambridge line which diverged from Hitchin just north of the station. The trackwork from Hitchin through Sandy and on to York was very flat, and regarded as a racing ground for all the north and southbound expresses. Speeds of 90mph with steam were quite common and on occasion even 100mph.

I have done two paintings in the same location to capture this period. In both, the standby engine can be seen waiting for an out of breath L1. This was one of the weaknesses in terms of cost in steam days, as tons of coal were wasted simply keeping engines like this in steam, to say nothing of the wasted manpower. In the top painting A1 Pacific 60136 'Alcazar' is racing south on a fine summer's evening. These engines were reputed to be somewhat rough riding. I had a soft spot for this particular locomotive as it was considered a rogue engine by the sheds which looked after it – that is until Mr Townsend of Kings Cross shed had it re-wheeled with a Gresley designed bogy whereupon it rode better than any other member of the class.

The second painting is of a V2 mogul, racing north in heavy snow. The only warm places are inside the carriages where the passengers can be seen insulated from the elements outside; the footplate might not offer the same level of comfort! The crew on the standby locomotive have probably found shelter somewhere off the footplate of their engine, which is so cold it has acquired a covering of snow on the bunker and cab roof. The heavy snowfalls of the early 1960s date this picture

Today the electrification of the East Coast line is complete and electric units of privatised railway companies such as GNR race through Hitchin as express trains always have, but without even the snarl of a Deltic engine. Their 150mph passing is silent apart from the noise of wheels on rail, and with continuously welded track even the clatter of rail joints has disappeared.

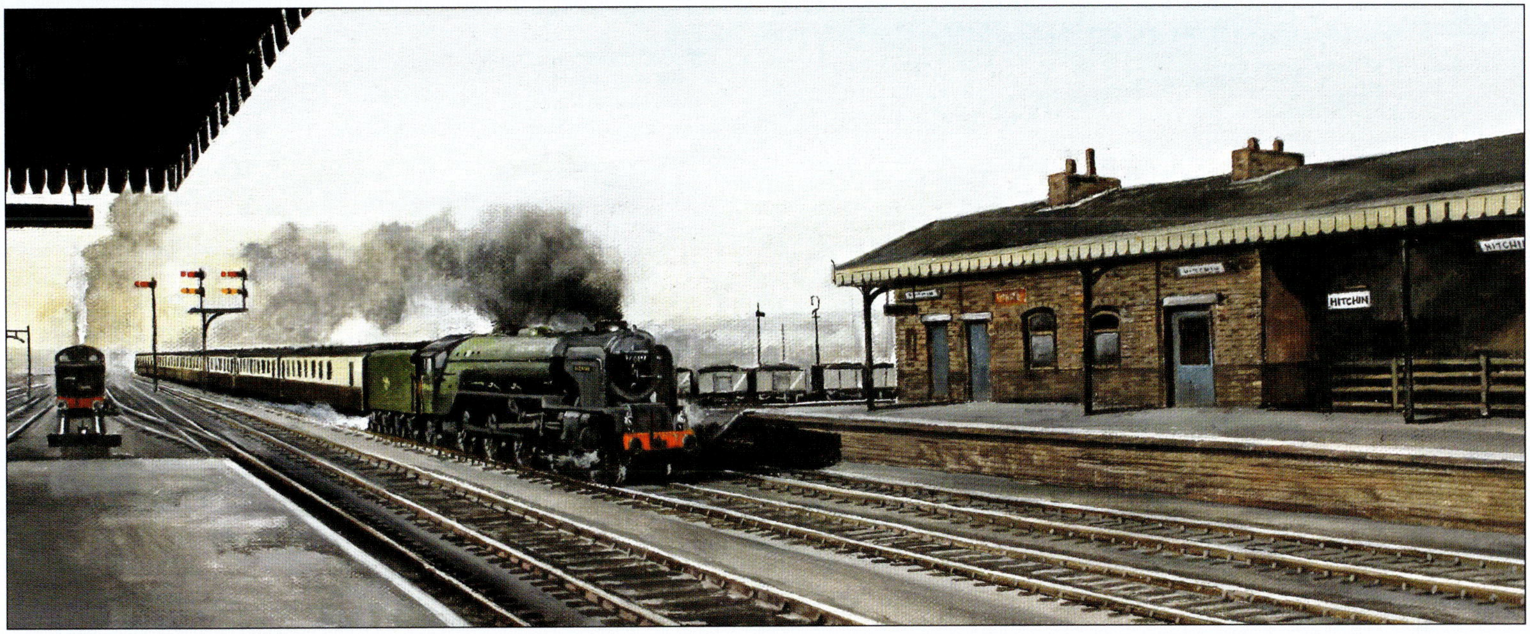
HITCHIN

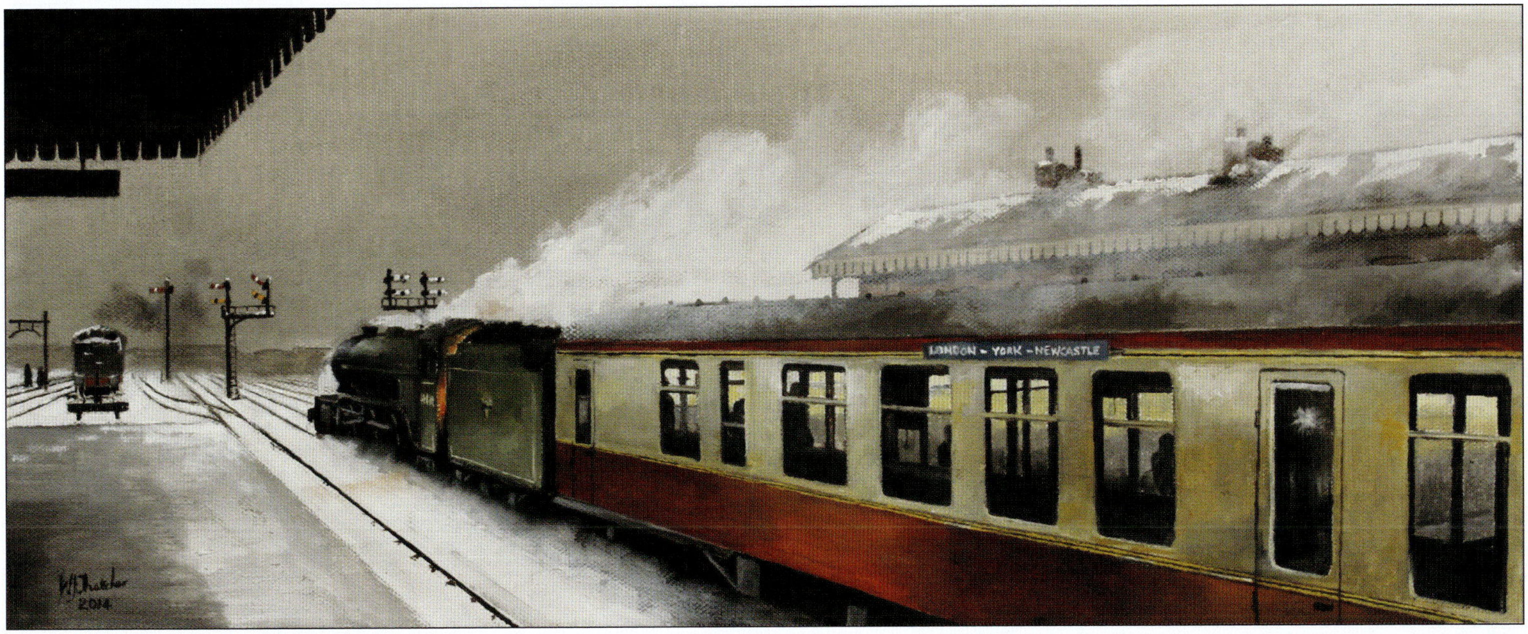
LONDON - YORK - NEWCASTLE

Liverpool Lime Street Cutting

I was employed as a post-doctoral Fellow in the Department of Engineering of Liverpool University in the early 1970s, and so became quite familiar with the railways around the city. Liverpool Lime Street Station was my gateway to south or north, and the long cutting immediately after leaving the station was always a fascinating mixture of sunlight and shade. I have done several paintings of the area around Edge Hill. I find it incredibly easy to associate it with steam days, for although the steam engine is long gone, the smell of soot lingers, as though it is determined to make sure the past will never completely fade.

Historically this is one of the most famous railway locations of them all, since the Manchester & Liverpool Railway was one of the first passenger carrying railways in the world. I use the expression carefully, because the line out of Whitstable in Kent ran it a very close second, and the Stockton & Darlington line *had* carried passengers, albeit in coal trucks! It was close to this location that the very first fatal railway accident occurred, to William Husskison, an MP no less, who failed to look behind him as other MPs have done since! The cutting was more open in those days, but with the increased urbanisation of Liverpool bridges were built which spanned the railway line. It was, and still is, possible to see right down the cutting from the very end of Edge Hill Station, although now spoilt by the overhead wires. The view is no longer obscured by the smoke and general murk which never disappeared in steam days.

Painting steam engines in dark locations is not as easy as it might seem. The human eye has an extraordinary ability to distinguish differences in shade, so any variations of black which are not quite right will show up. This is compounded by the digital photographs of today which lack the subtlety of old fashioned roll film and somehow render colours and shades in a harsh and brittle manner. It seems as though technology is trying to inject far more colour into everything than is actually there.

I have painted the cutting as it was, towards the very end of steam when enthusiasts (the Master Neverers Association) were cleaning locomotives for free so that they could take good photographs. This group of enthusiasts would often clean only one side of the engine, the side they intended to photograph, The railway shed staff treated them with great tolerance in the main but in some areas this amounted to indifference, as the sheds which saw out the end of steam were all of the Midland Region, which never did have a high reputation for keeping their engines clean.

Sunlight and shadow from alternate bridges and tunnels dapple the cutting wall and track bed, glancing off the Black 5 emerging into the daylight. Sometimes the shafts of sunlight are so bright it is impossible to see through them and the sudden emergence of a locomotive can be quite startling (especially an electric unit which has ascended the cutting in silence!).

The locomotive exhaust has a suitably sulphurous look to it, and it seems that the 'Neverers' have been at it, for it is unusually clean. Perhaps it was fitting that the last steam train to run for British Railways – the 15 Guinea Specials – were hauled by members of this class, and came from this area, which became the place both of the birth and death of steam

Alas, now electric locomotives and multiple units make their soul-less departure through these same tunnels – only the light and shade remain. The occasional steam special is allowed to blast its way up the gradient under the web of the overhead catenary. Perhaps the smell of soot and hot oil will always be there.

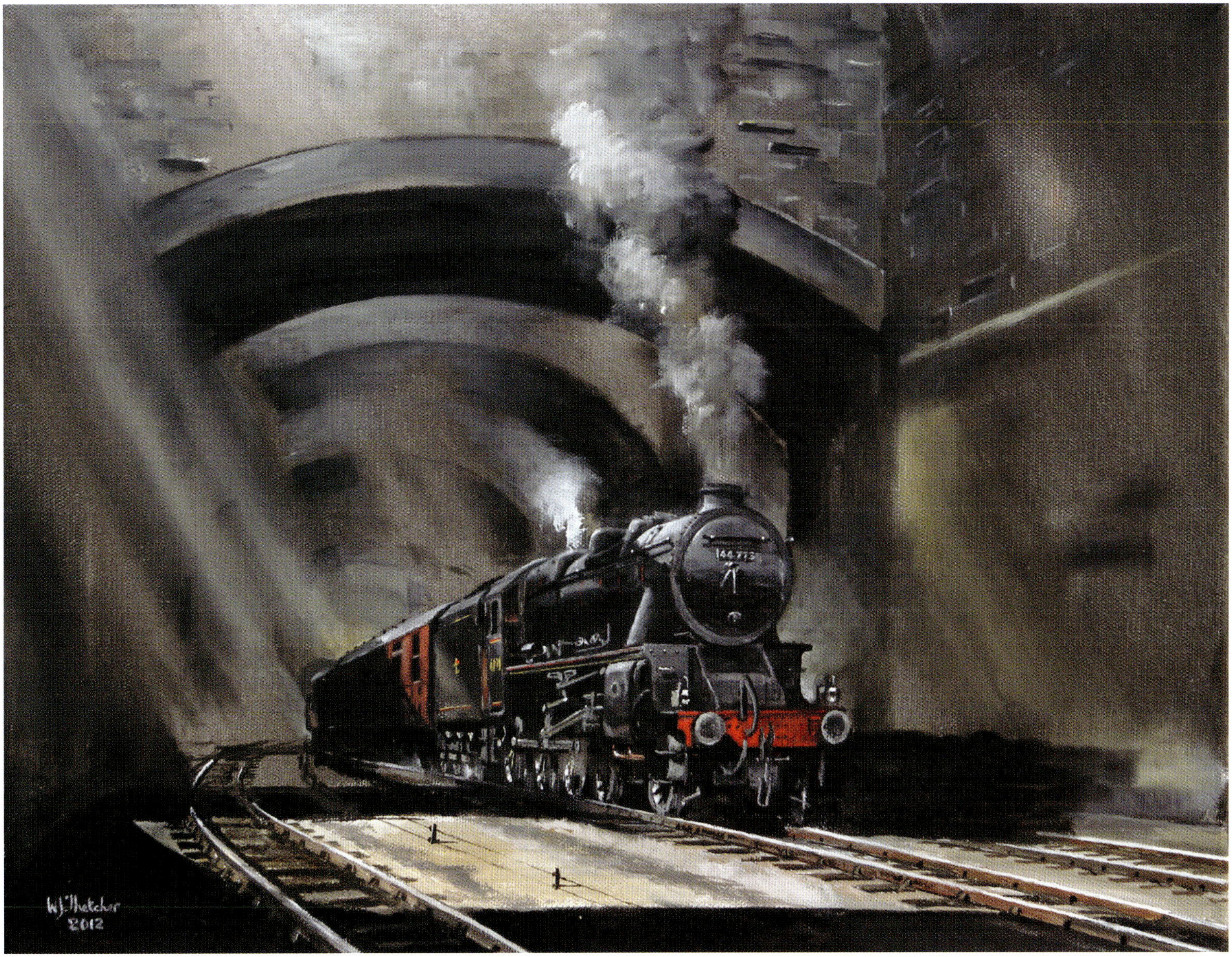

Sunlight and shadow in Liverpool Lime Street Cutting

Roughton Road Junction

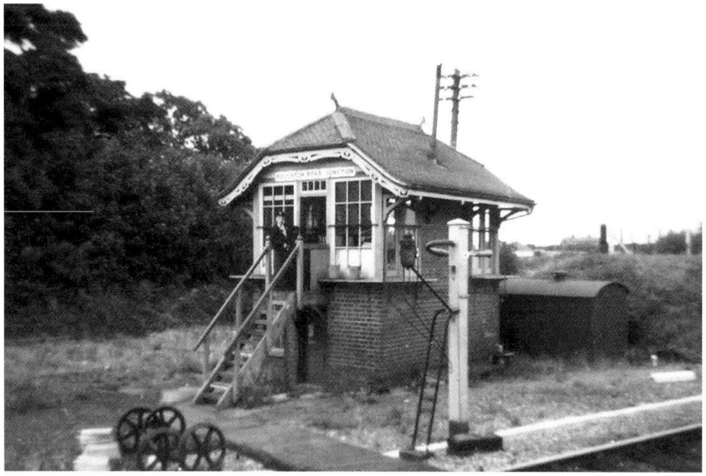

The location of this picture was so etched into my memory. I did not need any photographs to remind me, as I spent much of my time in Norfolk as a child inside that signal box. From about the age of eleven I would cross the railway line and spend as much time as I could watching the very low number of trains which passed from Cromer Beach station on their way to Norwich. Hard to believe this was once a thriving part of the old Great Eastern Railway system. The photograph above was taken with my box brownie camera in 1956.

The signalman was a young man named Barton, and he kept a shotgun in the box which he used, between trains, to poach pheasants from my step Grandfathers field opposite. I was his runner. Many of the birds ended up in the adjacent woods which were owned by someone else. The signal box was at the junction of the GE route to Norwich and the old MGNJR route to Overstrand and Mundesley, the track of that line having been lifted several years earlier. There was no toilet in the signal box, the old railway van, the wheels of which adorn the front of the photograph, served for that purpose. One dark evening in winter I was there when Mr Barton decided he needed to use that facility, instead of which he went down below to use the signal box wall instead. While he was so engaged a freight train coming from Cromer passed and the fireman, unable to see the signalman, held the train at the box. There was a heated exchange of bad language which I found quite impressive.

This whole area is now a housing estate known as Burnt Hills. It has its own halt but the signal box is long gone. The main line remains, and is still singled from this location into Cromer Beach station. Diesel multiple units shuttle back and forwards on an hourly basis where once B1s and B12s, along with an assortment of freight engines, made occasional journeys to and from Norwich.

I have caught the morning train to Norwich on a late autumn day, with the platelayer, who also spent much time in the warmth of the box, slouching alongside the track. Signalman Barton can be seen with the single line tablet behind him, having just exchanged with the driver of the B1. No problems this time!

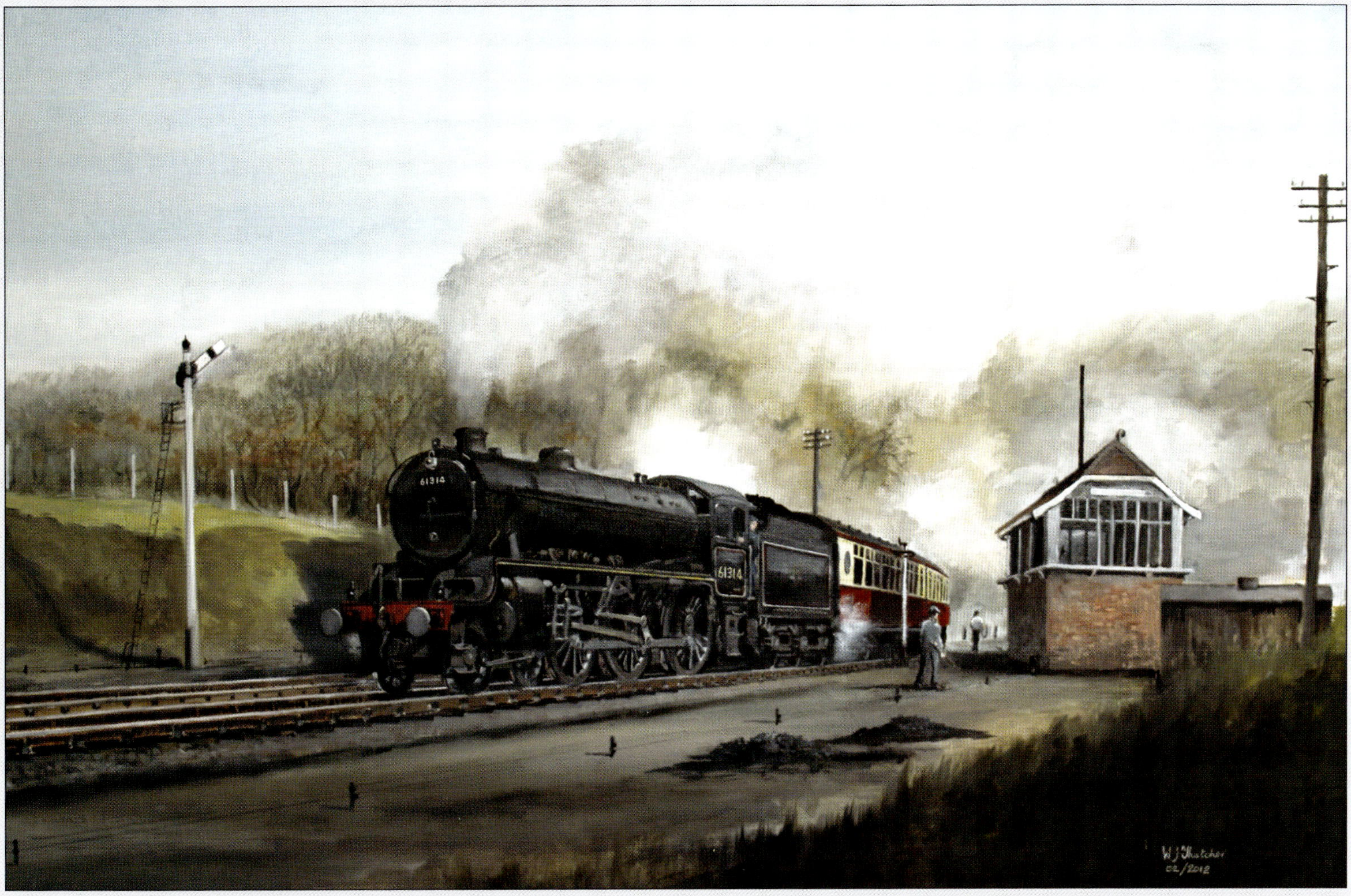

The Norwich morning train passing Roughton Road Junction

Evening at the Cross

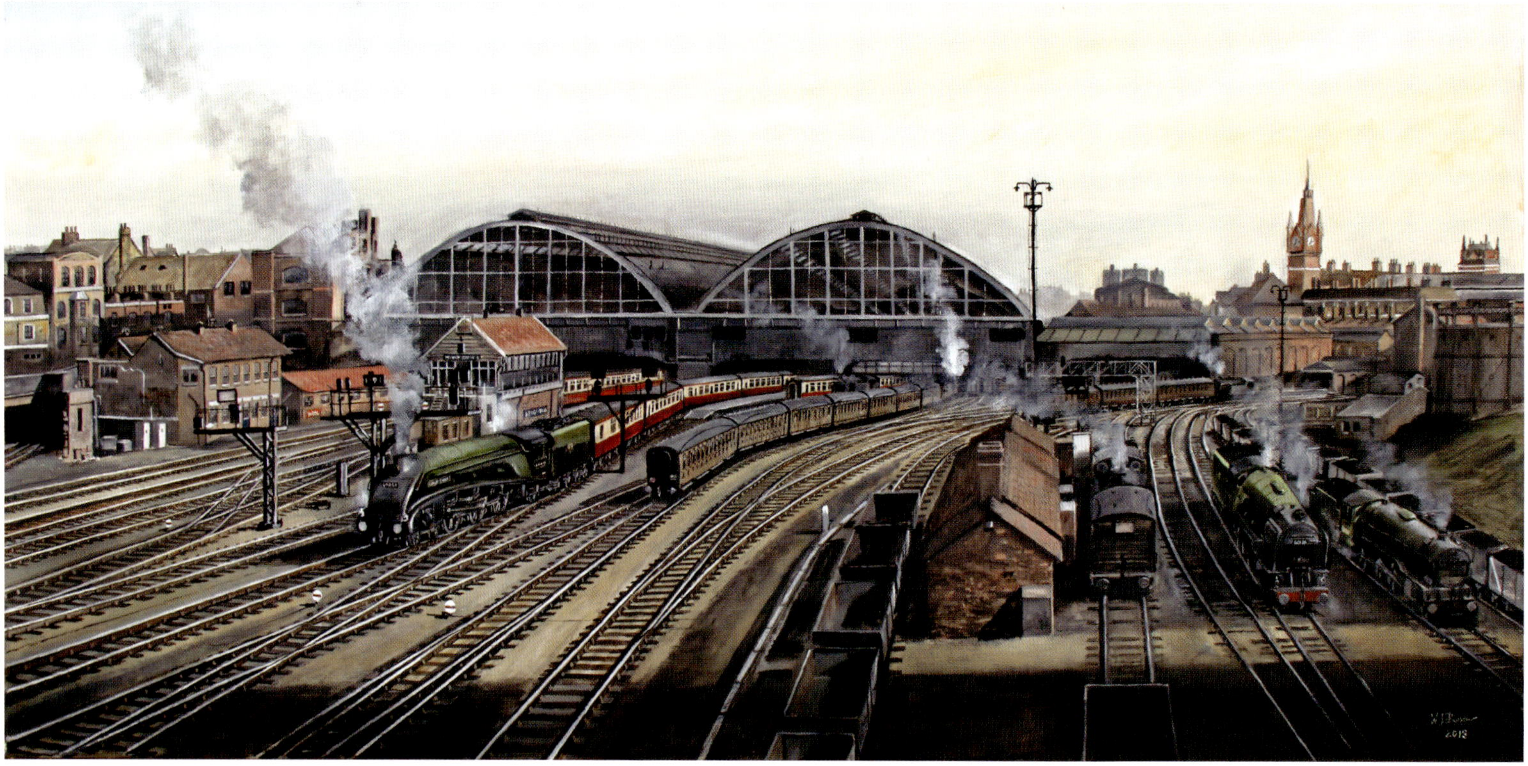

The area around Kings Cross and St Pancras is now so completely changed from the 1950s. Kings Cross was never the most salubrious of London's districts. The buildings were mostly tall tenements, flats, or factories, smoke-blackened from years of industry and the railways. Indeed there was a restriction applied to Kings Cross shed and station limiting the amount of smoke they were permitted to produce.

The painting captures the 'Cross' in a golden light which it saw too seldom. The multiplicity of tracks narrow down rapidly to enable trains to pass through gasworks tunnel, above which and to the right, the painter is positioned. To the right of the painting one can see the graceful clock tower of the Midland Hotel outside St Pancras. A4 60021 'Wild Swan' leaves with a train of red and cream coaching stock on its journey north. To the left is Kings Cross York Road platform, and the single line to Moorgate dives under the road.

Black 5 at Night

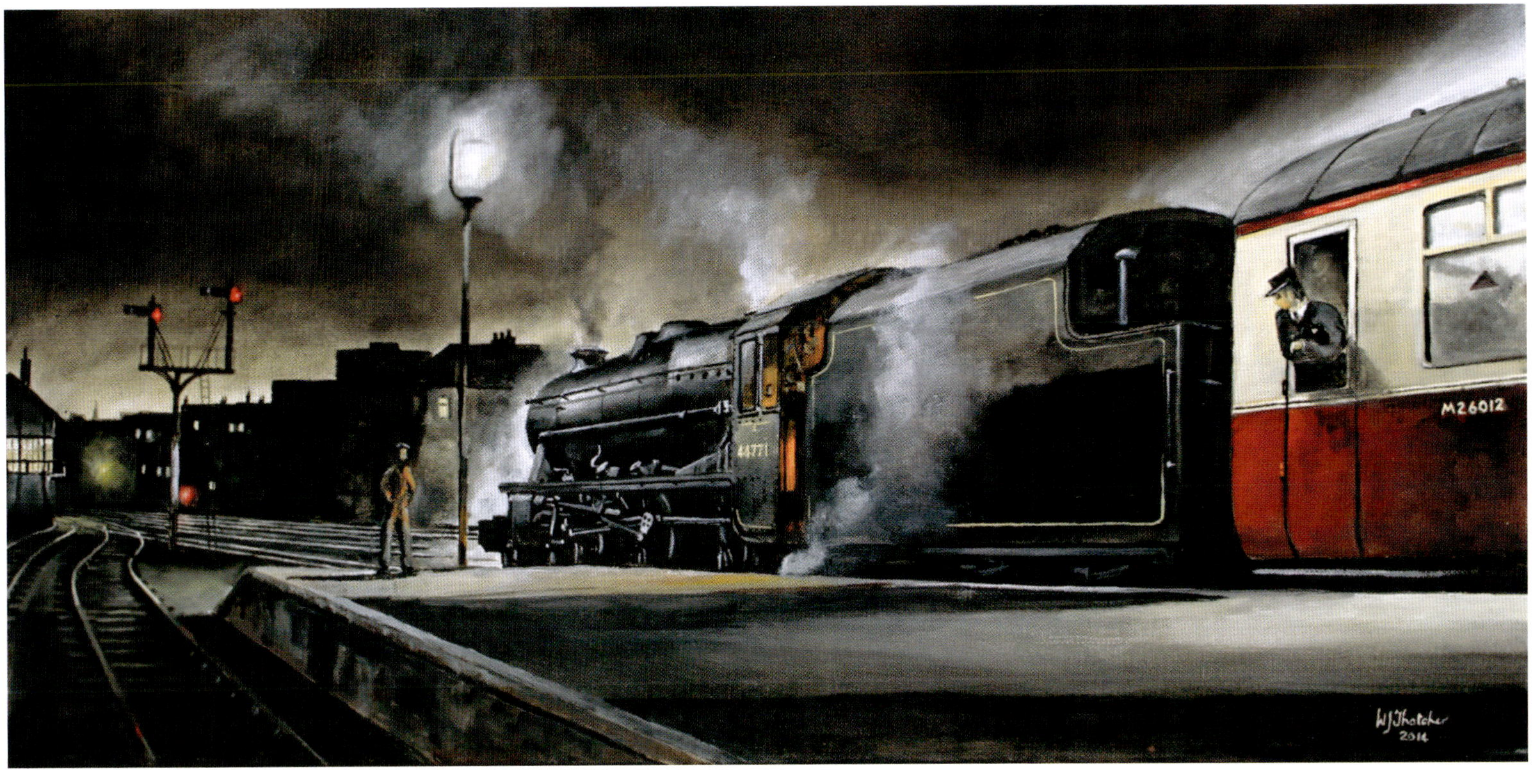

Just across the road from Kings Cross a Black 5 awaits departure time from St Pancras. The date is early 1950s as the semaphore signals have still not been replaced with coloured lights, but 44771 looks to be in ex works condition, while the guard looks resignedly out of his window. There was always someone who wanted to see the engine at the front before departure, and the glow from the firebox highlights the single observer.

Chilcompton

Chilcompton is a little village south of Bath. It is part of rural Somerset, although the houses there might give the visitor a hint of the town's past history. These are built in terraced rows from the local Mendip stone once a yellow pink and now as grey as Aberdeen granite. The colour is not due to natural weathering, but to the porosity of the limestone and its ability to absorb smoke and dirt. Chilcompton lay in the Somerset coal mining district along with other small towns such as Radstock and Midsomer Norton. For 23 years I was employed by Coates Brothers, a printing ink company, located exactly over the old Midsomer Norton coal mines. The land was cheap to purchase and much had to be done to make it a safe factory site, not least the protection of the embankment which bordered the Somerset and Dorset railway, the same line which passed through Chilcompton, the next station south.

The S & D was built to handle the coal traffic but also to provide a direct north to south route from the Midlands to the south coast. Unfortunately the line had been removed by the time I arrived, and all that remained was the ballast. To say the bridgework in the area was rudimentary is being very polite. The infrastructure as it is now called was of the make-do-and-mend variety and yet, in spite of this indication of the poverty of the line, many of the stations were gloriously well kept. Midsomer Norton won the best kept station prize on more than one occasion. The line was almost the sole province of that well known railway photographer Ivo Peters, at a time when photography was a luxury enjoyed mainly by privileged cameramen such as Maurice Earley and Ivo who were able to afford the best plate cameras. Ivo even had a Bentley which he used to chase the same trains all the way from Bath to Bournemouth. His Bentley appears in many of his photographs and is currently owned by the chairman of the North Norfolk Railway. Not surprisingly Ivo knew all the best photographic locations, and Chilcompton tunnel is certainly one of them.

Many of the tunnels on the line have now been blocked up to prevent vagrancy and to remove the risk to casual walkers or playing children; we live in such a 'elf an' safety' age. Some tunnels are now used as shooting ranges for gun clubs. I was lucky enough to find Chilcompton still open when I went in search of Ivo's locations. Apart from the absence of track, all was as it always had been. The immediate impression was that the tunnel was little more than an elongated and very low bridge. The Somerset & Dorset (Slow and Dirty to some) was famed for its low bridge and minimal tunnel clearance. Blowbacks due to the exhaust hitting the roof were common and caused serious injury on the footplate. It was the practice to shut off steam on entering the tunnels, then put it back on as soon as daylight was reached.

My painting shows a 7F freight built for the S & D, having just emerged from the tunnel. These machines were well liked on a railway line which had difficulty finding any other suitable engine; and it seems to have tried everything except Eastern Region engines including Midland Black 5s, 2Ps, Southern Moguls, Great Western Prairie tank engines; and finally it got hold of some Standard 9Fs which could do no wrong. A little imagination from the management might have pointed them in that direction earlier – the 7Fs were liked because of their high tractive effort and adhesion, combined with small wheels and an ability to take sharp curves and steep grades. The 7Fs held sway the longest of any class, and to me typified the line, which is why I chose them as the locomotive subject of the painting. My bicycle appears by the fence at the top of the picture. I never rode it any distance in Somerset – far too hilly! – and Chilcompton was on the edge of the Mendips. It is late on a summer's evening from the long shadows. At least the 7F has got over the worst of the climb, apart from Masbury summit, and now has a fairly easy run to Bournemouth where it will shed for the night.

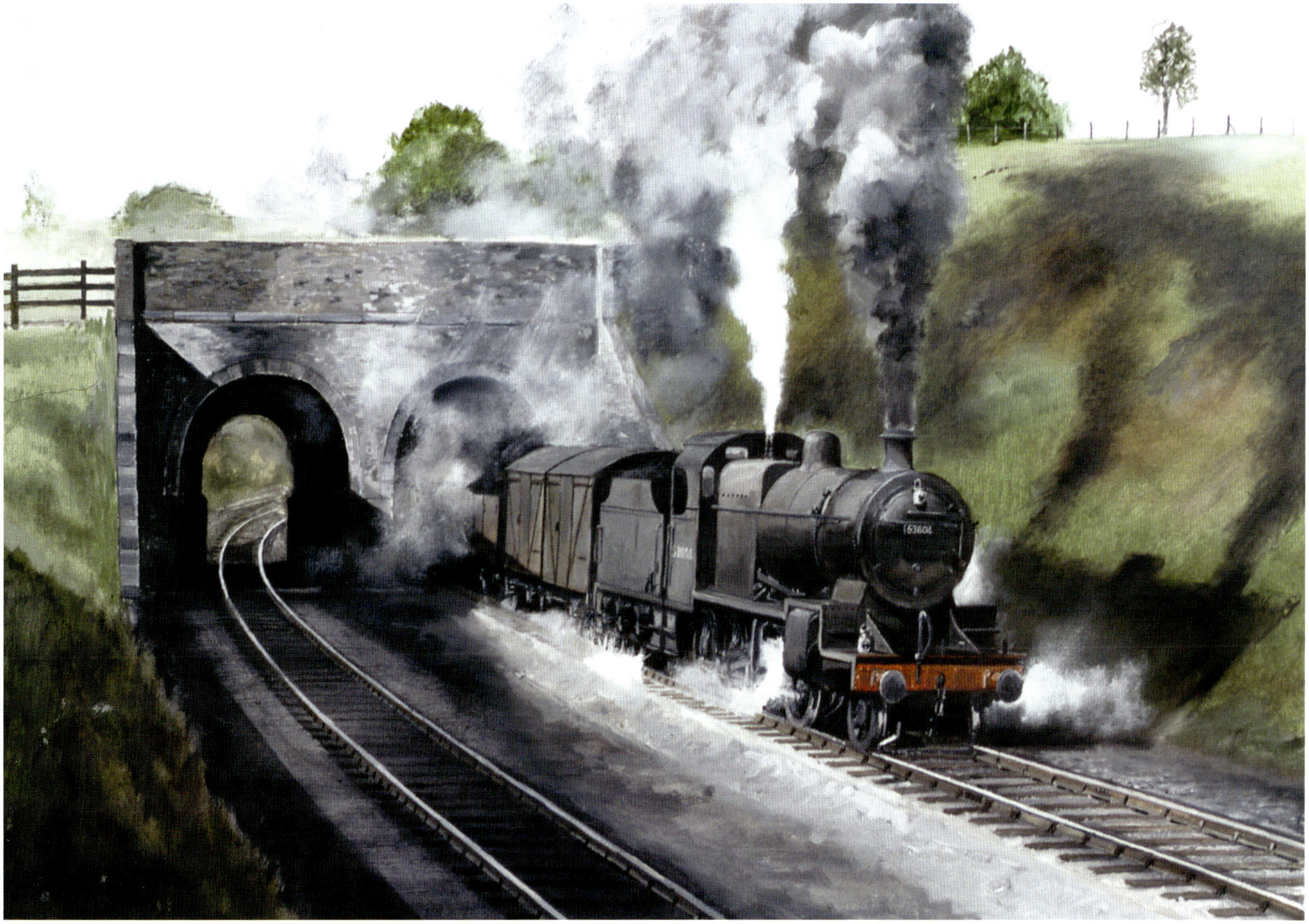

Emerging from the tunnel at Chilcompton, Somerset

Hatfield 1963 – The Decline of Steam

The winter of 1963 was one of the coldest on record, and the snowfall one of the highest. The fact that this coincided with the mass withdrawal of steam on the east coast route was coincidental. The following two years would see the complete cessation of steam south of Doncaster, indeed steam practically disappeared everywhere on the Eastern side of the country. The snow was several feet deep in the drifts and the biting cold seemed to go on for ever. My parents owned a dachsund, not the largest dog perhaps, but it managed to get lost in the back garden under the snow!

It was a glorious opportunity for railway photography. I had just spent what seemed a fortune on a Russian Zenith 35mm camera with an f/2 lens. This was considered to be one of the best in the business in those days unless you could afford a Leica. So it was that I waded my way through the snow two miles to Hatfield station, as rumour had it that steam was running because diesel oil was freezing up! The rumours were true! A run-down V2 clanked its way past making evil sounding noises for a steam engine but at least it was moving *and* providing steam heating for the passengers. Camera to the eye, I pressed the shutter and... nothing. It is the photographer's worst nightmare! A perfect set of conditions and subject matter, a unique opportunity and the equipment wont work. The shutter had frozen solid. Well would you credit it with a *Russian* camera? They obviously did not use them in Siberia. I stayed all day until the light faded, collecting numbers and trying to remember all that I saw. A few other photographers were about and I saw some of the results from their work in *The Railway Magazine*. I have done many paintings of Hatfield in these conditions since; I am trying to replace the lost images.

My painting depicts the sadness and desolation of both the winter and these events. In many of my paintings I seek to capture the feel and romance of steam and railways as I remember them. I recall all the content of this painting so well: the two platforms with three running lines passing between them, the footbridge where I practically lived as a child, the engine shed on the right with an N7 laying dead outside, its chimney sacked over prior to withdrawal, the elderly Gresley coach at the tail of a train for Welwyn Garden City even though its name board indicated Hatfield as the destination!

I took some liberty with the signal gantry which should really be behind me in the painting, but used it to frame the scene. There always seemed to be a WD locomotive standing in the yard, even when the much superior Standard class 9Fs became available. Indeed I have seen two 9Fs cold in the yard with two WDs happily pulling coal trains out of the sidings and heading for Hornsey. In later years there was an ever lengthening queue of N7s, their chimneys sacked over, standing dead underneath the footbridge. Every so often a 9F would come along and, in ones and twos, would tow them away to the breaker's yard. Then the WDs started appearing on the 'dead' line... Well I decided to resurrect one of them for this painting. The storm approaching from the east was soon to blanket everything in snow. This was only the second time I used such a low viewpoint on a square canvas to emphasise the sky. The yellow light made the cold seem even colder, as though the sun would never break through. If carbon dioxide is the cause of global warming, how did we have such cold winters then, when coal fires and steam engines emitted such vast quantities of it?

Later in this book other pictures depict the same period, especially the paintings 'Racing the Storm' (page 110) and 'Grantham' (page 141).

I am still cursing that camera!

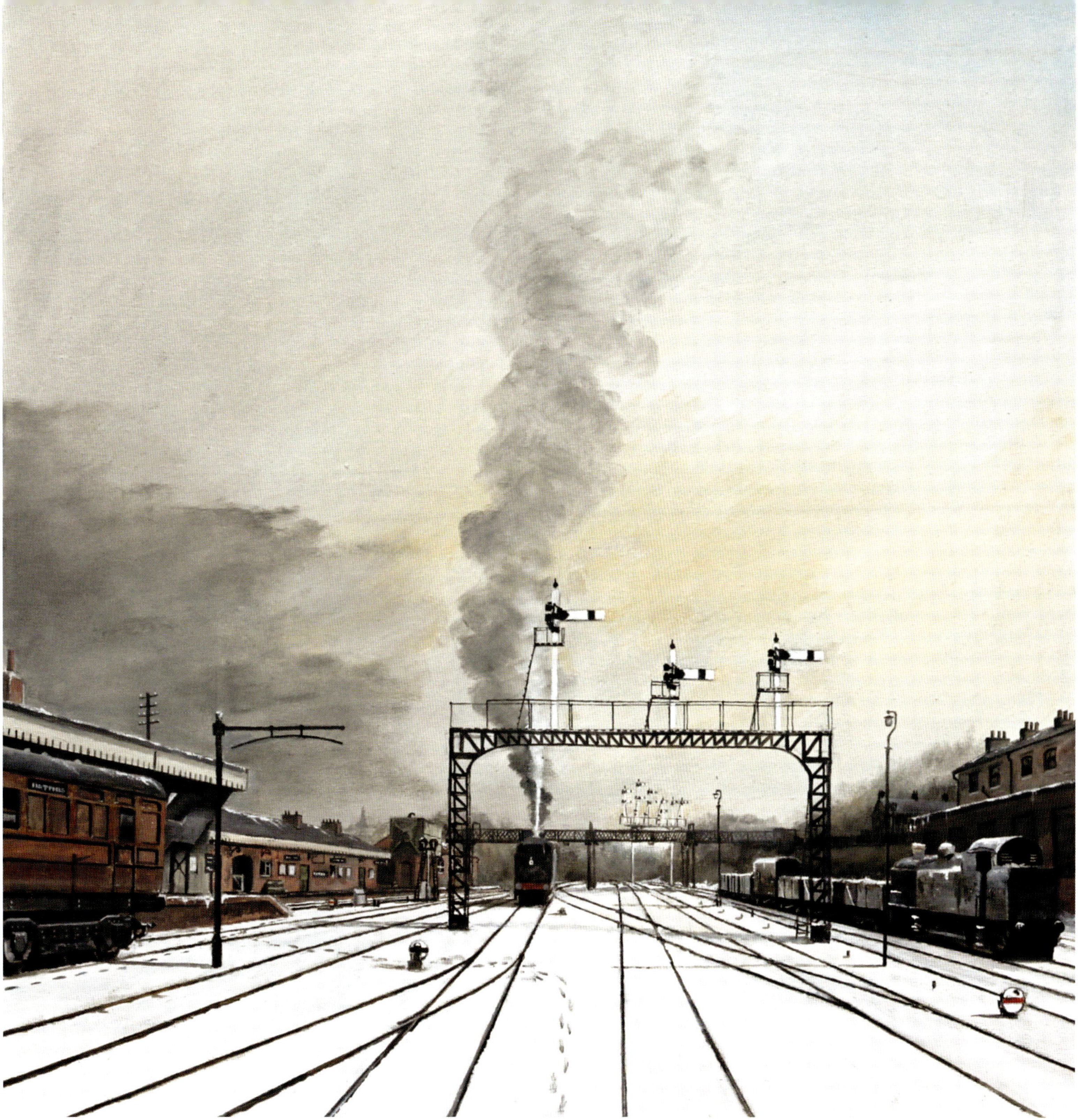

Holt

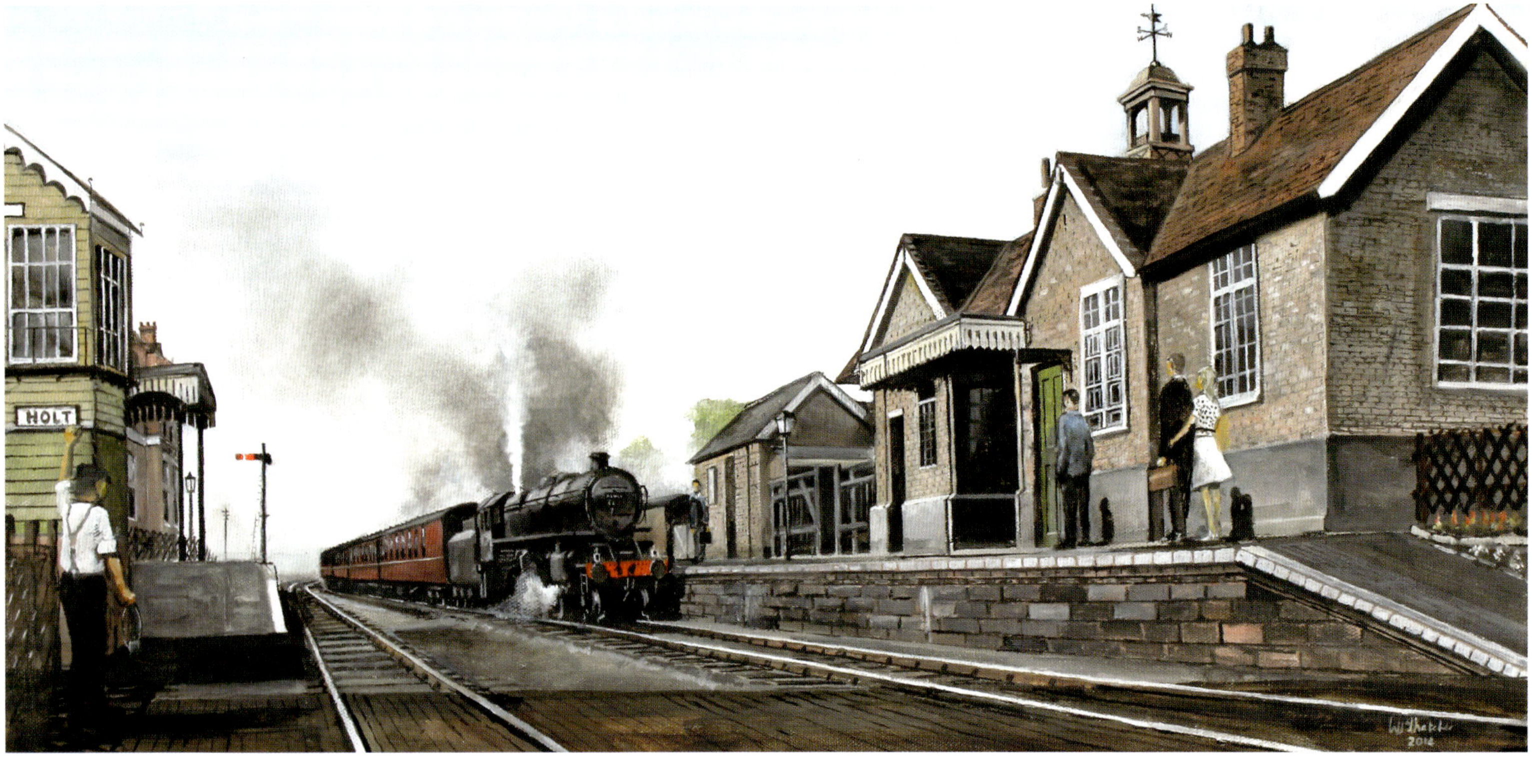

Holt in Norfolk lay on the old MGNJR. This line was pulled up even before Beeching, but it served a necessary means of transport for people and goods in a very rural area. Today the North Norfolk Heritage Railway has built a station in Holt, but it is a long way from the original which was located near the timber yard, to the left of the picture, and where the 'new' bypass runs. This is Holt as it was in the very last days of steam.

Temple Meads at Night

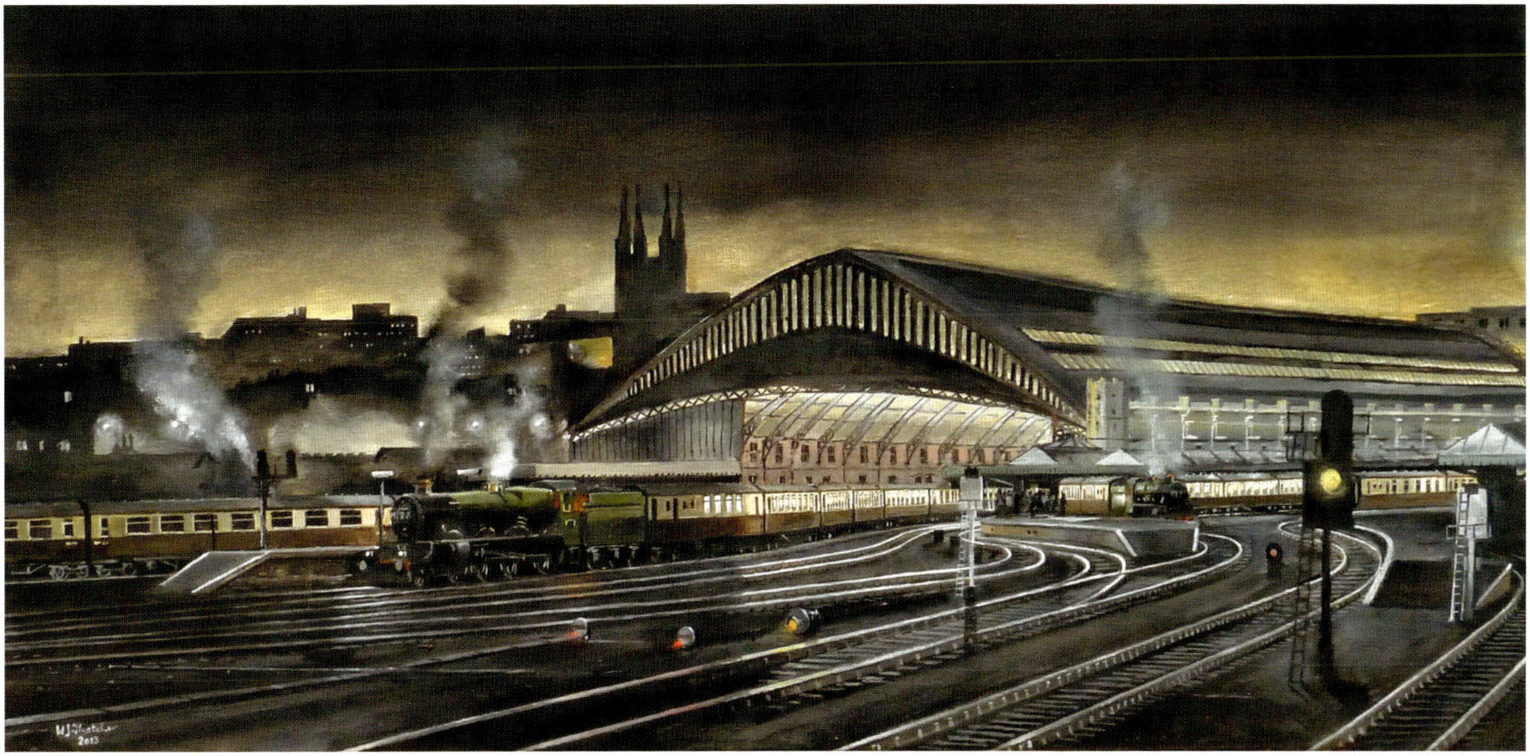

Bristol Temple Meads is a magnificent station, with its great curved train shed and the original Brunel frontage. It was, and still is, a focal point for rail traffic heading in all directions of the compass, and the track layout around the station and the junctions either side are one of the most complicated in the country. At night this was an amazing sight during steam days with trains from the West and from London passing through the network of tracks almost without a break. The view is of the westbound exit from the station beneath the London Road bridge. A 'Castle' and a 'Hall' wait for their respective signals.

The Brighton Belle

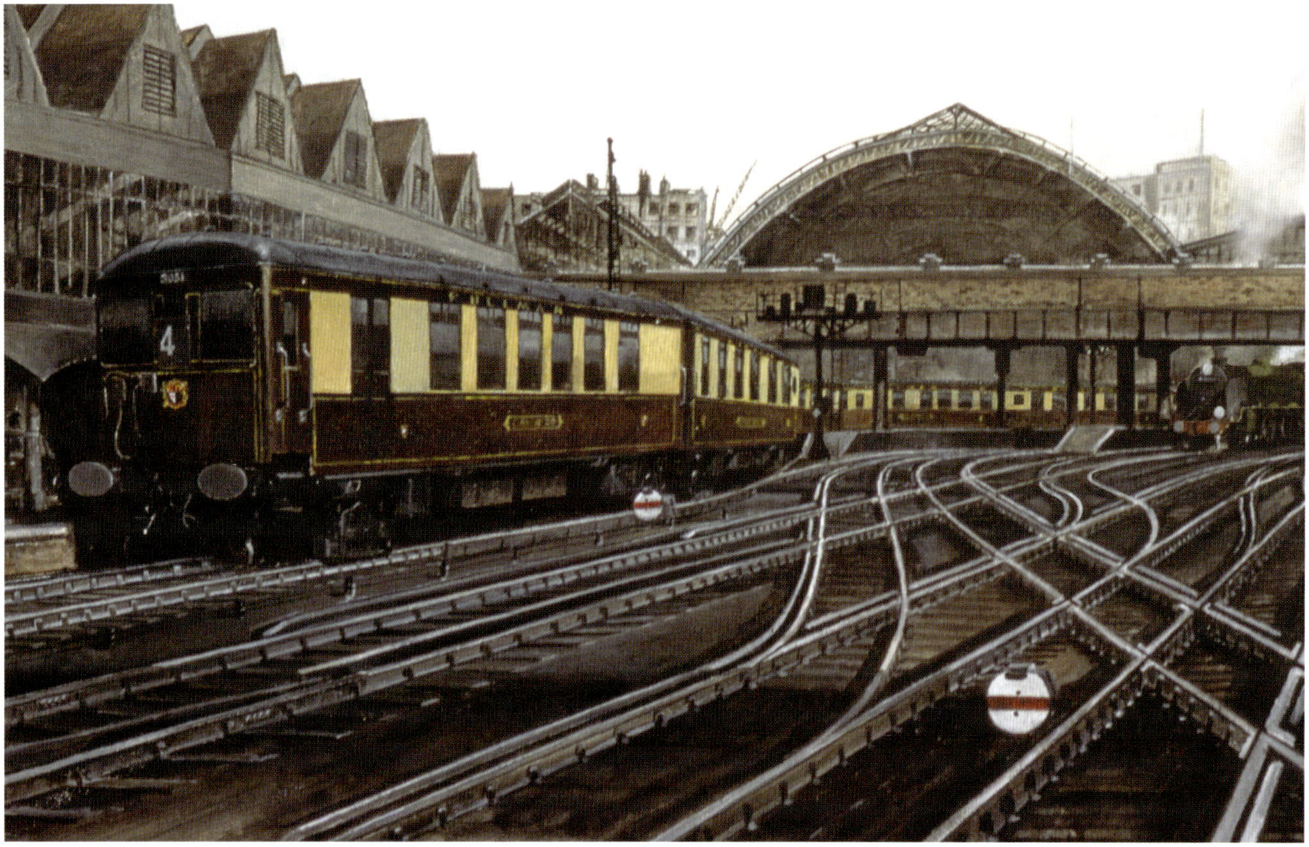

This was one of my earlier paintings, completed about 1980 as a commission for a gentleman in London. The period is the early 1950s hence the inclusion of this painting in the British Railways section. The all electric Pullman was a premium service and looked very smart in comparison to the variety of green-painted electric stock in use on the Southern at the time. It was considered to be the most famous electric multiple unit in the world. I often wondered what happened to this painting, for having despatched it to the address provided by the buyer, he then disappeared without paying for it!

Empty Stock at St Pancras

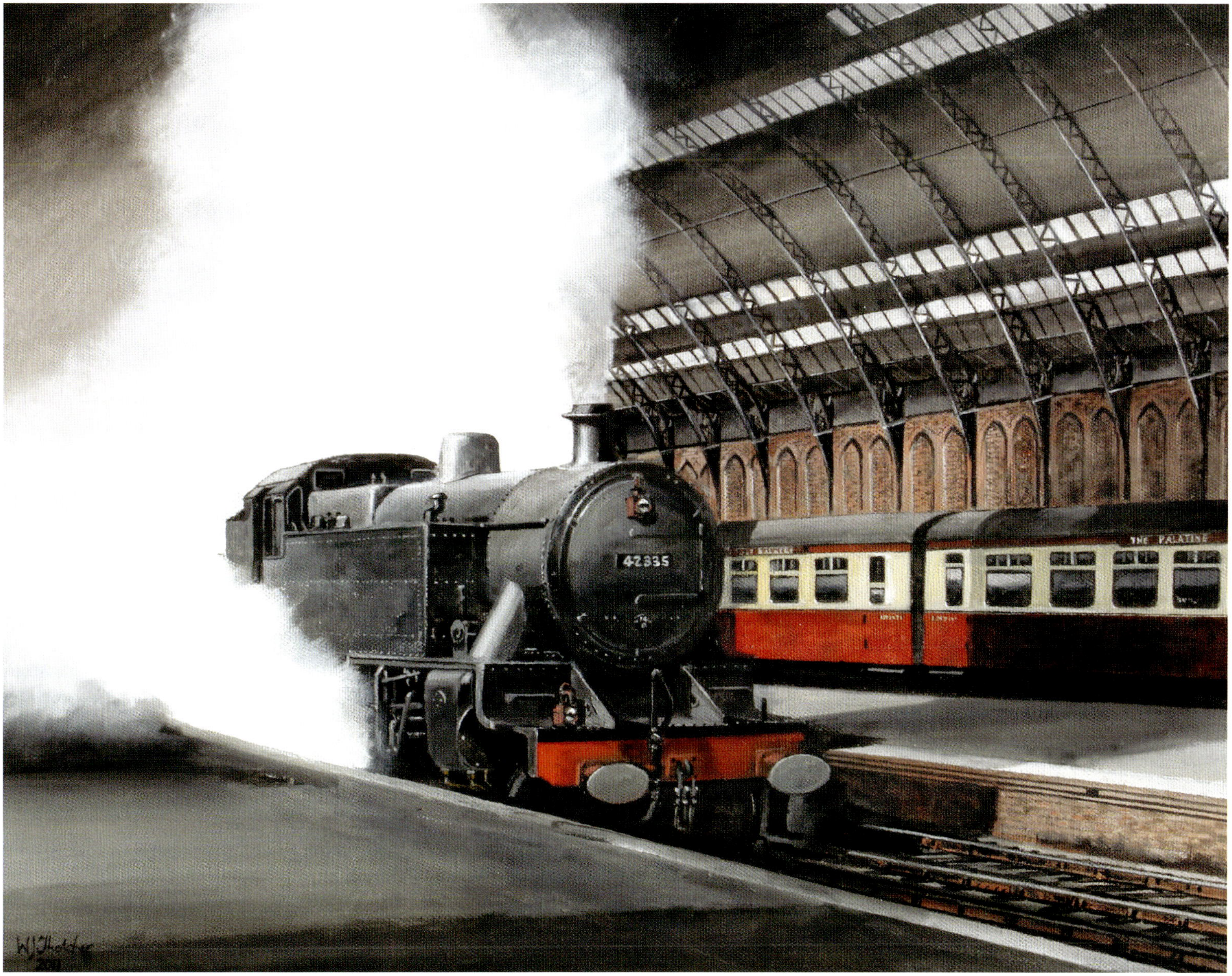

One of Fowlers – under powered 2-6-4T locomotives – removing empty stock from St Pancras in 1960. These engines were not popular with the enginemen as they were poor steamers. I frequently travelled behind this engine while it was in use on the Bedford to St Albans and St Pancras locals. It was usually in a filthy state and it usually lost time.

B12 at Weybourne

The following two paintings show the same engine, B12 number 61572, during British Railways ownership at Weybourne station, North Norfolk and again in recent years under the ownership of the North Norfolk Railway.

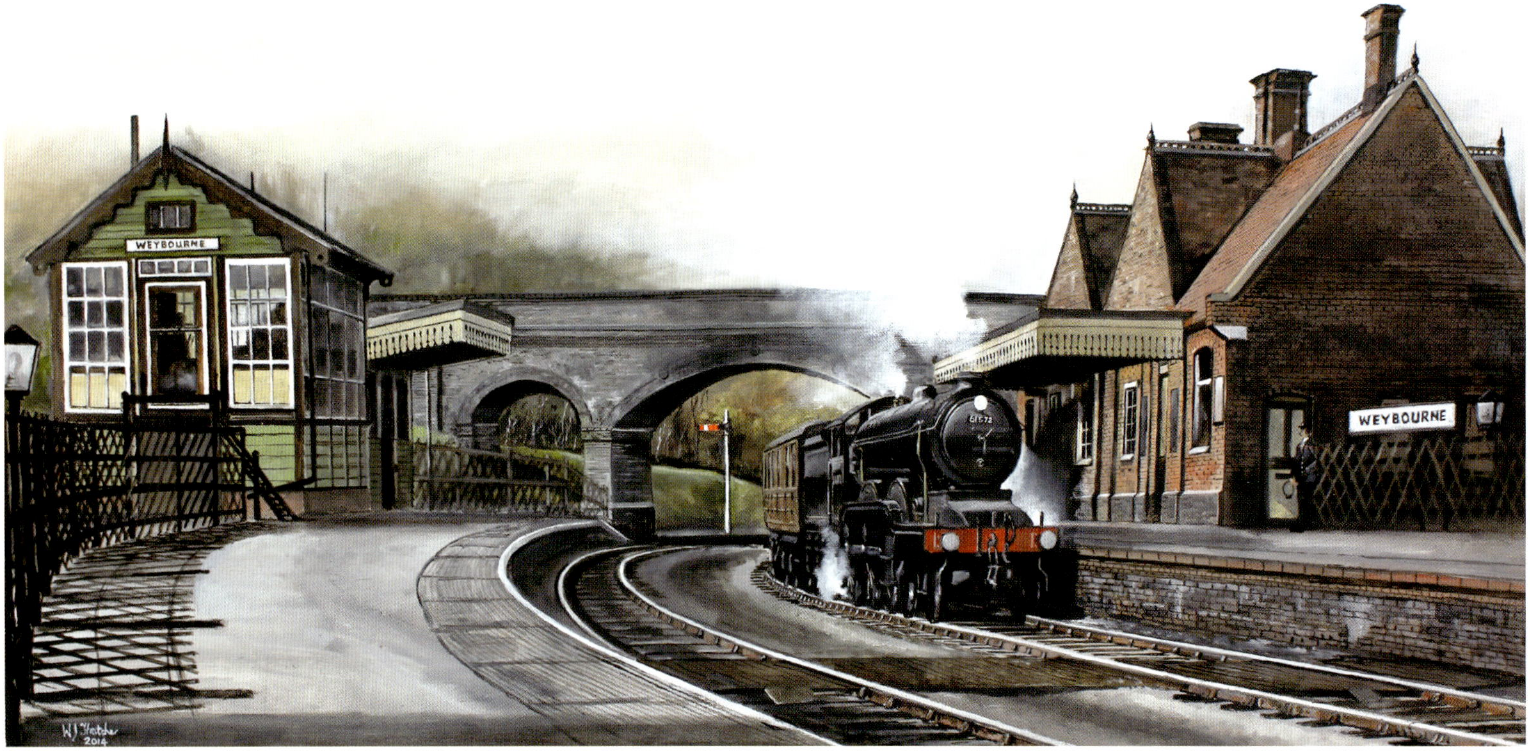

Note the shade of green used by the LNER is still applied to the signalbox. It differs considerably from the shade applied today; in fact there was much variation from station to station all over the old LNER system. Weybourne station is at least a mile from the village it is supposed to serve. Perhaps that is why only the Stationmaster occupies the platform ready to hand over the tablet.

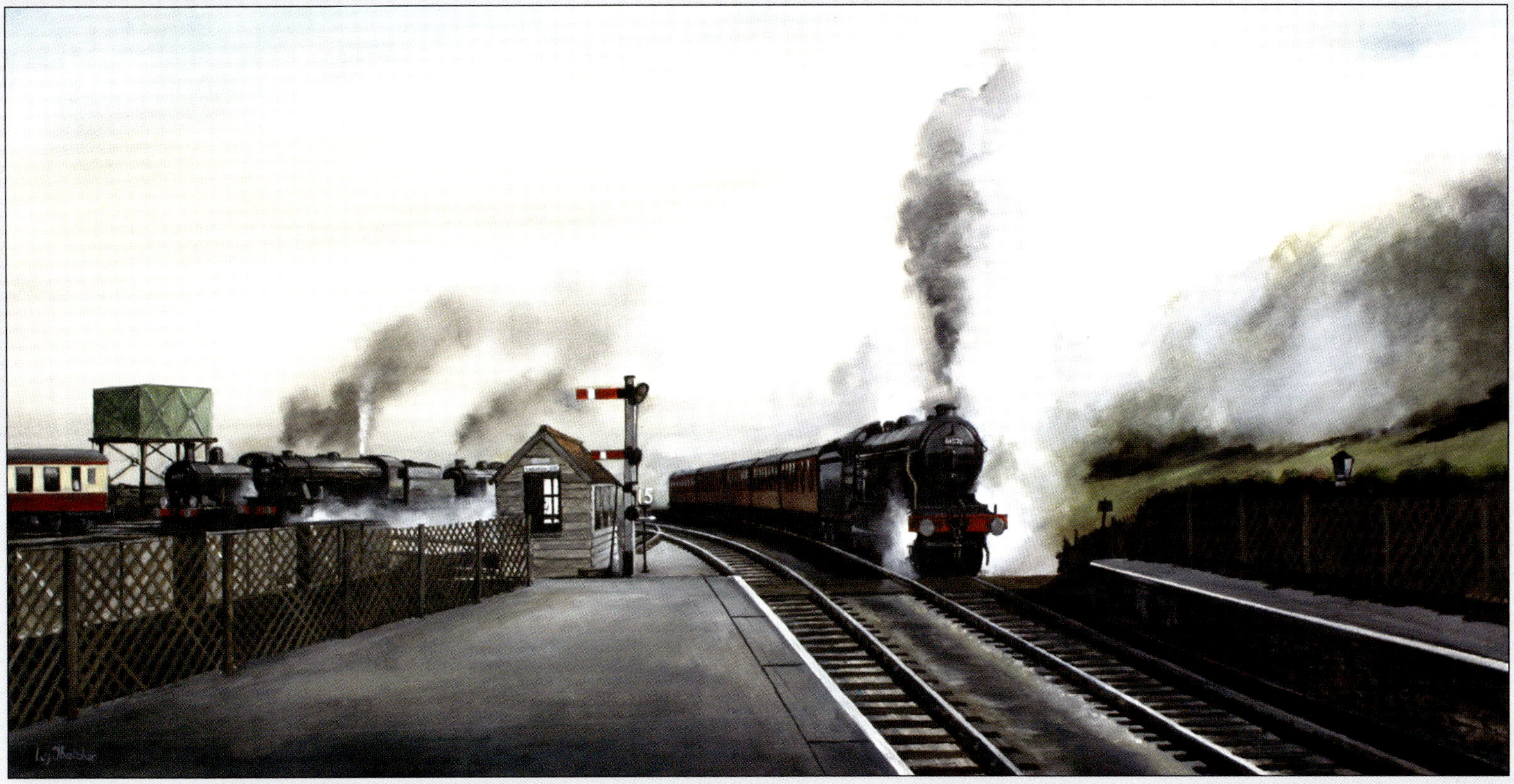

The only way one can see Weybourne so deserted now is to get on the platform outside the school holiday period in time for the first train of the day! The whole station has been beautifully and sympathetically restored. The engine shed is busier than it ever was before, too, being the location of a workshop for both locomotives and coaches. Here I have shown the other resident Eastern Region engines, N7, J52, and WD all in steam, waiting in the yard. It seems strange that Grandfather Jimmy Dennis stalled this engine in icy weather after leaving the station, on Weybourne bank, 60 years ago. He said he never liked the B12s and much preferred the J52 which he normally drove, claiming that it was much more sure footed. Perhaps he was at the wrong end of a lot of mess room jokes involving stalled B12s!

The Jacobite

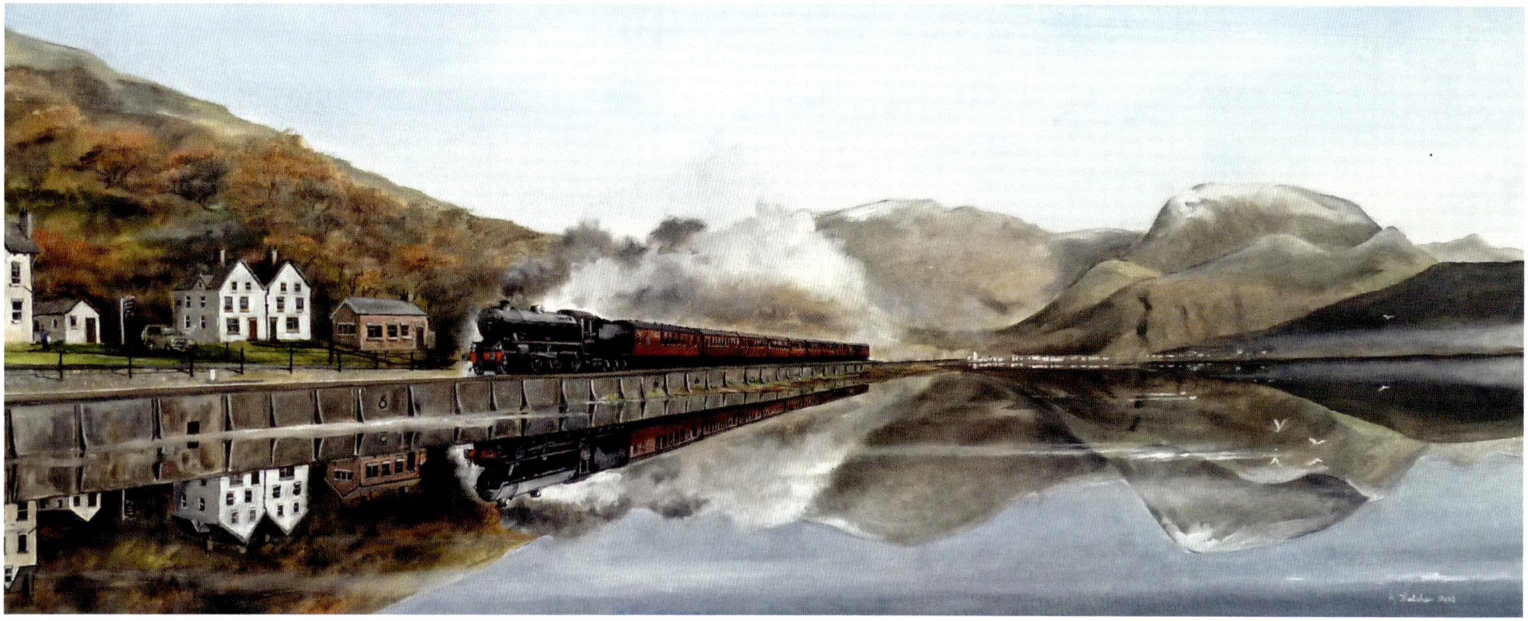

Another painting of a preserved locomotive, but this time on the main line. The journey from Fort William in Scotland to Mallaig is one of the most beautiful railway journeys anywhere in the world. In the author's opinion only the journey from Durango to Silverton in Colorado comes close to it. The authorities in Fort William realised the tourist potential, and reinstated a daily steam-hauled service which they named 'The Jacobite'. I have never travelled on this train when it has had an empty seat! Leaving Fort William the train skirts Loch Eil where it is shown here on a lovely calm autumn day. The looming mass of Ben Nevis can be seen reflected in the perfectly still waters, and the paper mill and town of Corpach seen apparently at its foot, although actually several miles in front of that well known peak. Several different locomotives have, at various times, hauled this train which consists entirely of West Coast Railway Mark 1 stock. Here, K1 class locomotive 62005 heads the train on its westward journey. These locomotives were ideally suited to this line, having a small wheels and good adhesion needed for the tortuous line ahead.

Skipton

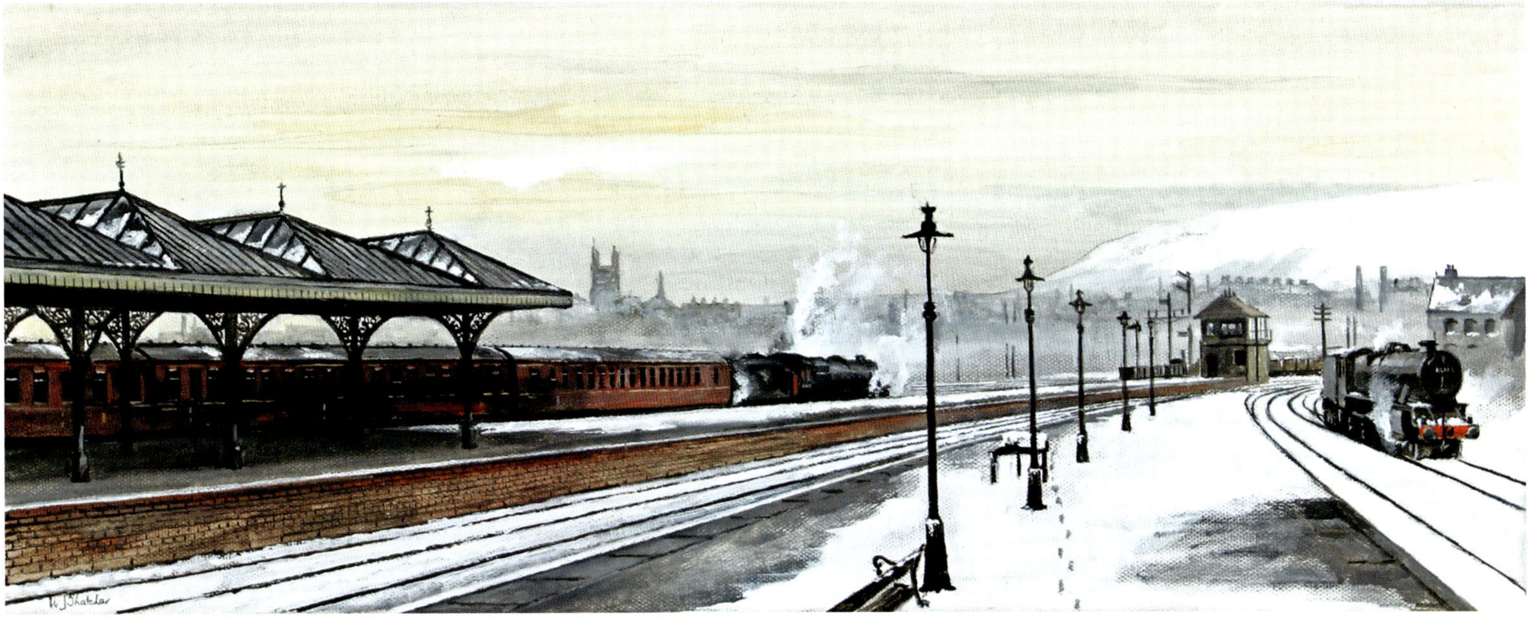

In complete contrast to the previous painting, and this time in the North of England, it shows a bitterly cold day in the market town of Skipton. Unusually, although I have travelled the Settle and Carlisle line many times, hauled by a variety of steam locomotives, in sunshine and in snow, I was never lucky enough to see it in clear winter conditions like this. The painting was inspired by that great railway photographer Henry Priestley, whose photographs always incorporated the feel of the surroundings, the architecture, and all the little details which make our railway heritage so memorable. The snow has fallen and covers the Pennine hills in the background. It is so cold the carriage heating has made no impression on the snow-covered carriage roofs, while the attempts to clear the platform have just resulted in a layer of sheet ice. Two Black 5s struggle to maintain a service in these arctic conditions. My last journey through Skipton was just as cold, but barely visible through the falling snow; unfortunately the station was in a semi derelict state but the class 5 locomotive at the front end maintained time through a January blizzard. These locomotives seem to be the toughest of the breed, for I have never been let down by one which is more than can be said for some of their more illustrious and pampered Pacifics. ;Princess Elizabeth;, and A2 ;Blue Peter; have both failed on this route while I have been in the train, while Stanier's Moguls and Black 5s have battled the elements and won!

Edge Hill Freight

The painting shown earlier in this book of a Black 5 emerging from Lime Street cutting gives the reader some idea of this location. At the top of the cutting is Edge Hill Station. It is not a very imposing station but comprised six platforms at the time this painting was done. These platforms were sharply curved at their westward end, and viewed towards Manchester the extensive engine shed which housed Liverpool's allocation of locomotives could be seen to the left, although more often than not the emerging locomotives were obscured by a variety of wagons, disused carriages and the breakdown train. The yard to the right was similarly obscured which probably accounts for the fact that very few photographs have been published looking in this direction; a situation which is rectified later in the book, but not here! Edge Hill yard box was just visible from the platform ends, but of course totally out of bounds to the public. Only a lucky few were able to get permits to photograph trains reaching the top of the climb out of Liverpool, and the most famous of these was Bishop Eric Treacy who was for many years Bishop of Liverpool. This painting is based on my memory and backed up by his photographs. The sheds were actually aligned with the line as it emerged from Lime Street cutting but I seem to have turned them round slightly more than they should be perhaps by as much as 45 degrees. The signals however stick in the mind quite clearly. They always seem to have been incredibly stubby, with massive circular counterweight discs attached to each arm.

The weather in my painting is clearly not good! Liverpool was a very wet place (weatherwise!) to live and the advent of The Beatles may have brought sunshine to the lives of the rock and roll generation, but did nothing to prevent the need for good waterproofs either in Lord Street or higher up on Edge Hill platform. A storm is advancing from the south-west, which shows up the smoke from the Jinty busy shunting the south yard. One of Stanier's ubiquitous class 5s can be seen struggling upgrade with a fitted freight, possibly a pigeon train which would may have started from Lime Street. Most other freight would have been assembled in Edge Hill yard.

Facing downhill is one of Fairburn's elegant 2-6-4T tank locomotives. They always appeared to me to be the most powerful tank engines for use on suburban stock. Of course there were plenty of muscular freight tank locomotives such as the Great Western 0-8-0s and the Southern Region's W1s, but those engines were quite unsuitable for the operation of fast suburban traffic. The cutaway frames in front of the cylinders enabled the observer to differentiate between this class and the Stanier equivalent. It was surprising to discover that Edward Thompson's feeble-looking class L1 tank engines on the Eastern Region were given a higher power classification. The Fairburn machine in the painting must have been ex works, for I never saw them as clean as this! I observed that the further north I travelled, the dirtier the locomotives seemed to be. The Midland Region was not famed for its cleanliness and Edge Hill certainly conformed to that standard.

However, this painting was intended to be all about atmosphere. The lighting, the yellow patch in the west indicating either better weather to come or more likely the last hope of sunshine for the day, combined with the brooding clouds, helps make the odd splash of colour from the signals and from the glowing fire visible in the Fairburn tank engine all the more noticeable. I should think that Bishop Treacy, with his heavy tripod and plate camera, would have long run for cover in the circumstances.

Today this has all been swept aside. The yards have been decimated, the signalbox and semaphore signals demolished, and a new central control box miles away covers all the traffic. Electrification has brought overhead wires so that much is obscured by the gantry work, but steam *has* returned and once again it is possible to see unnaturally clean Black 5s, Coronation Pacifics, and even some foreign looking engines from other regions pounding their way up towards Wavertree with enough energy to cause the overhead catenary to bounce up and down from their exhaust as they pass.

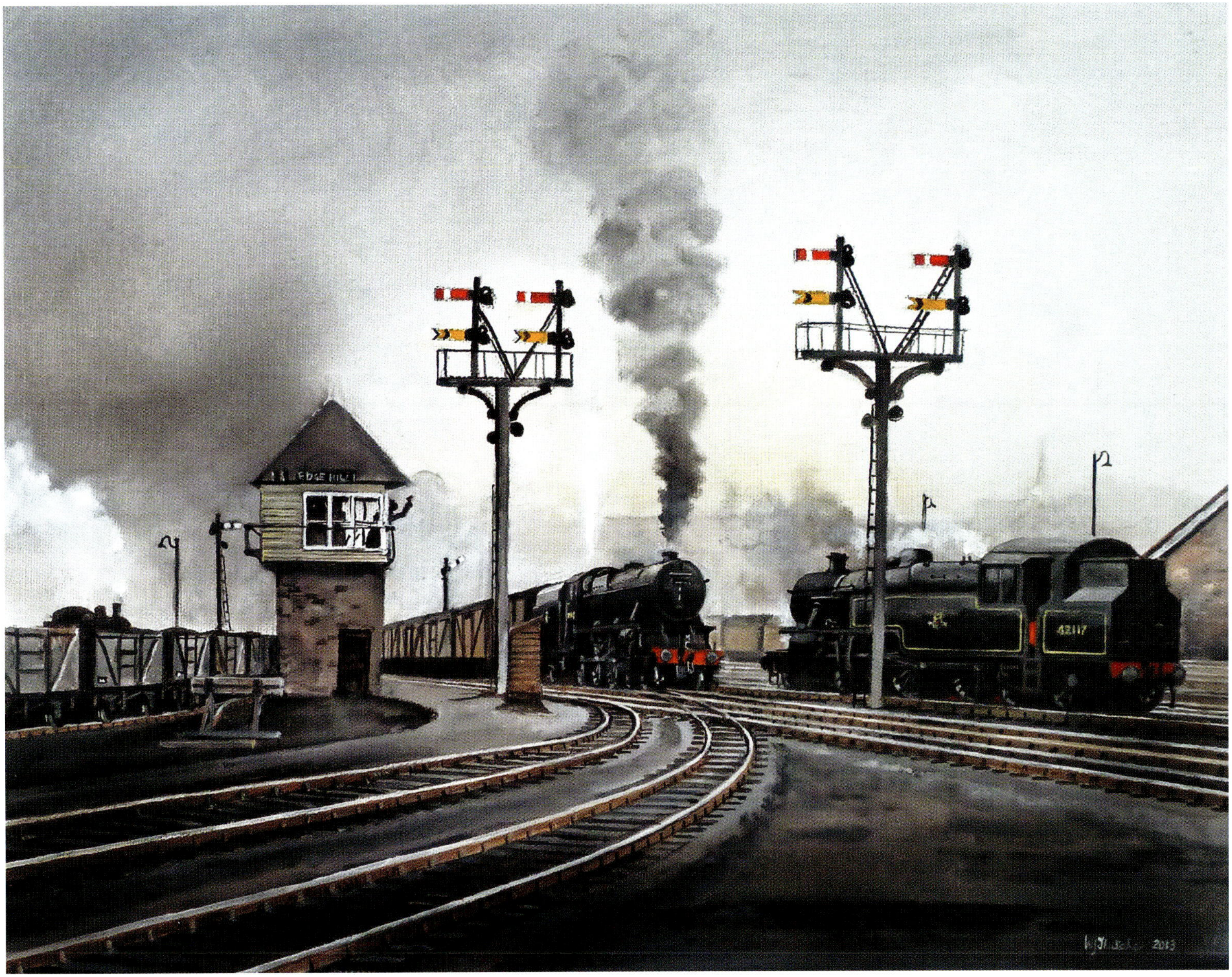
EDGE HILL
42117

Sheringham

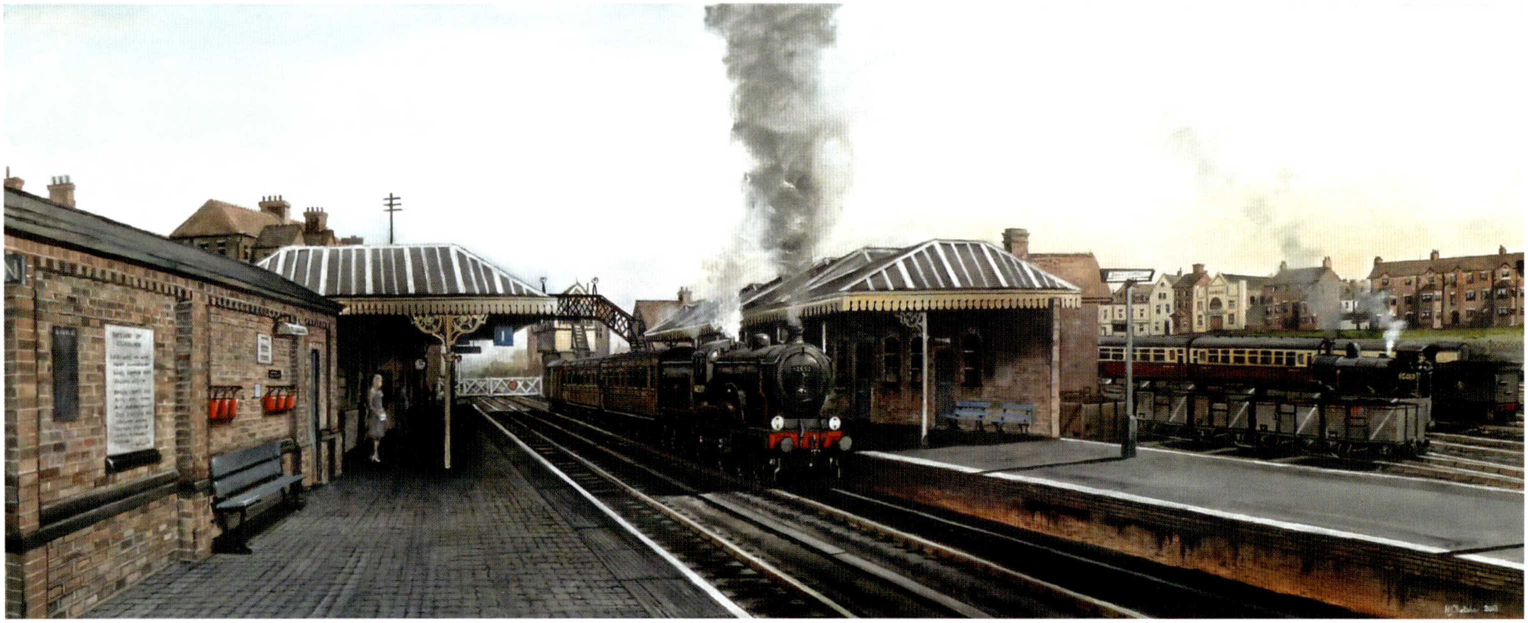

Sheringham is a small town on the North Norfolk coast. It was, and still is, a fishing town, famed for its lobsters and crabs; nowadays the tourist industry is the main source of income. The railway was once part of the Midland & Great Northern Joint, known locally as the 'Muddle and Go Nowhere'. Sadly that is what has happened. The line now lies at the end of the network rail system from Norwich where it is linked by the level crossing seen in the painting to the North Norfolk heritage railway. The painting depicts the station in its final years under British Railways. In fact the date can be discerned by the poster announcing the closure of the Mundesley branch line. In the painting the railway yard is still intact and an elderly J15 in clean condition can be seen shunting there. Both station canopies and the footbridge are still intact in the painting and the signal box and fire buckets are in their original locations. All the houses to the right today are as they were then, but the Odeon is now a Masonic lodge. Although the goods yard has been tarmacked over, and is now a car park, and the right hand canopy has been removed, all the rest of the station has been sympathetically restored. Sadly no member of the D16/3 class has been restored, but one of the vintage carriages serves as a tea room outside the neighbouring town of Holt.

North London 1948

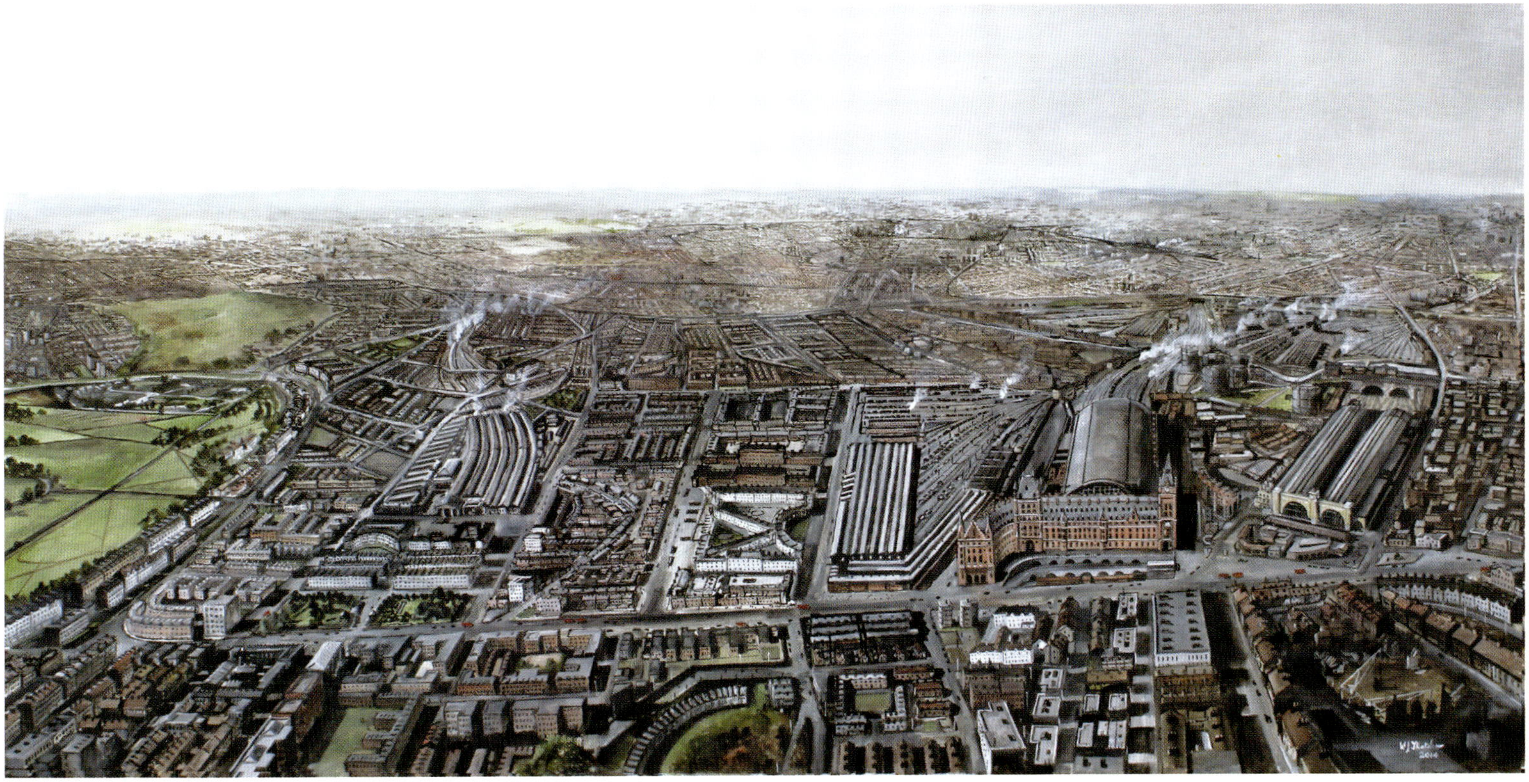

Viewed from an imagined elevation south of the Euston Road, the northern suburbs stretch to the horizon, from Elstree to Enfield. The war has not long been over and rebuilding can be seen to the south of Kings Cross Station. The proximity of all the northern stations can be seen, including the Doric arch outside Euston, and the magnificent Midland Hotel outside St Pancras. Alas, the so called 'African Village' has already sprung up outside Cubitt's Kings Cross. The extensive goods yards around these last two stations are still intact, whilst noticeably absent from Euston.

Out of Waterloo

Following on from the painting of London, I have tried to capture the environment around major stations in London. I have a lot of feeling for the city which has changed so much and continues to change, sometimes at an alarming rate. It is where I spent a lot of my childhood and later where I studied at University. London is so distinct in its different districts, or at least it was. The area around Kings Cross and Liverpool Street were so very different from the area around Paddington. South London suffered some of the worst bombing during the war, and nowhere was this more evident than around Waterloo Station. Waterloo was, and is, the largest and busiest of the London stations. The rationale of moving Eurostar to St Pancras was entirely political, and to my mind irrational as it meant the Channel Tunnel was further away; otherwise the margin of size between Waterloo and the rest would have been even greater. Waterloo was never built with a single plan in mind such as the great masterpiece of Brunel at Paddington or that wonderful roof at St Pancras. Waterloo evolved, a piece at a time. Gradually all the pieces were joined together, and an overall roof constructed, which soon became too small for the ever-increasing number of lines weaving their way into, and latterly past, the main station building.

My painting depicts Waterloo in the early 1950s. Rebuilding the embankment is still in progress as can be seen from the cranes to the left of the painting. Behind the cranes can be seen some bomb clearance work, and in the foreground a half blown-apart building that extraordinarily remained standing until late in the twentieth century. The left hand side of the painting is a reminder of the residues of war, the housing seedy, run down, and coated in soot; areas of ground are cleared for building but rapidly acquiring the status of a rubbish tip. The entrance to Waterloo station from the south was just about as unglamorous as it can get, a glorified hole in the wall inside which a ramp elevated the foot passengers or their cars (not too many of them) up towards the main station concourse.

Under the bridge, and nearer to the city, things have started to improve. The Red Lion Hotel has had a facelift and been largely rebuilt, while the shops in the high street look as though business is starting to return. Rationing is still in full swing however and it will be a while before crowds return to the pavements. In the meantime the train is still the main source of transport, and Waterloo serves not only the South London districts but the whole of the South of England – as well as the 'withered arm', the name given to its long line (the old LSWR) down to Devon and Cornwall.

Under its excellent management, particularly that of Sir Herbert Walker, the Southern was the most efficient of all the post grouping railways. That is it lost the least amount of revenue. This was largely due to the third rail electrification it employed which enabled fast and frequent trains to leave the station during rush hours and even clear the bottleneck of Clapham Junction where all Southern lines converged. Several hundred trains an hour left these termini between 4 and 7 pm in the weekdays, and still do. Electric light signalling, rapid acceleration, and an early form of safety – the dead man's handle – enabled this. Yet in amongst all this efficiency, some lines were not electrified! The Kent Coast was still steam hauled and so was the 'withered arm'! Steam therefore continued to run out of Waterloo right up to 1967. It must have been a nightmare to the operating staff clearing the steam-hauled trains out of the way of the Emus.

Here we can see two of the dinosaurs, a Maunsell 4-6-0 leaving with a train to Southampton and a Bulleid West Country Pacific waiting to back down on to a West Country express, both of them clogging the bottleneck at the station throat. Notice the variety of coaching stock. The view from the block of flats was popular with trainspotters who were chased away by the flat owners as soon as they were spotted themselves. It gave a wonderful panoramic view which I have tried to capture by showing the angular change of the track's sleepers.

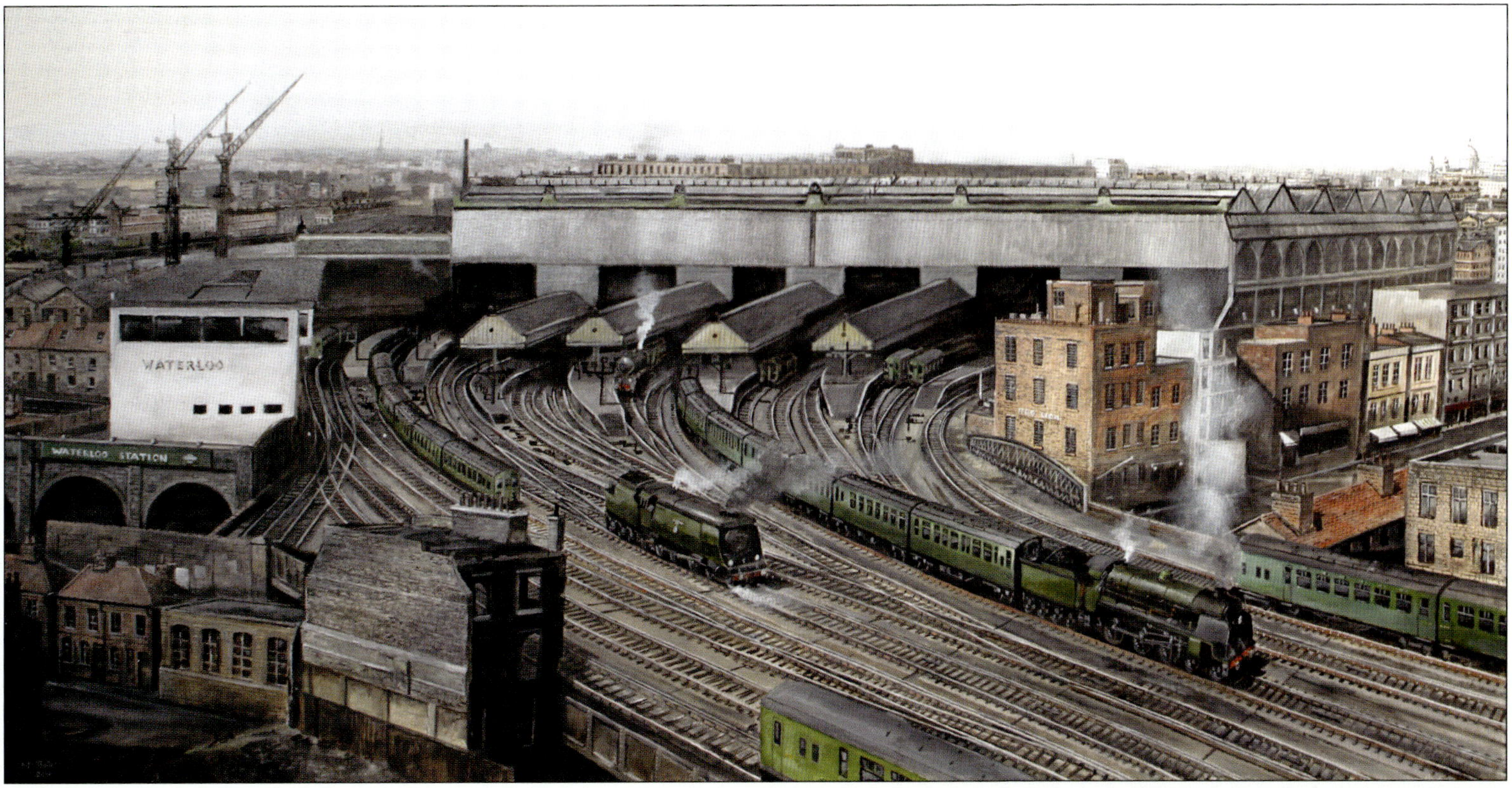

Panorama of Waterloo Station, early 1950s

Paddington Station

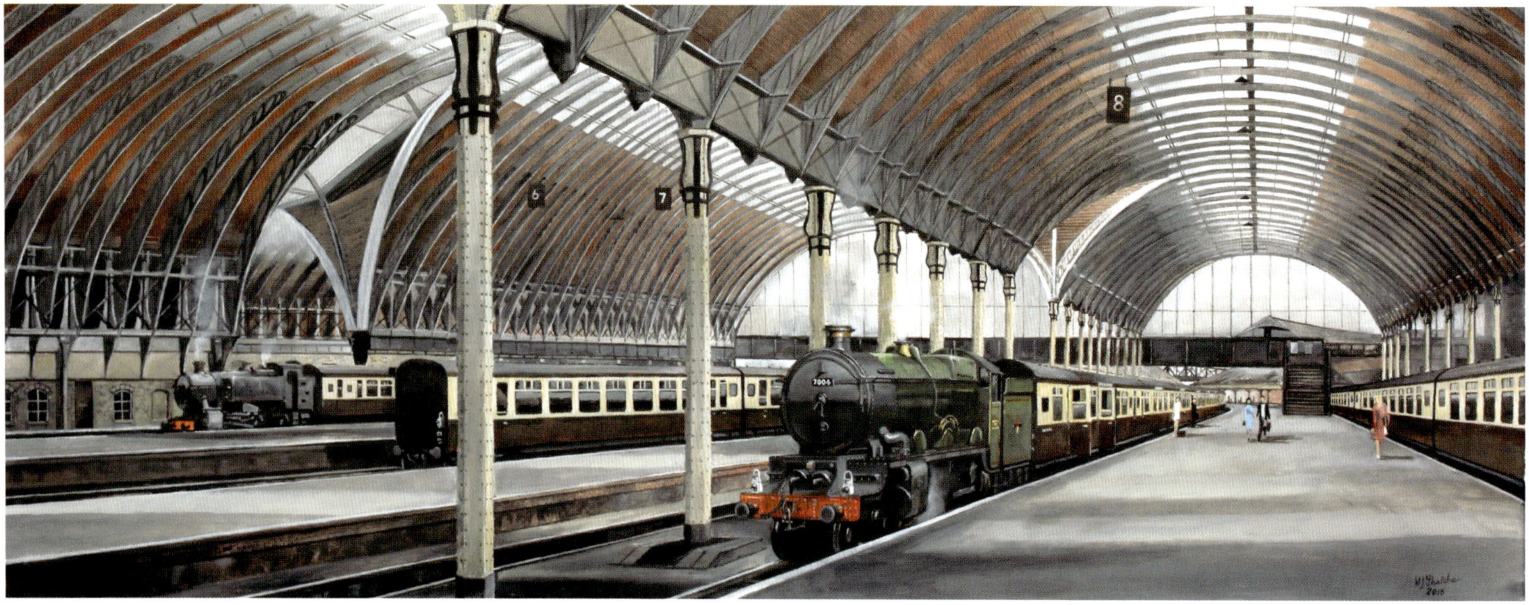

Sir John Betjeman will be remembered for his poetry. More people are now aware of the role he played in saving the magnificent gothic architecture and the train shed roof of St Pancras station in London. But his interest in railway architecture was much wider than that, and is revealed in one of his lesser known publications *London's Historic Railway Stations*. This book contains an outline of the history of each station together with Betjeman's appraisal of the magnificent buildings which were perhaps the greatest architectural achievements of the Victorian era. Lets face it, most Victorian houses lack style, but the Victorians *invented* the railways, so their stations are the defining structures we associate with that mode of transport. Of all the London stations Brunel's Paddington station had the finest interior. It was always a cut above the rest – he intended that it should be so! Even in the last days of steam, as shown in this painting, it looked cleaner and more genteel than any of its contemporaries. The directors of the GWR wanted an enormous conservatory in a railway cutting... and as Betjeman observes, that is what they got.

Eastleigh

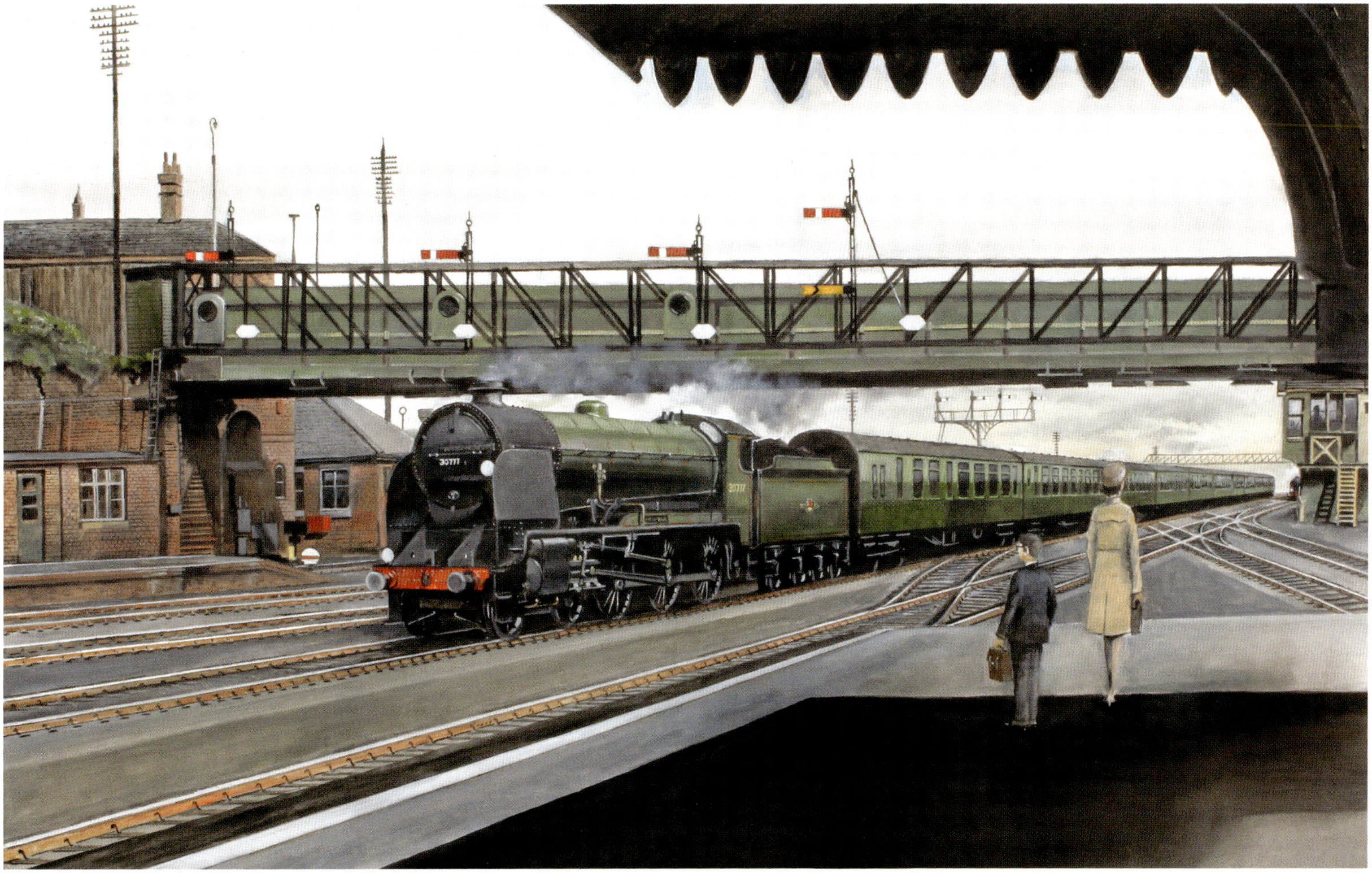

I have done fewer paintings involving Southern Region locomotives or locations than any other, for the simple reason that there were few locations on the Southern that had any really grand architecture in the style of Paddington or of York for example; there were no locations as gloriously dirty and romantic as Liverpool Street, and worse, the South of England was sanitised by the early adoption of electric trains which, while efficient, were completely soul-less to me! This painting of Eastleigh was one of my rare exceptions!

Huddersfield

During the time I spent in Liverpool in the 1970s I had to drive across to York on business. Of course it was a perfect opportunity to visit York railway station. I am not sure exactly when the National Railway Museum transferred from London to York, but I never had time to visit it if it was there at that time, which I think it was. The drive took me through the heartland of industrial Lancashire and Yorkshire, and left a permanent impression. Coal was still a major source of energy in those days and the sight of the chains of power stations visible from that route sending clouds of steam and the smell of coal dust into the atmosphere will never be forgotten. I looked down from the Pennines on to Halifax and Huddersfield. Here was heavy industry; here were steel works, foundries, coal mines embedded in a dark smog so that only the tops of the tall chimneys were clearly visible. There seemed to be no end to the chimneys. It was not pretty, not even particularly photogenic, but it had atmosphere and I have set out to capture that atmosphere in this painting.

I visited Huddersfield station only once, and was disappointingly ordinary, looking very much like a rural station only covered in dirt, and probably the most untidy station I have ever seen for litter. What did impress me was the very tall buildings adjacent to the station which I presumed to have been linked to the milling industry at some time but were by then being used as warehouses. They were black with soot except for the odd brick which had split at the face and showed a bright orange! Brickwork and windows were of the old style – that is brick arches were used to support the wall above window frames instead of the modern practice of using lintels. You could easily tell where windows had been replaced, for they were topped with concrete lintels.

The master of photography in these industrial surroundings to me was always Colin Gifford. Malcolm Dunnett was another but his pictures did not always contain the detail I sought, although they capture the dirt and gloom to perfection. I used photographs from these master photographers to provide me with the details I needed for this painting.

The austerity WD 2-8-0s were the only freight locomotive that could symbolise this industrial heritage. At a distance there is a slight resemblance to the front of an A3 Pacific, but close to they resemble no other locomotive from the Big Four. The only time one could see a clean WD was ex works. Usually they could be heard making horrible noises plodding through industrial areas such as this. The rather brutal look of the WD seemed more appropriate than the 02 which was the only other freight locomotive indigenous to the area. It was a machine with absolutely no frills and not much grace or elegance either, whereas the 02 had a graceful cab and a slim boiler which belied its power classification. To make amends I included the tender and cab of one of these fine machines on the line adjacent to the head-on WD. The towering warehouse on the left is just as it was in my memory. It shut out the daylight and dominated everything especially the station. The only sky visible was then a dirty yellow in colour. The sulphurous smell of coal was everywhere and accounted for the yellow colour of the sky.

This kind of painting can be one of the hardest to create, certainly the sort with the greatest potential for going wrong. With all my paintings the smoke is put in last. The detail behind the smoke is completed so that I get a feeling for how the smoke should blend in to the picture. The smoke has to be semi transparent at its edges but dense enough elsewhere to convince the viewer that the engine is working hard and that the fireman is not sitting down! Getting the smoke wrong at the end of a lot of very detailed work is catastrophic! It does happen every now and then, but industrial scenes like this still keep attracting me. They are, I think, the railways as so many of us remember them.

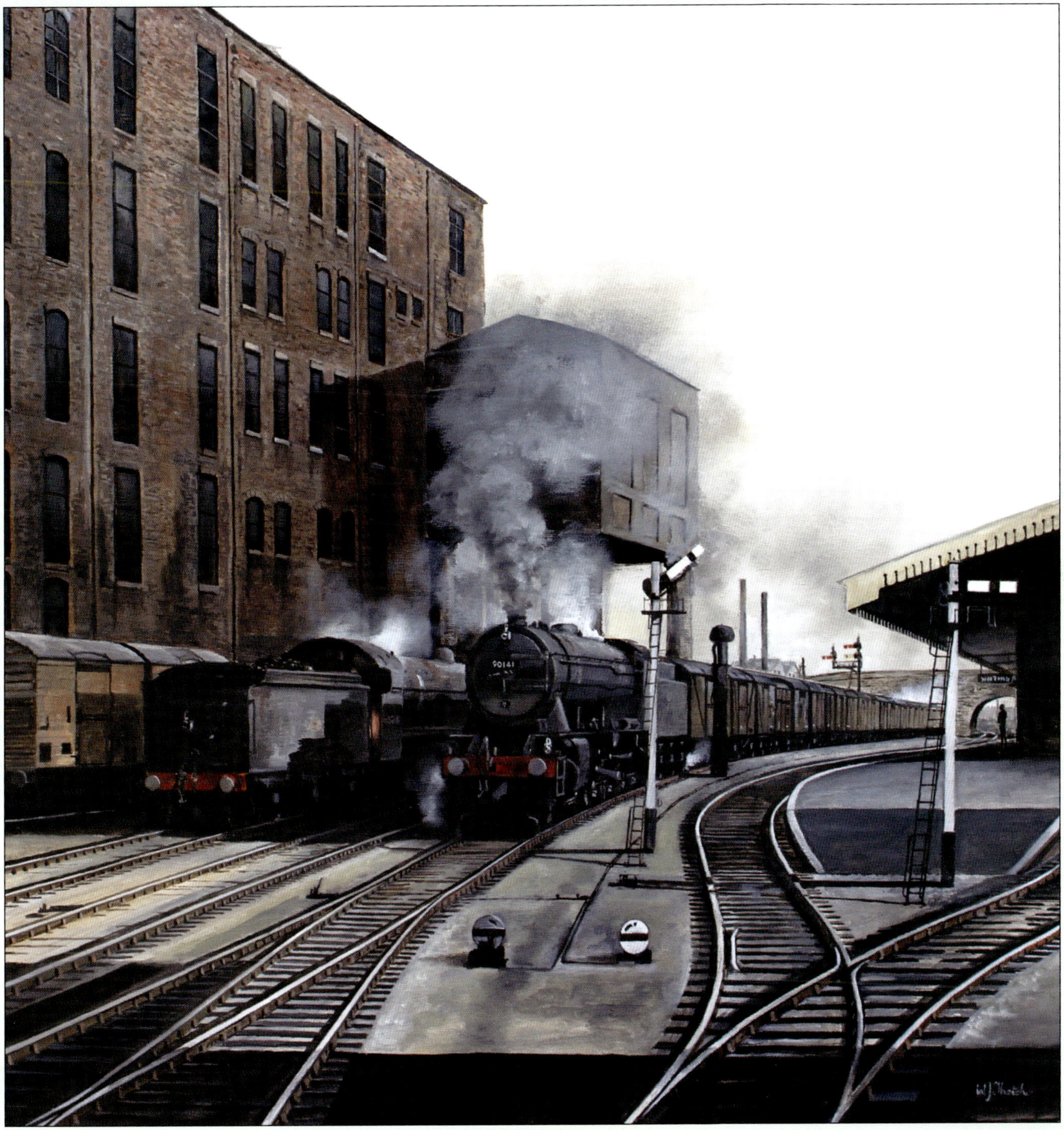
90141

Ribblehead Autumn

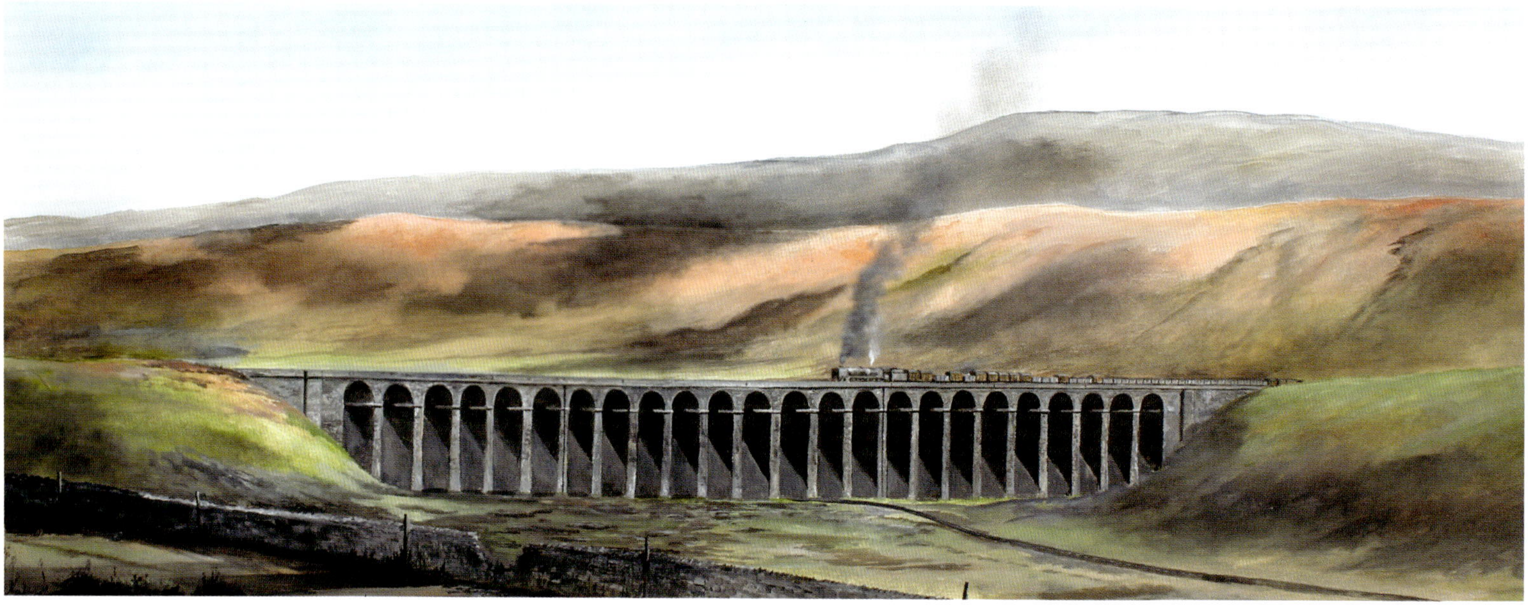

This, and the painting opposite, are intended to be seen together. They illustrate the dramatically altering mood of the Pennine Hills through summer and autumn to winter. I have travelled the line in all weathers before the threat of closure and after the repair of the mighty Ribblehead viaduct and the reinstatement of the line. It was one of the triumphs of society over a government intent on ignoring the needs of the local community, on the grounds of cost. Thank goodness society won, not only because sights like this would have been lost for ever, but because of the re-emergence of the railways which has meant that this route is now essential both for tourism and for freight, relieving the congestion on both the East and West Coast main lines between London and Scotland.

It has to be said that autumn days like this in the Pennine Hills are very rare! My experiences are more often clouded with memories of rain which comes at you horizontally, driven by howling winds strong enough to blow a heavy tripod over. My first photograph taken here of 'Clan Line' on one of the first steam specials bears witness to this! But when the sun does shine it is one of the most remotely beautiful areas in all England. In the painting a 9F trundles a freight train southwards in perfect conditions.

Ribblehead Winter

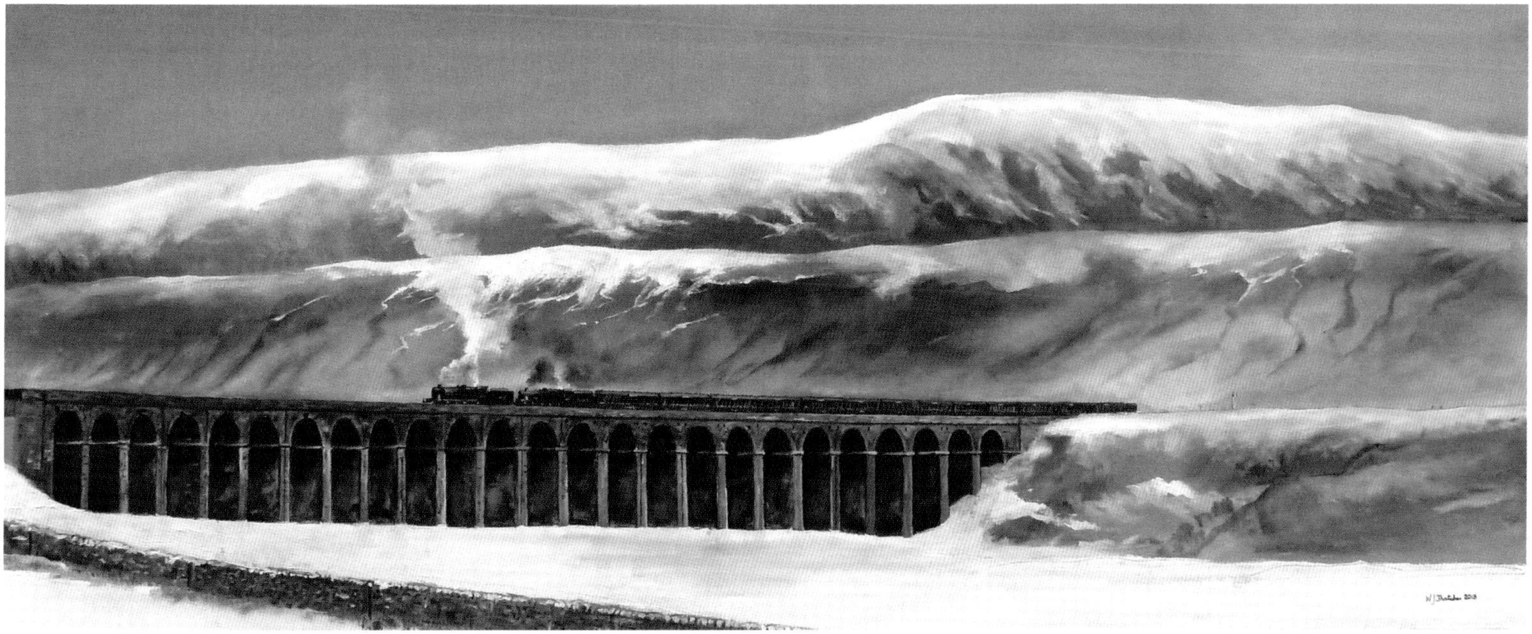

Now these are more familiar conditions! The first time I crossed over this viaduct with snow on the ground was actually idyllic; the train was one of the Past Time Railways specials from Preston to Carlisle, and was hauled by the secretive little Stanier Mogul; an engine perfectly suited to this route and it put up an amazing performance. On that occasion the sky was blue and the snow-covered hills were pure Christmas card stuff!

The last time I travelled the same route was behind a Black 5. The sky was leaden, just like this, and the driving snow obscured everything, even the buttresses on the viaduct. That the train kept time was due to outstanding handling by the engine crew.

I have depicted the viaduct in LMS days with a double header (the Midland never got it out of their system!) comprising a red Jubilee being piloted by a Black 5. Had the authorities realised it, a single Stanier Mogul could have done the job just as well!

Out of Paddington

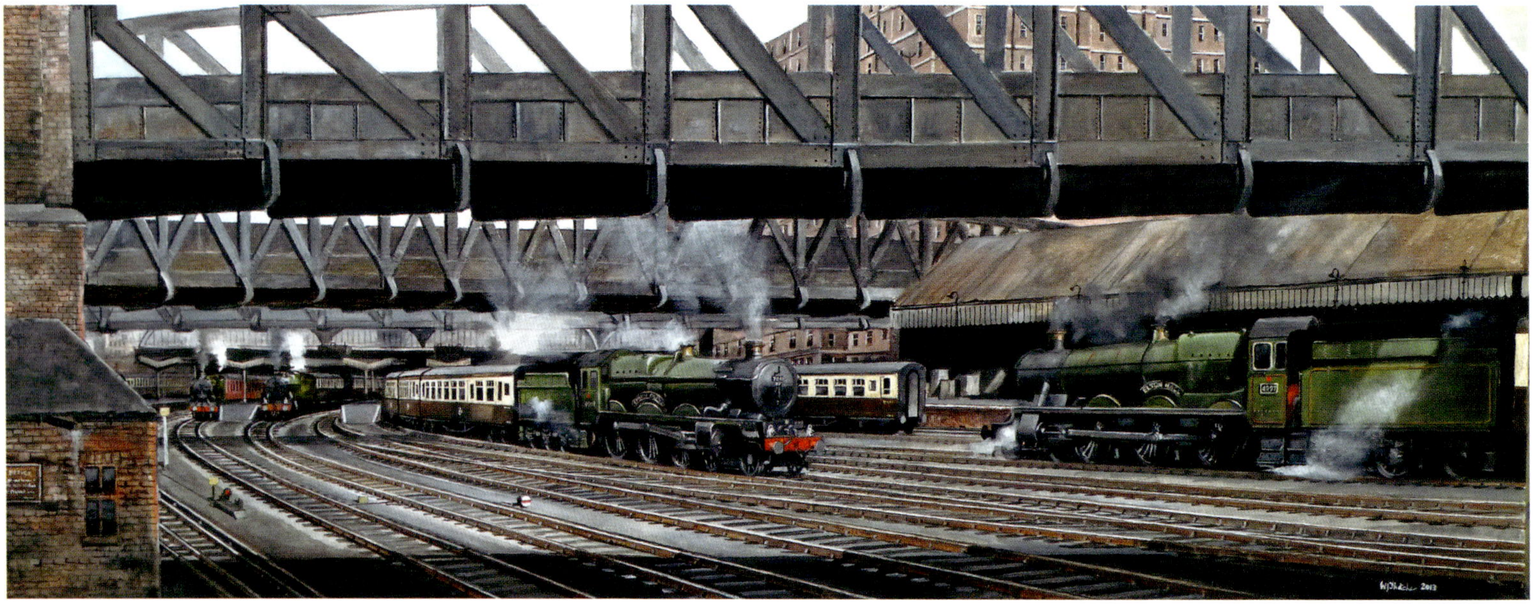

In the theme of Out of Euston and Out of Waterloo paintings, the western exit from London was dominated by Paddington. It was very difficult to get photographs of trains leaving Paddington, although easy enough to get them arriving. The reason for this was the Stationmaster at Royal Oak, a station served by the Hammersmith and City underground line. As soon as anyone who looked like a trainspotter turned up on the platform it was 'Oi! Get off out of 'ere'. I managed to get a few photographs from this location by hopping on a tube train leaving Paddington at the same time as a main line departure, hopping off at Royal Oak, grabbing a quick shot, and hopping back on the next London bound tube! On one occasion I managed two photographs before Adolf, as he was un-affectionately known, made his appearance. The composition here is entirely imaginary, as I was never lucky enough to get a photograph like it, but the photographs at least enabled me to get the infrastructure right. A Castle class locomotive can be seen leaving with a West of England express, while a Hall makes its way into the terminal.

Holbeck

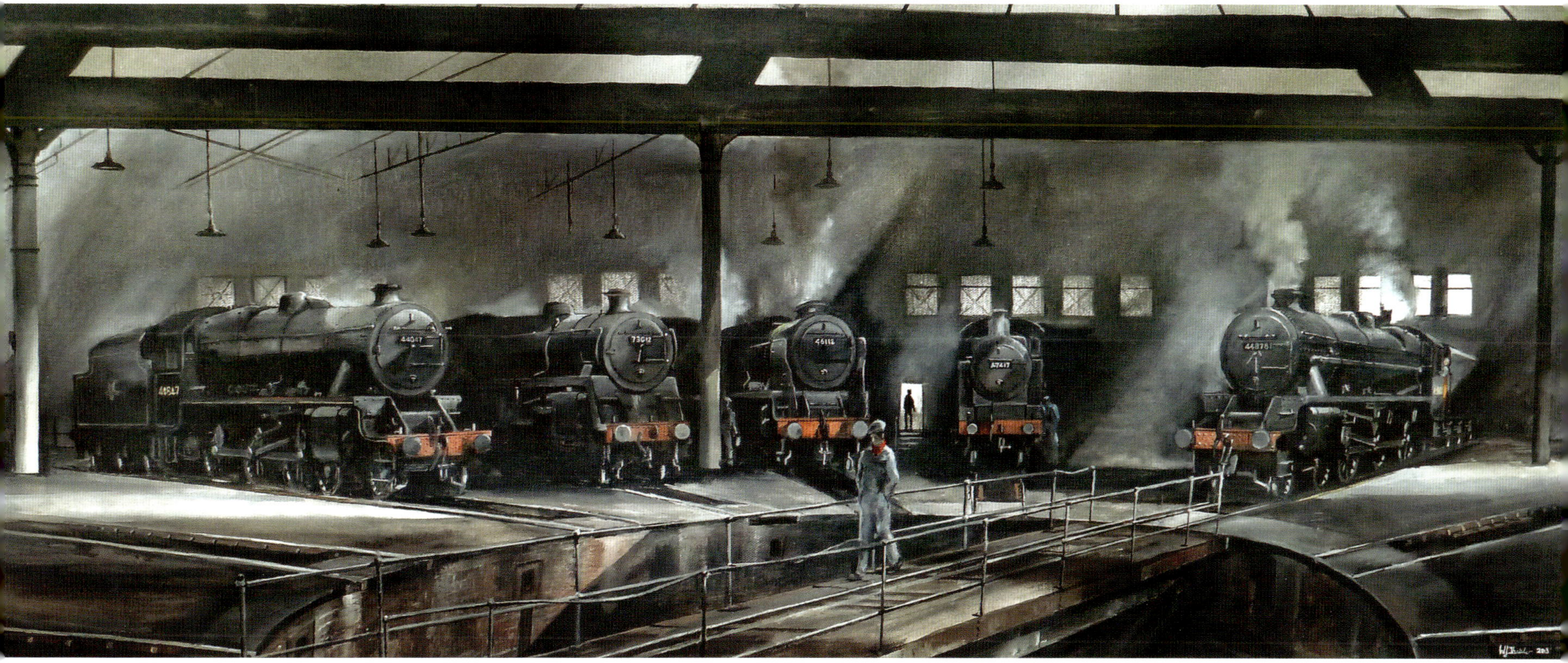

By the time I saw Leeds Holbeck shed, it was being used to stable diesels. The front of the shed was partly demolished; at least it was in such a disgusting state that is what it looked like. Inside the smell of steam engines still lingered even though polluted by the smell of diesel oil. I do not suppose I am alone in the ability to smell a steam engine anywhere. It certainly was not difficult here. The soot from their passing coated every brick. The windows, uncleaned for years, were quite opaque to the outside world, but then many of the diesels seemed to be emitting as much smoke as steam had done twenty years earlier and the acrid stench seemed a lot more harmful.

So this painting filled in the gaps as so many of my paintings do. The distinctive windows define the roundhouse, while two Black 5s frame a standard class 4, a rebuilt 'Scot' and a Jinty tank engine. Someone is escaping for some fresh air in the doorway, and the engineman crossing the turntable, with railings bent and battered from feet being placed where they shouldn't, doesn't look to be in too much of a hurry as he guides the Black 5 out of the shed.

Leeds

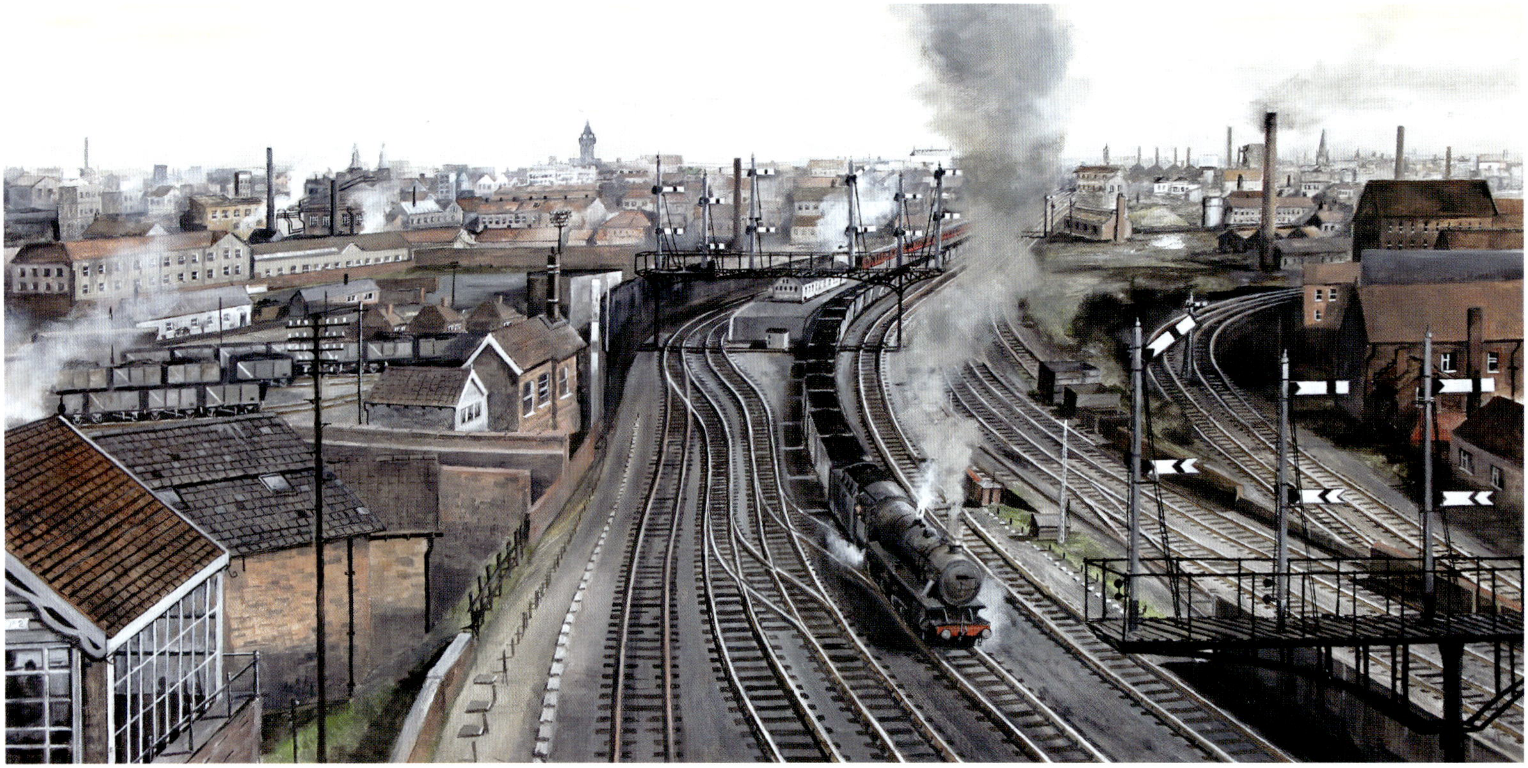

Leeds really was the crossroads of the railways in the North of England. The trans-Pennine line brought Midland railway traffic into the city while both East and West Coast trains found their way there via York. The city was, and still is, a maze of railway tracks. It is as industrial as Huddersfield but not so closed in and claustrophobic. In the centre of this picture is Holbeck high level station. The elegant clock on the town hall can be seen on the horizon. As with the painting of Huddersfield, it seemed that the only engine which would look right in this environment would be a WD on a coal train, the locomotive emitting a suitably sulphurous smoke screen as it heads west.

Four Bridges of the Tyne

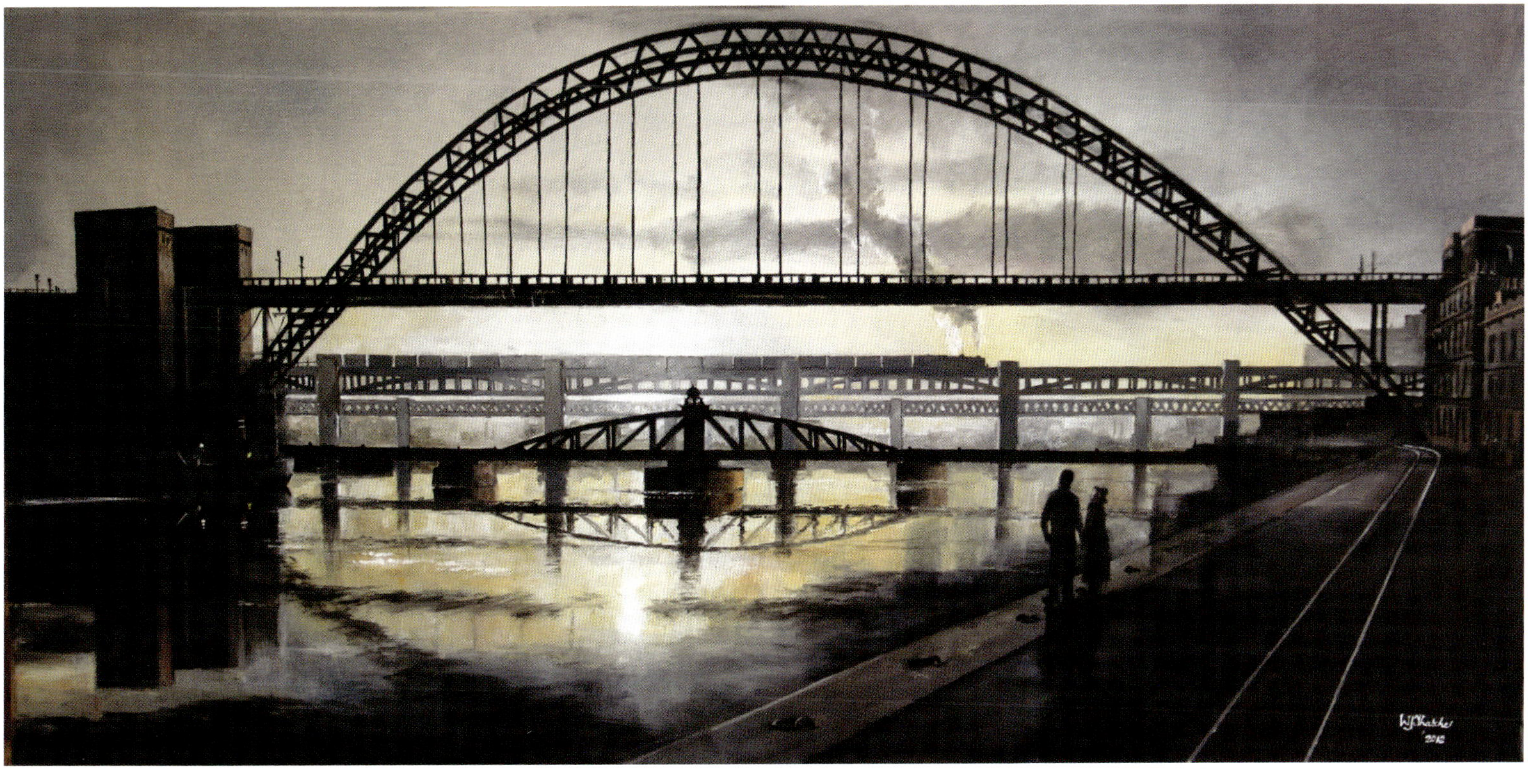

Moving still further north we come to the city of Newcastle. Tyneside was the birthplace of the railways and, like Leeds, the railways have dominated and influenced every industrial event in the area. It was coal that brought the railways here but Newcastle seems to have shed all its heritage, for the modern city looks nothing like this picture which can be dated around 1930 from the V2 crossing the high level bridge out of Newcastle Central, and from the bonnet worn by the lady on the quayside. Are they a courting couple? We will never know! A light railway system served the dock front here for a hundred years. It is now a riverside park.

‘Kittiwake’

Staying in Newcastle, A1 Pacific locomotive 60120 ‘Kittiwake’ has brought the Queen of Scots Pullman service from Kings Cross into Central station. This is a well known location and hundreds of wonderful photographs exist of it, alas, none of them mine. I had to travel there behind a Deltic to see the station, and get the atmosphere (if one can forgive the comparison), of what it must have been like in steam days. Even the Deltic looked good in the perfect setting of light and shade, with shafts of sunlight penetrating the gloom, mostly from broken panes of glass in the otherwise soot-encrusted class canopy. Newcastle Central was designed and built by Robert Stephenson. It was opened on 29 August 1850, an opening attended by Queen Victoria. It is now a listed Grade I building, its arched roof being the first of its kind. To the north-east of the station, the diamond crossover is the largest of its kind in the world.

Newcastle always puzzled me. I have mentioned earlier that this was the birthplace of the railways, and yet there seemed to be little affection for them here amongst the few railwaymen and station staff that I spoke to. Even as a young spotter it was well known in the south that Gateshead engines were always the dirtiest locomotives on the line, frequently so bad that it was impossible to see the numbers. This was in sharp contrast to Kings Cross or Edinburgh Haymarket. Central station was the same. Certainly ‘Kittiwake’, which was a Southern area A1 at the time, was well kept, and one which I saw frequently pounding up and down the East Coast main line, so that was the engine I chose for my picture. Although this is one of my earlier paintings it is still one of my favourites. The light on the boiler seems just right, and the locomotive exudes a brute strength, an impatience to get on its journey, with smoke lifting from both nostrils. The curvature of the platform in Newcastle Central is perfect for displaying the train without having to shorten the view to the first two or three carriages (which never looks good) while enabling a full size depiction of the engine itself.

The Pullman trains were the most prestigious on the East Coast, providing fast and comfortable journeys mainly for businessmen. An excellent description of these trains can be found in Dave Peel’s book entitled *Locomotive Headboards*. It is interesting to note that ‘Kittiwake’ has not got her headboard on. Towards the end of steam there was a tendency not to bother, as they required fitting and removing at the end of the day, work that was deemed unnecessary. Even the Western Region stopped using reporting codes on the front of their trains. It seems to me that this was symbolic of the lack of pride in the operation of the railways everywhere which was most evident at the end of the British Railways era.

Newcastle is now completely changed. Investment in the city centre has produced areas such as the Metro Centre, a smart modern shopping arcade and entertainment complex. Newcastle Central station has undergone a transformation. It serves stations as far apart as Penzance and Inverness. 7.8 million passengers passed through the station in 2013 and many more did so without getting off their London or Edinburgh bound trains. A £20 million facelift is currently in progress. The platforms, once dirty and litter covered, are now faced with tiles which look like marble.

Modern shops and restaurants flank the platform concourse, while high speed electric trains of the multiple unit variety glide effortlessly into and out of the station under the electric catenary. In 2015 the station reverts to the care of Network Rail as successive governments privatise then re-nationalise the railways.

It is a very far cry from the sound of A1s or A4s slipping violently as steam roared from their chimneys while trying to get some adhesion on that sharp curve out of the station.

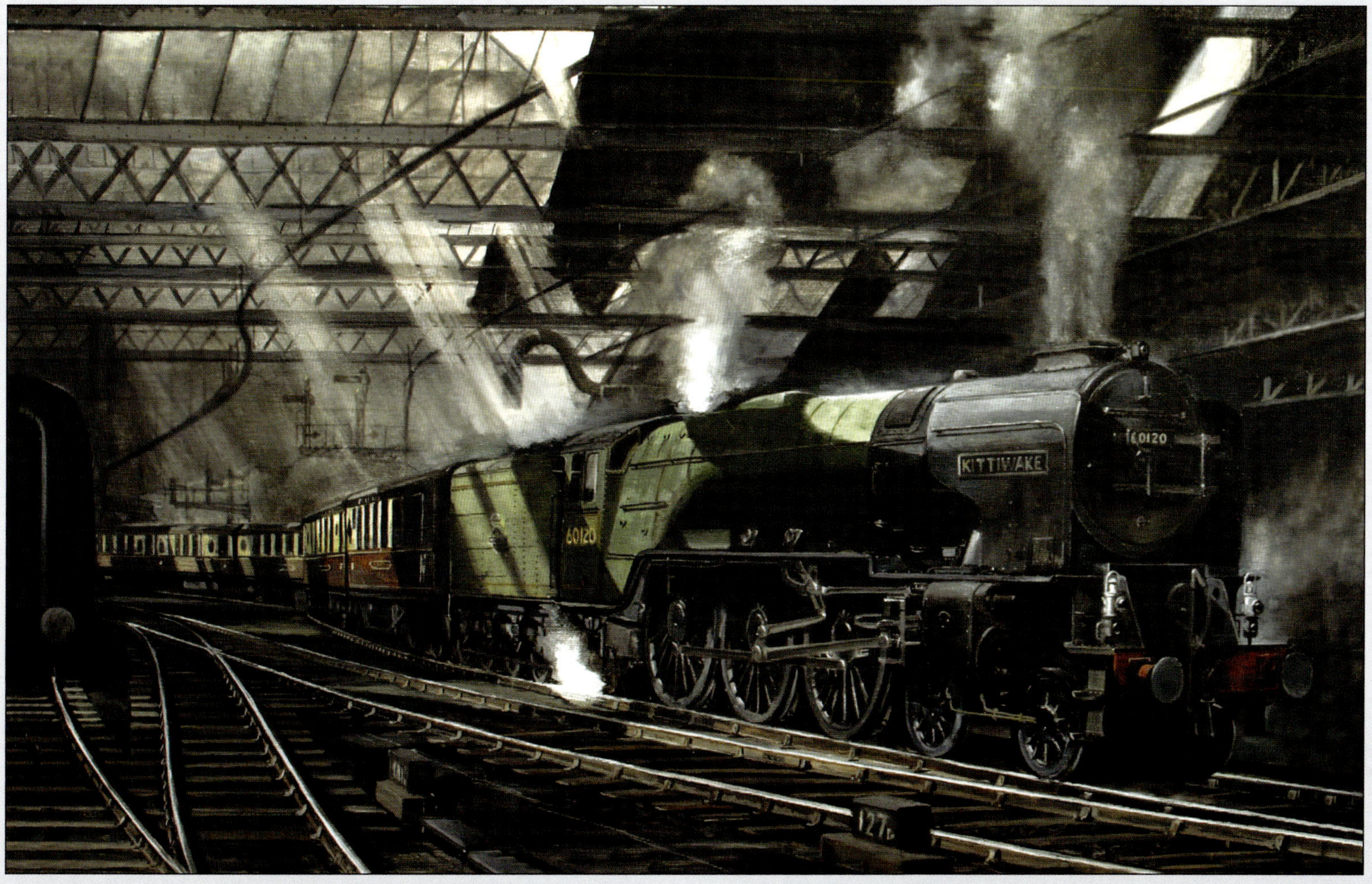

'Kittiwake' entering Newcastle Central

Norwich

In complete contrast to the previous painting, several hundred miles to the south of Newcastle lies the old market town of Norwich, now the principal city of this mainly agricultural region. There were originally three stations serving this small city, Norwich Thorpe, the present station, Norwich Victoria which closed in 1916, and Norwich City which served the old Midland and Great Northern Joint Railway and remained open until 1959.

It seems that the stations in Norwich were developed along the same lines as its much larger contemporary, Waterloo in London. Everyone who built a railway line built a new station, or at least new platforms in existing stations! That may go some way to explain the absence of any great architectural style about Norwich Thorpe – it was always being altered to accommodate some new development. Even today one cannot help but notice that while the front of the station presents an air of grandeur, the inside is little more than a truncated booking hall.

I very much wanted to find some angle to paint this station and show it to be the equal at least of some of its urban counterparts, but alas, look as I might, I could not find an aspect which achieved this. The main reason is the change in the length of trains using Thorpe station. When it was first built, these were no more than two or three coaches long, and the 'booking hall' accommodated them. Even in the Victorian era, trains such as the Cromer Express with up to ten coaches used this station, and yet no shelter was built for them; instead the platforms were merely lengthened so that disembarking passengers could scurry down their length to find shelter in the 'booking hall'.

By the time British Railways were building their Britannia Pacific locomotives, eleven and twelve coach trains of Mk I stock were normal and the platforms had to be lengthened again. It is a great shame that a city as wealthy as Norwich was, or is, could not build a suitably impressive railway station to advertise itself in the same way other cities have, even if the old Great Eastern Railway, which was permanently short of cash, could not afford it.

The Britannia's mentioned above were a phase change in locomotive power available for the Norwich to London services which were becoming increasingly important at the time. Named trains such as The East Anglian, The Norfolkman, The Easterling and the Broadsman, all conveyed an important business traffic to and from the capital. Previously these trains had been hauled by little 4-6-0s of the Sandringham class. Capable little machines in their own right, they were really suited to local semi-fast trains and struggled with a load over seven coaches. Both my Grandfathers drove them at various times, as both were employed as drivers by the LNER and later the Eastern Region of British Railways. Their view was that the B16s were under boilered; they raised steam well enough, but did not have enough capacity, requiring the fireman to fill the box continuously on a journey of any length.

The Britannias were an eye-opener to them and every other driver on the Great Eastern network. They had a huge firebox which could be loaded with coal and left (although like most engines they performed better with a thinner hotter fire). They had lots of power, and although very noisy and sometimes rough riding on poor track (the Norwich to London Line is continuously being upgraded even now!), they could run.

The travel time for the crack trains to London Liverpool Street came down to two hours via Ipswich; slightly longer via Cambridge to Kings Cross. Nowhere in Britain were these locomotives more appreciated, which is a shame because the East Coast main line had hundreds of powerful Pacifics or V2s but no thought was ever given to building a powerful lightweight Pacific for East Anglia.

My painting show one of Norwich's immaculate Britannia class locomotives 'Coeur de Lion' leaving the extended platforms of Norwich Thorpe. The saving grace of the station was the signals at the end of the platform which gave some sort of 'railwayness' to the location, signals which should have been mounted off the platform for safety reasons but which seem to have been overtaken by platform extensions!

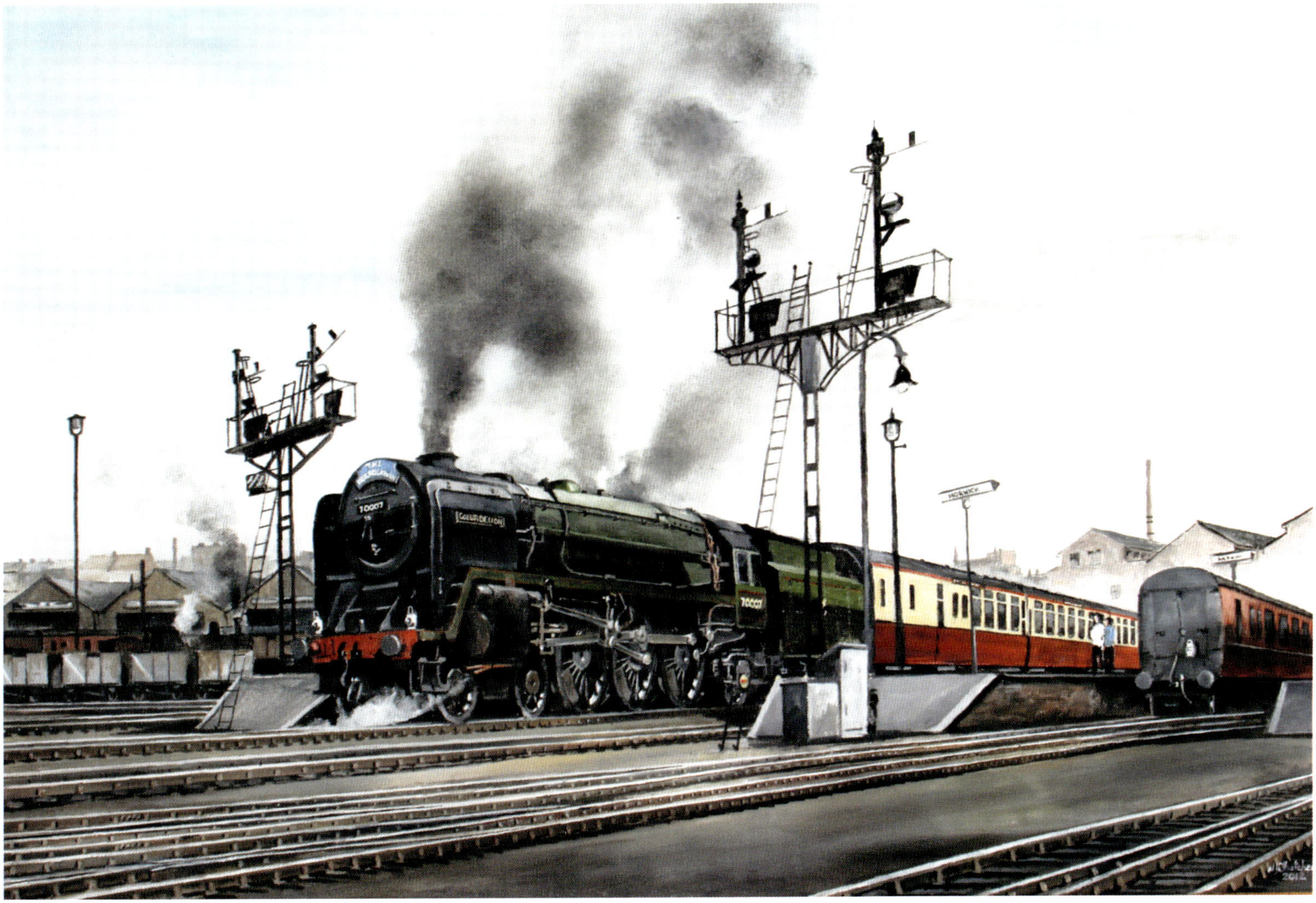

'Coeur de Lion' about to leave Norwich Thorpe Station

Newton Abbot at Night

I have always had the greatest admiration for those railway enthusiasts who spend nearly all their spare time helping restore engines rescued from the Barry scrapyard of Dai Woodham. Some are little more than shells, and it is difficult to see how they can ever be turned into operational steam locomotives again, let alone the pristine machines which end up hauling 400 ton trains at 75mph on our congested main lines. 'King Edward I' is an example of such meticulous engineering work. I was privileged to be able to travel behind this fine machine together with my friends Bob and Mary Tout on a steam special running from Bristol to Penzance and return. It is easy to underestimate the distances involved; one can travel from London across the borders into Scotland in the same time as one might reach Penzance, so KEI as it is commonly known put up a mighty effort to take the return Cornishman unassisted from Bristol that day with twelve coaches fully loaded with day trippers and enthusiasts. The biggest obstacle on that journey is of course the notorious Devon banks of which Dainton and Hemerdon are probably the worst. The southbound journey is not quite so bad, especially on Hemerdon Bank, because the engine is fresh, and so are the crew.

The return journey is one to be feared from the footplate or enjoyed from the comfort of the coach (or from a good photographic location on the line side!). There is absolutely no respite once the level crossing has been passed out of Plymouth at the eastern end of the station, for the long steep ascent of Hemerdon begins immediately. On the occasion of our journey all began well as we departed, but it became apparent that all was not well after about a mile-we were travelling much slower than the speed needed to breast the summit. Eventually KE1 sat down (the enginemen's way of saying refused to go any further!). The air brakes which were driven from a specially installed Westinghouse pump on the footplate of the engine at Network Rail's insistence, had failed, and the brakes had slowly but surely brought a 2000 horsepower locomotive to a stand in the worst possible place. Here the skill and determination of the Driver Burns, the crew fitters and mechanics in the support coach really showed itself. In a matter of about 15 minutes they disconnected the air brakes and connected up the original vacuum brake pipes which all steam locomotives are equipped with. Hey Presto! Now all the engine had to do was start a 500 ton train on a grade of one in fifty-five!

And it did it! Slowly and surely it not only started without a slip, it accelerated up that fearsome grade and proceeded to sail over Dainton and the other banks as though nothing had happened. With some very fast running over the Somerset levels (what was the speed restriction?) we reached Bristol Temple Meads three minutes early! We were fortunate that the return journey was at night and nothing was held up by the incident, but it enabled us to see just how much power a 64 year old steam engine could produce.

My painting is a direct reminiscence from that journey. I chose to paint a Castle rather than a King, because I much prefer single chimneys on the Great Western engines and the Kings had double chimneys by the mid 50s. The rest is as I remembered it, supported by some very poor quality photography with an early digital camera which could not cope with the dismally poor lighting. The coloured aspect signals were replaced in the painting with the original semaphores. I am not sure whether the buildings in the left distance were there in the 50s but they looked right and gave balance. One cannot stand next to a steam engine at night without a sense of the energy being transferred from a white hot fire into steam. The noise and the heat are testimony to that. Unfortunately in a painting all that can be captured is the colour and luminance of an open fire hole.

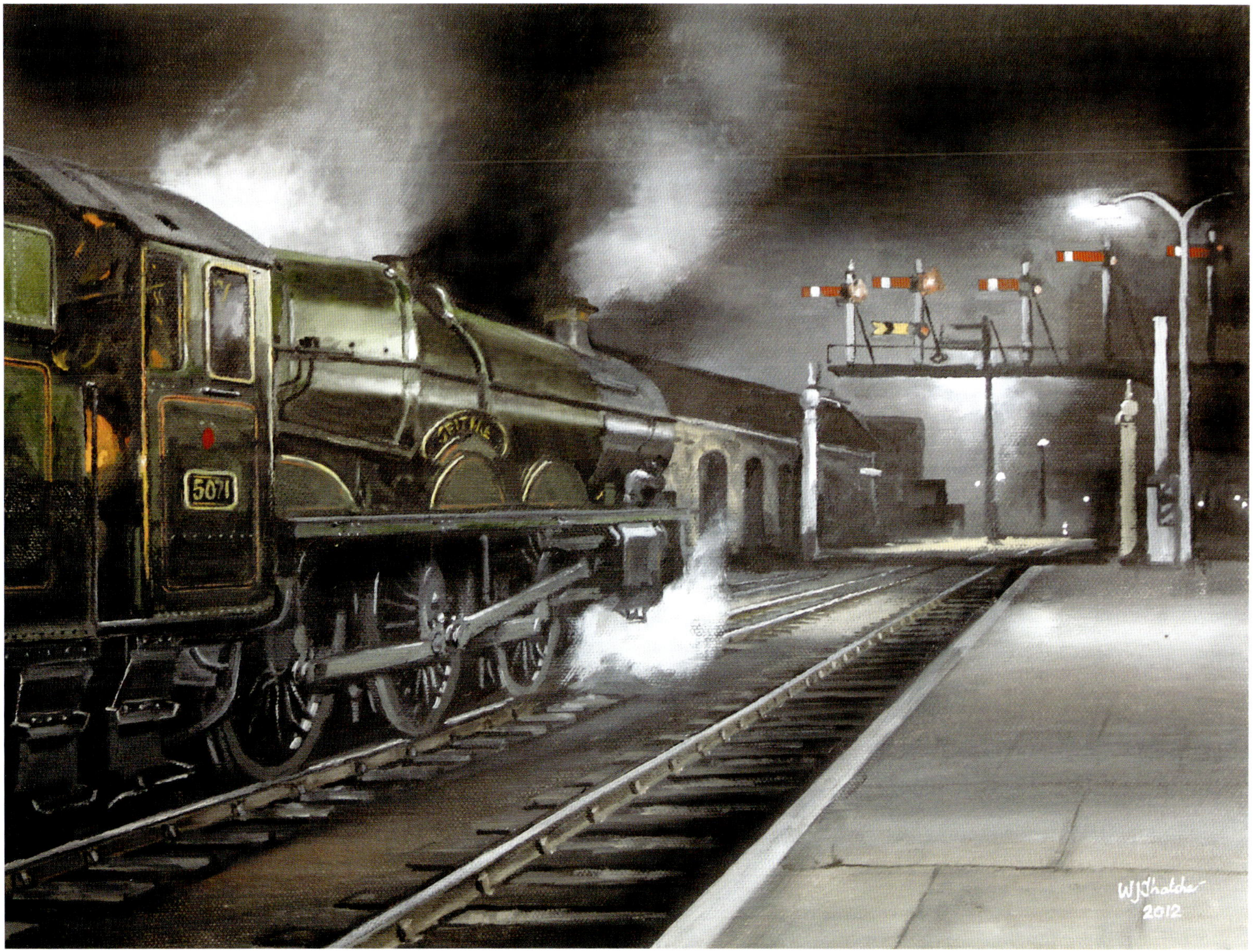
5071
WJThatcher
2012

Colwall

The Great Western route from Paddington to Worcester is something of a contrast to the severely graded Devon to Cornwall line. The only hills of any note en route are the Malverns, an isolated pocket of upland which look impressively mountainous as it rises above the Herefordshire plains. No attempt was made to climb these hills, instead tunnels were bored at Colwall and Ledbury thus maintaining the easy grades which had prevailed since leaving London. The tunnels were constructed between 1856 and 1861 when they were opened on the 15 September. Unfortunately the bore of the Ledbury tunnel was so small that it resembled the tight fit of the tunnels on the Somerset & Dorset Railway; with negligible clearance it was possible to have a blowback if the locomotive was worked hard. Furthermore there was only room for one track, which has a sharp curve and a moderate grade at the north end (suggesting that the tunnel builders did not get their alignment right when starting from both sides!). This, combined with a problem with constructing ventilation shafts due to the steepness of the Malvern hills, meant that the atmosphere in the tunnel during steam days was decidedly poor.

Colwall is a tiny hamlet built into the side of the Malverns, just above the mouth of the tunnel. The nearest station is in the market town of Ledbury, a few miles away from which trains direct to Paddington, Worcester, and Birmingham still run. The bottleneck which prevailed during steam days still does so today. Typically there are four to five trains a day to the major cities. Ledbury is one of the few places in the UK where rail traffic is falling. A mere 197 000 passengers used the station in 2013, a fall from the previous year.

Colwal remains a very pretty and much photographed village. It typifies the non-industrial image of the Great Western, and since my in-laws lived in Ledbury I had ample opportunity to watch diesel multiple units crawling their way through the narrow bore and asphyxiating their passengers with their carbon monoxide-laden fumes. The transition in my mind to steam was not difficult. The driver of the Castle class locomotive emerging from the narrow bore has 'opened up', no doubt glad to be in the fresh air again. The immaculate state of the engine is indicative of its local shed; Worcester Shrub Hill was famed for the state of cleanliness of their engines – none on the entire Great Western did it better, The tradition was carried through to British Railways days. Dirty Castles were unheard of until the Midland Region took over whereupon cleanliness took an immediate dive.

The hamlet of Colwall can be seen above the tunnel mouth. I have not been there for many years now but hear that some development has been allowed and the hamlet has now become a village, while Ledbury has lost its engine shed, its branch line, its goods yard and even has a privatised ticket office not even based on the station.

That's progress!

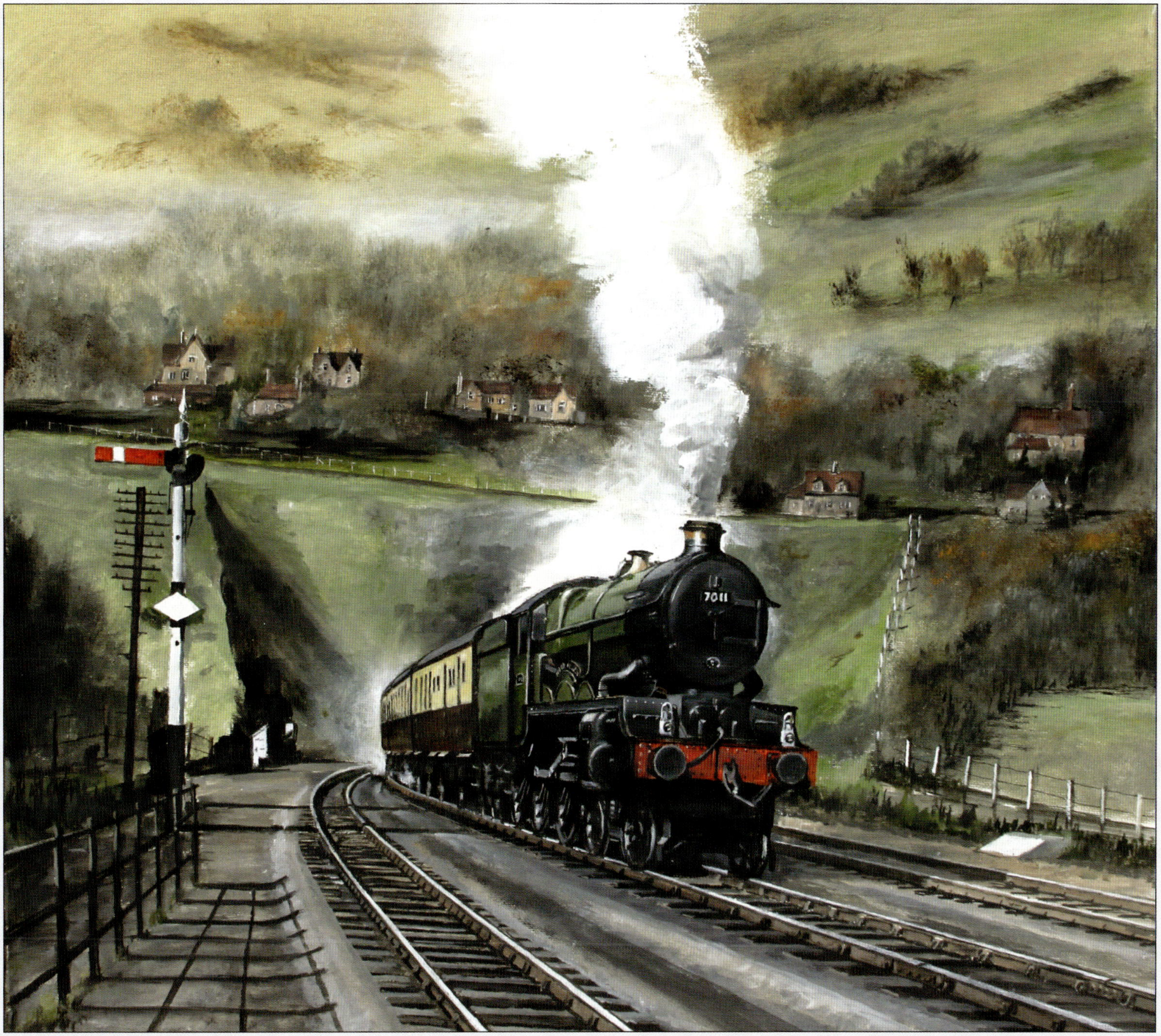
7011

A 9F in Monsal Dale

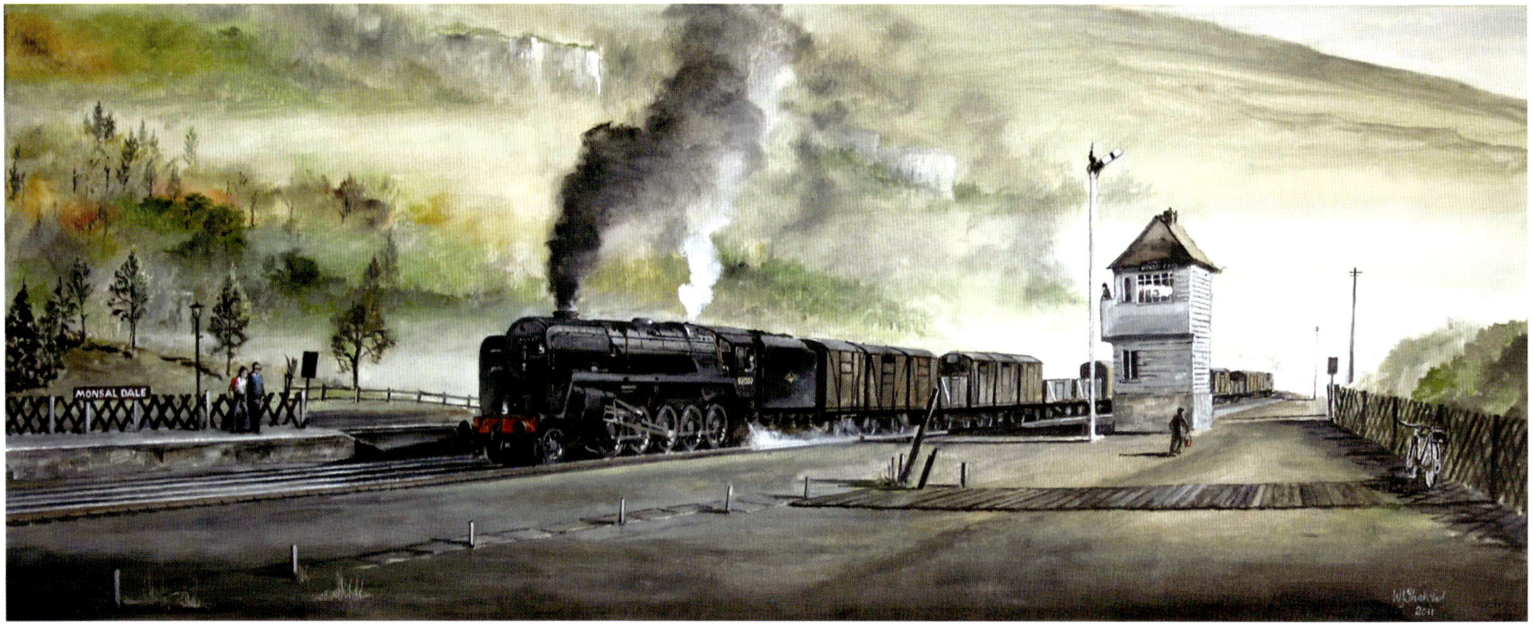

This painting was the result of a commission requesting a number of combinations which I had to research quite hard to satisfy! The desired locomotive was a 9F in rural surroundings so eventually I found some photographs of Monsal Dale where this class, indeed this locomotive, actually did run right up to the end of steam. Not much chance of getting a sighting of this location today as it is an overgrown cycle path under the care of Sustrans. Such a pity the cycle track could not have been built alongside the railway which used to connect the Midlands to Manchester.

No problems finding the bicycle in this one but I wonder where the gentleman with the fire bucket is going. I have exaggerated the width of the track bed where lines have already been removed to give the picture space, as a huge engine such as a 9F looks hemmed in and completely wrong on single lines or narrow cuttings, especially as it was essentially an industrial machine intended for long distance main line work.

Monsal Dale in the Autumn

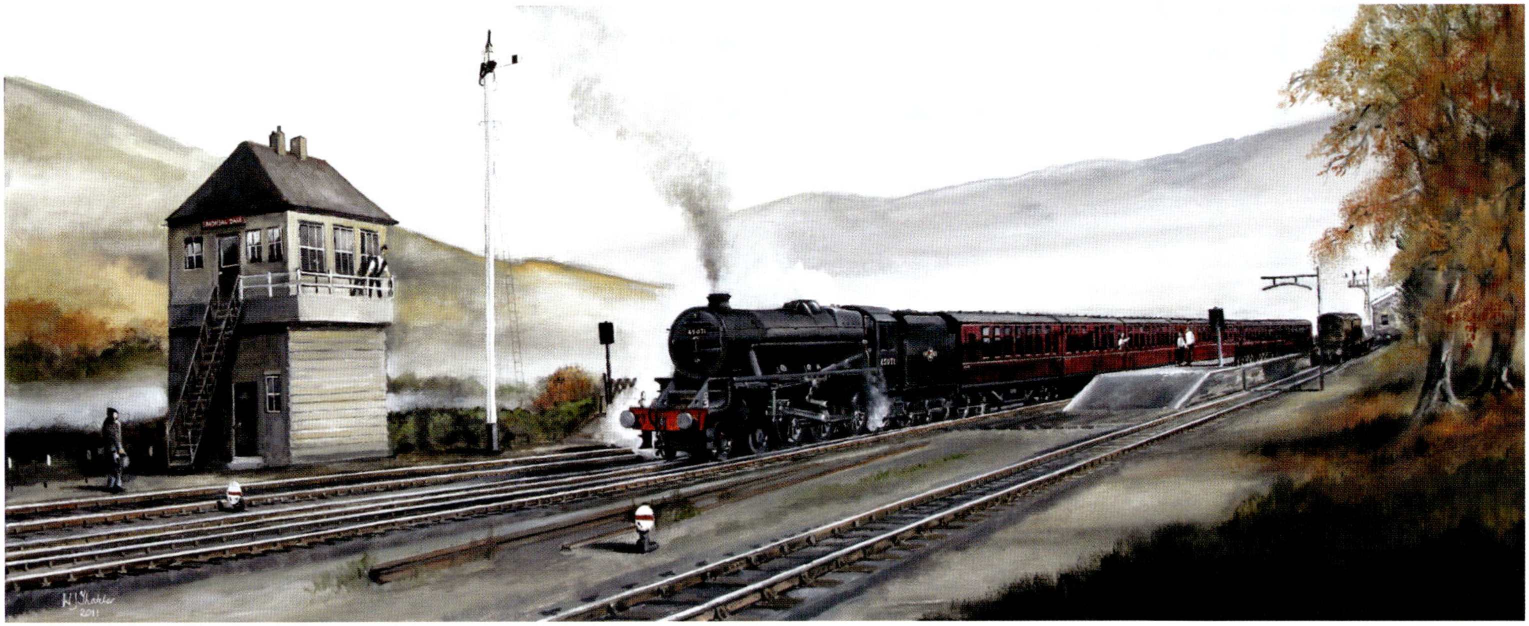

The research into Monsal Dale convinced me that this would have been a very attractive place to photograph or paint trains, with beautiful scenery as well, so I switched my mind around and viewed the same location as the previous picture from the other side of the track. This time I have shown a Black 5 about to depart with one of the last trains to stop at the station before the track was finally lifted. It must have been cleaned by the Master Neverers, a group of enthusiasts who liked their engines to be clean when photographed! A passenger is waving goodbye to the persons seeing her off, while the signalman is doubtlessly having a word with the driver. The gentleman with the bucket is still there but at least it is not a fire bucket this time.

Not only was this the season of autumn; the end of the line is very near with tracks already lifted lying in the foreground. The wide space behind the box has been reduced to its true dimensions, but has anyone noticed the signal?

Racing the Storm

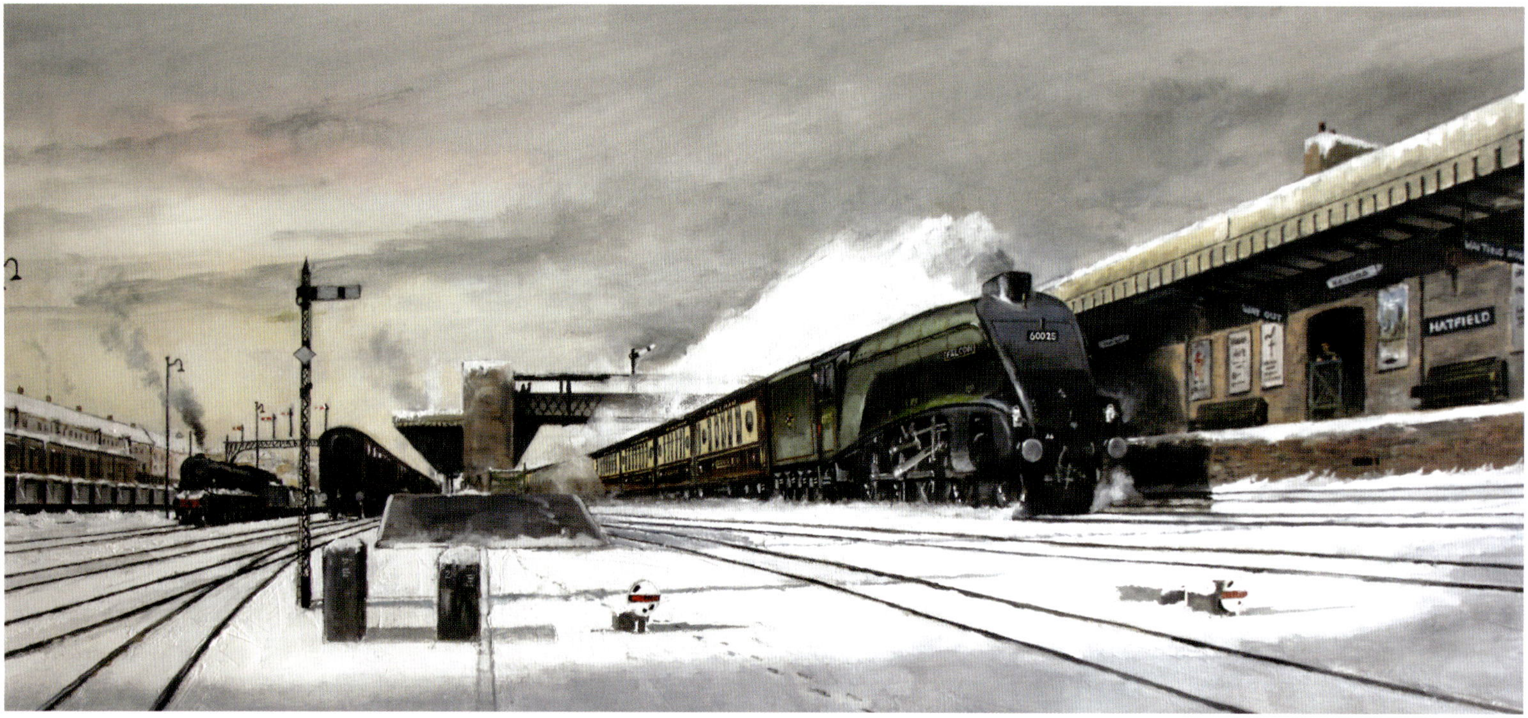

The season has moved on to winter, and the winter of 1963 has been mentioned before. This is Hatfield again on the occasion when my camera froze solid, but viewed from under the footbridge to the south end of the station, a position I was very unlikely to have had access to! Footprints show the route of my would-be trespass, as a London bound A4 races through the station trying desperately to get to London before the gathering storm clouds above the station deposit a fresh load of snow on already icy rails. A WD lurks in the yard, its boiler having no affect on the snow-covered running plates.

Kings Lynn

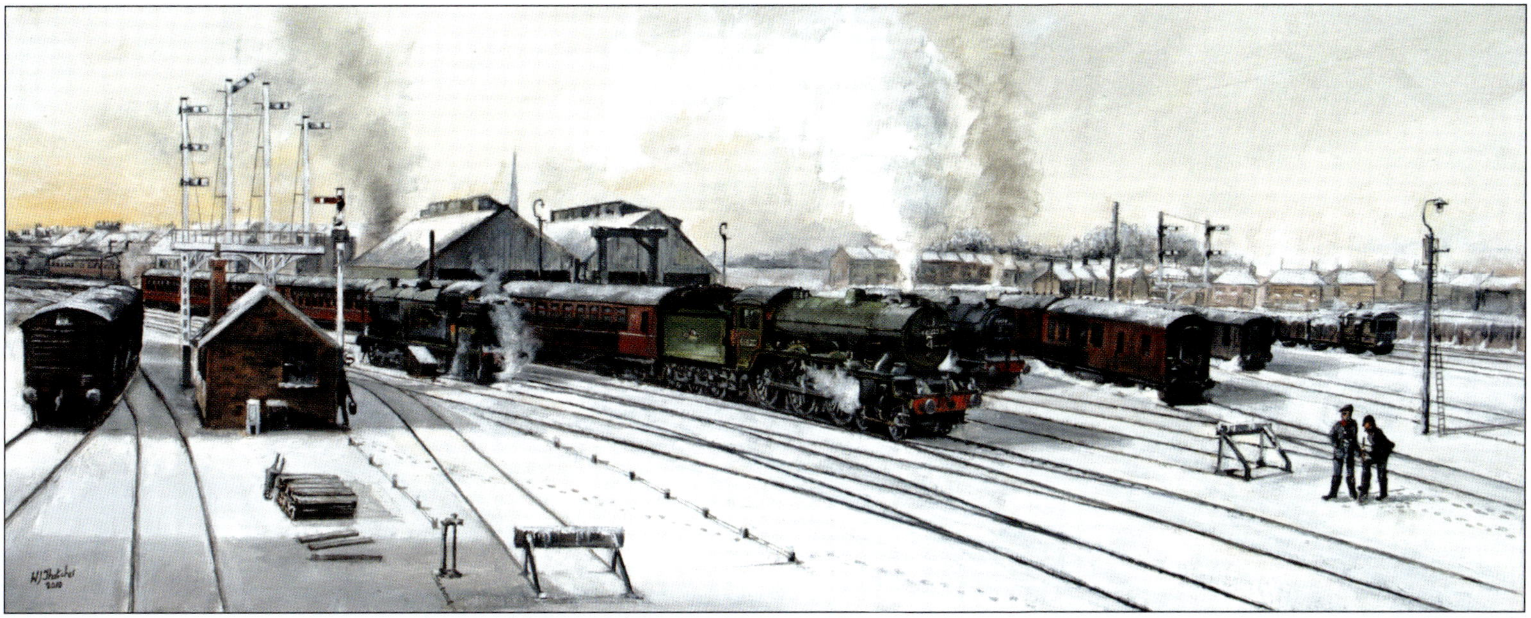

The winter of 1958 was also bitterly cold and heavy snow fell over East Anglia and most of southern England. This is Kings Lynn with a mantle of snow which helped to hide the usually scrappy and untidy area around the shed. New houses were being built adjacent to the station and signalling was still by semaphore signals on a rather splendid gantry just outside the shed. Engine 61620 'Clumber' – a Cromer engine which Grandfather Jim sometimes drove – has been honoured with a Cambridge express. This engine was in such a dreadful state internally and externally I doubt it would have made it to Cambridge.The workmen digging a hole in the snow are paying attention. I wonder what that gentleman is taking into the building on the left. Coal from the N7 perhaps?

Painting snow is not as easy as it looks. Notice the variations in colour with the reddish tinge reflecting the wintry sunshine. Today this scene has totally disappeared beneath an untidy mess of tarmac, surveyors' horrible orange mesh fencing and abandoned cars.

Hornsey

Hornsey is a suburb of north London. It is a mere nine miles out of Kings Cross and about the same distance from Hatfield where I used to live. I did not visit it very often. There seemed little point when Kings Cross and all the London termini were so close. In hindsight I wished I had cycled there more often or even caught a local train, rather than taking so many photographs around Hatfield. Hornsey was an immense network of rails, as far as the eye could see. The station was very similar to the other suburban stations at Harringey and Wood Green, but with one advantage, Hornsey had a very long footbridge spanning some twenty tracks giving an excellent view of all the traffic in and out of Ferme Park yard and Hornsey engine shed which housed all the N2 and N7 tank engines used by Kings Cross. The footbridge, just like the one at Hatfield which I have mentioned before, was inscribed with the graffiti of hundreds of trainspotters, with such phrases as 'died here waiting for Silver King' (well I never did see that engine!).

Ferme Park sidings were the location where all the coal trains from the north left their loaded wagons, turned around and took a train of empties back north again. In hindsight it was a massive conveyor belt hauling coal into the capital. Watching from the line side at Hatfield, these long freight trains received little attention, with the procession of A4s and other Pacifics passing so frequently. At Hornsey the true value of the railway became much more obvious. The incoming freight locomotives were housed at Hornsey for the night; and used to clear the empties not only from Ferme park but also New Southgate and even as far afield as Hatfield.

The painting depicts Hornsey as I remembered it from my last visit. It was a particularly vile autumn day, and I must have been mad to attempt it under the grey skies which threatened rain all day. Worse, I saw very few suburban engines which were not already underlined in my Ian Allan ABC combined volume. The arrival of this freight train provided the best entertainment of the day. The sky, always brighter on the horizon, showed no signs of improving where I was, The long freight train hauled by the inevitable WD clanked into sight making the cacophony that only a WD can make. This was before the 9Fs made their considerable presence felt and rendered the WDs redundant at a stroke. The driver and fireman of that WD must have had a hard day, for they shut off steam earlier than most engines going into the yard, hoping no doubt, to drift in under light steam. They immediately paid the price, as the wagons, squealing and clanging on the curve, brought the train to a halt. The driver I assume, then compounded one mistake with another by opening the regulator too quickly to overcome the recalcitrant wagons resulting in one of the most spectacular slips I ever saw!

And this is the result. It took several seconds for the regulator to be closed and a more gentle approach tried, but the smoke stack was tremendous. Alas it was far too dark for my Kodak box brownie 127 camera, and all I got was a black bottom half to the picture with some smoke silhouetted against the sky for the rest. So that is the history behind the painting- an attempt to resurrect a scene which I could not record at the time. I included another WD in the painting as they always seemed to be hanging around the yard . Sometimes as many as a dozen of these beasts of burden could be seen coupled together waiting for the next call. I also included an express rushing north, the carriage lights visible in the gloom.

Sadly the last I saw of the Hornsey WDs was their removal to the scrapyard. A 9F would haul three of these machines at a time up the slow line through Hatfield heading north; the sacking over their chimneys seeming rather pointless. I wondered at the time if collecting the numbers of an engine without coupling rods was allowed. Such was the innocence of the age, and the speed of the demise of steam.

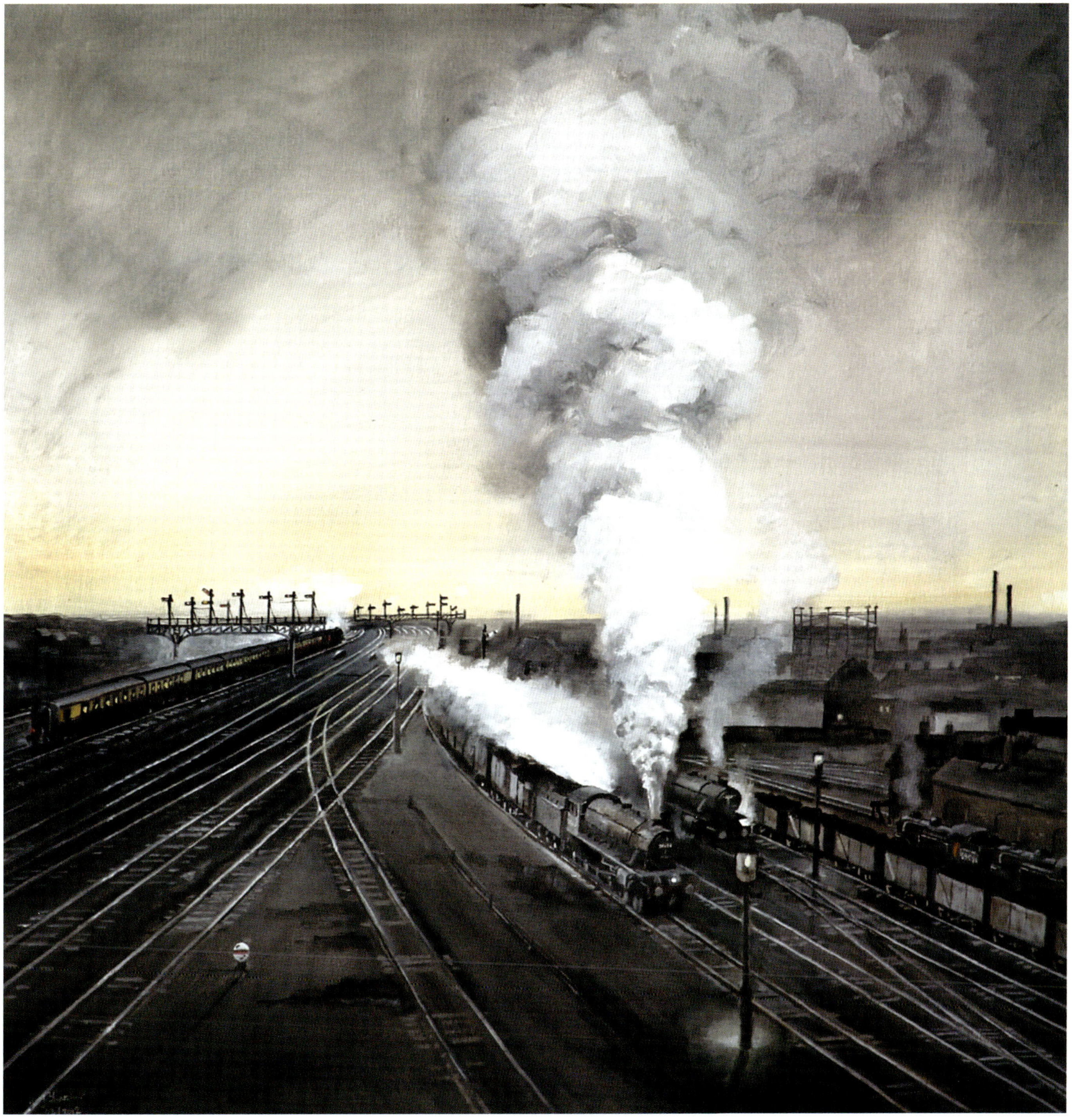

Chatham: Hop Pickers' Special

I seem to have done fewer paintings of the Southern than any other region, probably because of my prejudice towards my home environment of the East Coast. That said, I had just as much opportunity to visit the southern termini in London as I did the others, but my Ian Allan shows that I spent relatively little time in Victoria or Waterloo. I think the relatively short journeys of the Southern had something to do with it – there was not the romance of the long routes to the North or via the Great Western to Devon and Cornwall. Of course, like so many before me, I considered that latter route to be the preserve of the Western, and ignored the withered arm of the old LSWR.

The few memories I have of the Southern from my early childhood arise from my aunt and uncle who lived in Herne Bay in Kent. At the tail end of the war my twin sister, Penelope, and I were moved to Herne Bay to escape some of the bombing, mainly V1 rockets, which Germany was firing at random over the London area. I have vague memories of being bundled under the stairs in the home of my grandparents in Bishops Stortford when there was a flying bomb attack. I do not know why my parents thought Herne Bay would be any safer. They certainly did not want us with them in Stroud in Gloucestershire where my father was doing design work related to aircraft production, since that was a regular target for the Luftwaffe. My uncle and aunt would take us to Herne Bay station or sometimes nearby Swalecliffe which was a curious affair perched on stilts by the side of the Kent Coast line embankment. From there I watched Oliver Bulleid's curious streamlined locomotives which were either painted black or so dirty they were black anyway, hauling long trains to Margate and to Dover. I also remember Uncle Joe having an argument with someone over us being there – of course I did not realise that at the time this was related to troop movements, much of which was still supposed to be secret.

Later visits to these same relatives meant that I got to see a lot of the same locomotives in better condition, and as the 1940s turned into the 50s trains began to run from London loaded with people who had come from London for a fortnight's holiday picking hops in the Kent orchards. These Hop Pickers' Specials ran all sorts of unusual routes, and the Southern region had a set of headcodes which depicted the destination, giving the railway buffs the opportunity to see some equally unusual locomotives. Mostly, however, the Hop Pickers' Specials were hauled by King Arthur 4-6-0s or by the West Country Pacifics, the larger Merchant Navy class being restricted in its route availability due to its weight (although I seem to remember the odd one on the Kent Coast).

The painting shows a Hop Pickers' Special pausing in Chatham which is some thirty miles or so from Herne Bay. The train had originated in north London, but it is most likely that the engine was changed as soon as it reached Southern metals. Chatham used to be a pretty station, and was regarded as part of the Kent countryside in the 1950s. Today it is still tidy but forms part of the suburbs of London, having joined hands with Rochester & Gillingham. The third rail electrified line system made the operation of steam over any route where it was in existence especially hazardous for the railwaymen who had to watch where they put their feet when descending from the cab. It always surprised me that the water which invariably leaks from the slacker hose beneath the cab did not cause a major short with the live line.

I chose to use a West Country locomotive in the painting viewed at an angle three-quarters front, because this gave the best impression of these machines which were somewhat irreverently called Spam cans by the spotters. They were continually being modified in their earlier years because the streamlining seemed to worsen the problem of smoke obscuring the driver's view. The locomotive as shown was in its final streamlined form although what that particular form of streamlining achieved I fail to understand.

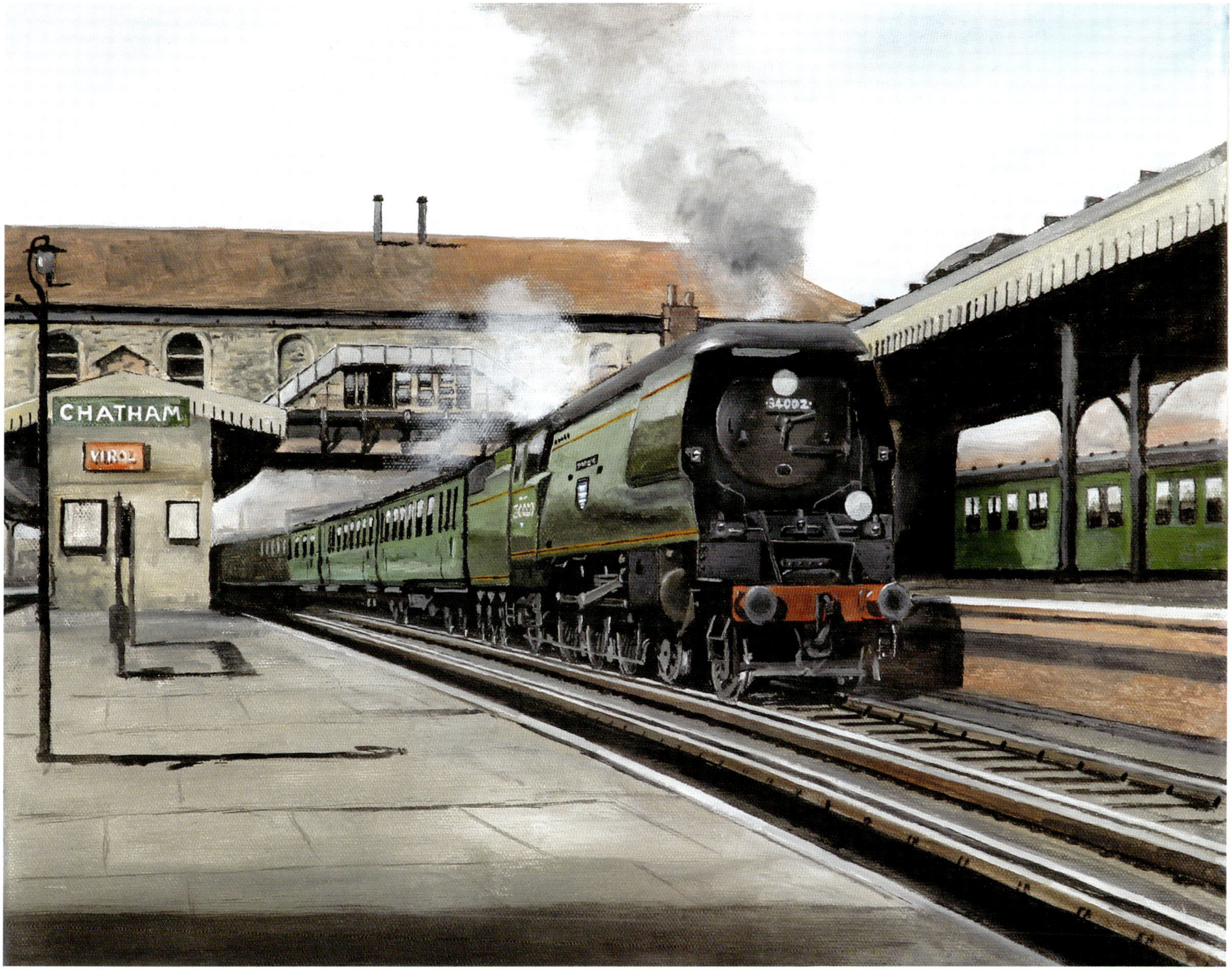

The Hop Pickers' Special standing at Chatham Station

British India Line at Stewarts Lane

By contrast the rebuilt Merchant Navy and West Country Pacific locomotives were in my view some of the most elegant machines to run on British railways, a view which seems to be shared by many when one notes the number of the class which have been rescued from the Barry scrapyard and restored to full running order. The rebuilt locomotives combined the best of Oliver Bulleid's innovative design and eliminated the worst. Out went the streamlined casing, which was absolutely useless, obscured the drivers view, and added to the weight of the machine. Out also went the dangerous chain-driven valve gear which ran in a totally enclosed oil bath. This eliminated the leakage of oil which would sometimes soak into the boiler lagging of the streamlined engines and catch fire! Happily the beautiful Boxpok wheels were kept, together with the magnificent all-welded steel firebox and boiler, probably the best designed of any steam engine.

It has been written that Bulleid was furious at the rebuild propagated by British Railways and carried out by R Bond. He had never been receptive to the many complaints of the original locomotives passed to him by the inspectors whose job it was to ensure that the railway ran efficiently and modifications were made to minimise maintenance. In fact Bulleid always blamed the problems on poor workmanship and never on poor design, resulting in very poor relationships, and almost no communication between himself as CME and the running staff. The original Merchant Navies were thus the heaviest on maintenance of all the British Railways Pacifics. One can begin to understand the problems that Sir Nigel Gresley had suffered when Bulleid oversaw the design of 'Cock o' the North' on the LNER!

The fact remains that the rebuilt machines were vastly superior to the originals in terms of maintenance, and almost matched the Peppercorn A1 Pacific locomotives of the Eastern Region. The rebuilding had been brought about by the failure of the crank axle of 35020 'Bibby Line', at speed. Luckily nobody was hurt, but inspection showed seven other Merchant Navies were similarly afflicted, and it was the final excuse needed for the rebuilding of these problematic machines. No longer were shed staff straightening out bent coupling rods by using a jack against the engine shed wall as reported by Colonel Rogers in his book *Bulleid Pacifics at Work*, although the author has a very vivid recollection of rebuilt Merchant Navy 'Clan Line' slipping so violently at Salisbury when starting a special (The Solent and Sarum) that the coupling rods had to be inspected. The same engine has acquired the reputation of being the most reliable preserved steam locomotive on the main line. It is always turned out in immaculate condition, and I have seen it on all the regions of British railways and travelled behind it many times; the only time I have ever seen it late was due to a railway enthusiast trespassing on the track. The rebuild has a great similarity in appearance to the Britannia Pacifics of BR design, but looks better, i.e. more powerful thanks to the lower running plate.

Because of this elegance of design I have depicted one of the class 'British India Line' outside Hamptons at Stewarts lane, a location which will be very familiar to the railway enthusiast. Originally the locomotive was on the turntable at the run down location of Nine Elms, but the surroundings were so depressing for such a magnificent machine, I recanted and placed it in the location shown. Two enginemen are leaning back admiring the rebuilt locomotive – or perhaps they are criticising the change, for railwaymen are notoriously conservative and change is never accepted at face value!

All of this has now gone. Look at the painting of the W Class tank locomotive in the same location (page 29), and notice the changes that Hamptons continuously underwent. The rebuilt Merchant Navies were among the last express steam engines to be scrapped. Oliver Bullied could have been proud of this testimony even if he did not like the rebuilding.

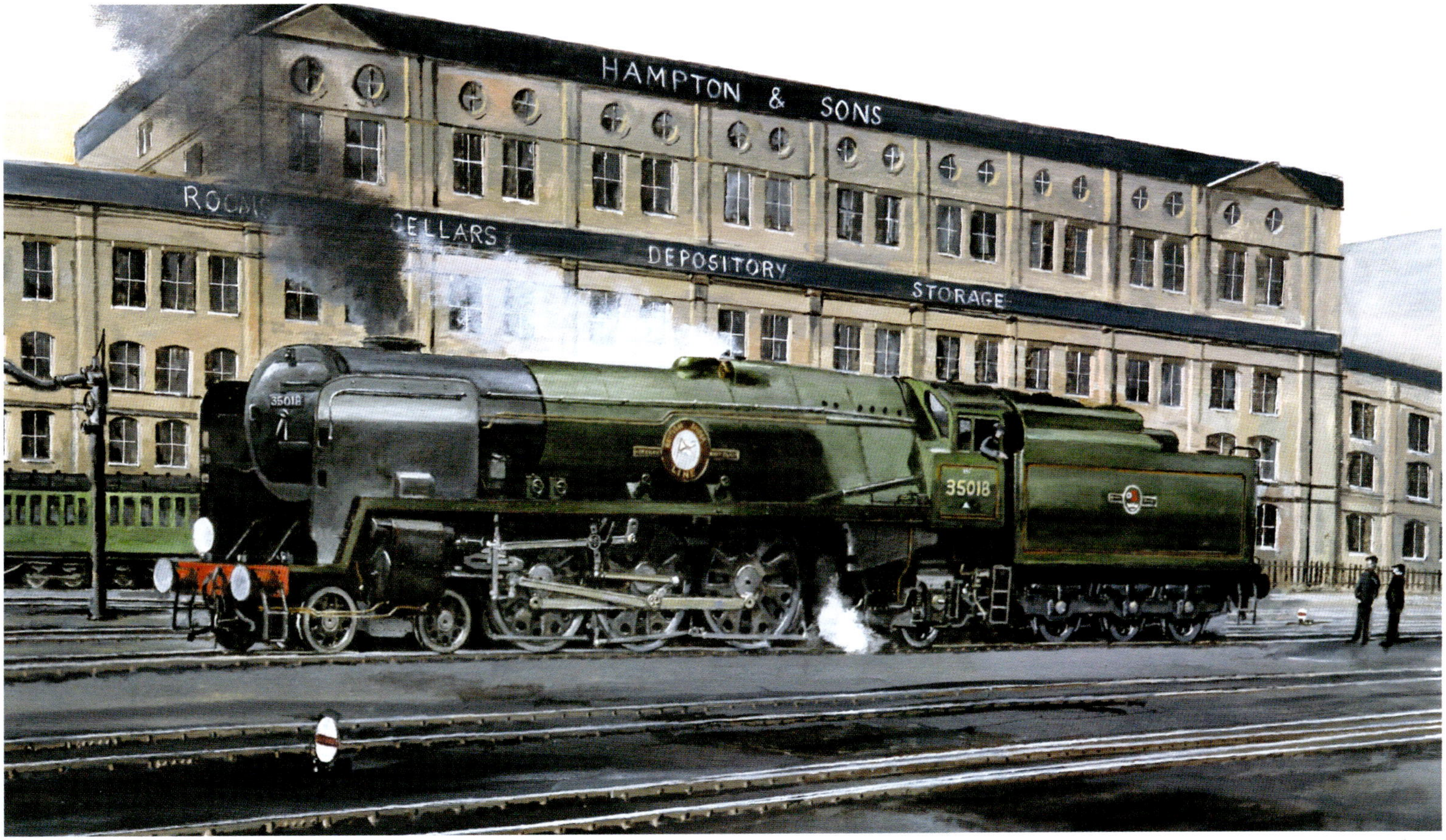

'British India Line' at Stewarts Lane

Edinburgh

I moved to Fife fairly early in my career as a lecturer in the University of St Andrews. This gave me ample time to visit Edinburgh and in particular Princes Street and Waverley Station. It is an impressive station and was much more so then than it is now. Situated in a cutting adjacent to a park and with the North British Hotel (now renamed) dominating it on one side while the castle did the same on the other, it was easy to overlook the considerable space on the castle side of the station given over to storing carriages and shunting goods wagons. All of this has gone now, swept away in the name of progress, and Waverley looks sorry, and the more untidy, for it.

Edinburgh was an important railway centre, serving as it did all the major cities in Scotland with direct connection to all the east coast cities of England and of course London. Most people think of Waverly as a terminus, which it was for some services, but it was actually a through-station lying on the line which connected Portobello (on the East Coast main line) via St Margarets, past Princes Street Station, on to Haymarket and Glasgow. Alternatively the line through Turnhouse and Dalmeny to South Queensferry and the Forth Bridge provided access to Dundee, Perth and Aberdeen. Railway buffs will instantly recognise the names of St Margarets and Haymarket, for it was here that the engines which served Edinburgh were stabled. Most of the East Coast main line engines were cared for at Haymarket, and cared for is the appropriate word. I recall a gentleman who wrote under the pseudonym 'Toram Beg' recording the activities of Haymarket and in particular 'his' A3 locomotive, 'Spearmint'. The pride of ownership is written in every line. Waverley station was a little like Haymarket. There was certainly pride in ownership. Built in 1891 by the North British Railway Company, it was the largest station in the UK. And the station was very modern in concept too. Ticket machines were in use as early as 1938 and even platform tickets at 3d each. It was actually cheaper to get a local train to Abbeyhill at 2½d return! The station concourse and booking hall for long distance travel was a most beautiful area with mosaic floors and a domed glass roof, but it was all pulled down in a modernisation purge in time for the 1970s Commonwealth Games. The things that are done in the name of modernisation! Today the booking hall looks as though someone has thoughtlessly dumped a half eaten doughnut in the centre with kiosks randomly scattered around it.

The painting, done from a location above Calton Tunnel to the east end of the station, utilises the same technique I used for the London 1952 painting (page 61), but this time there were more substantial photographic records to draw on. Edinburgh has not suffered the frantic changes London has in recent years, although the locals will tell you they are bad enough. In the painting the signal box installed in 1930 has been replaced with a new power box. Semaphore signals have been replaced by electric lights, and nearly every short-haul local train has been cut from the timetable, so there are no more local trains making their way into the outer suburban platforms. In 1910 there were 186 stations served from Waverley under fifteen miles distant. In 2010 there were none.

I could not resist putting my father's Humber Hawk in the picture with him standing beside it. There is an old fashioned Morris post van there too. The railway is still as shown in the painting except that you cannot see it. It is hidden under a maze of wires and supporting structure while East Coast electric trains glide in and out of the station to the east, bound for the south, or west, for Dundee and the north. There are no more B1s waiting for work in the yard, or V1s lurking behind redundant outbuildings. Gone are the procession of V2 2-6-2s, or the A1 waiting to depart with a London-bound express, and appropriately named after the city in which it stands, 'Auld Reekie', the name for Edinburgh in less salubrious days. It is a painting of nostalgia and historical record.

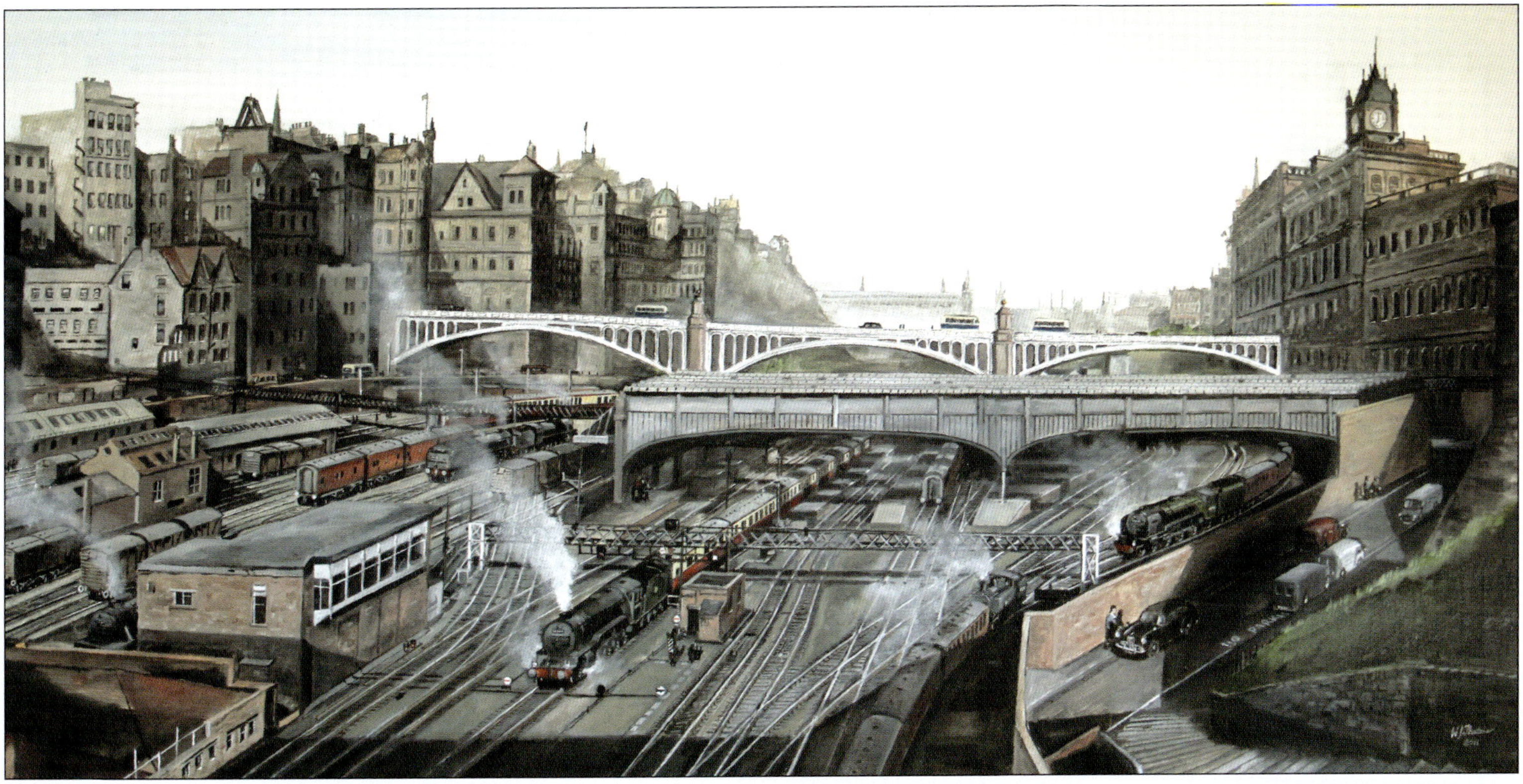

Looking out over Edinburgh from above Calton Tunnel

The Liverpool Street Pilot

This was always one of my favourite paintings, and also my favourite location. Liverpool Street station, London, was a smoky smelly dirty cathedral of steam, heaven for the steam railway enthusiast. The station was built by the Great Eastern Railway Company, a business that was perpetually short of money. Even though the Great Eastern served the City, sponsorship from banks for the Eastern Counties Railways was not forthcoming, and was not helped by some of the railway directors' perverse decisions. In 1870 a Victorian writer described Liverpool Street station and the Eastern Counties line as '...feeble, struggling, unprofitable and impecunious'. The Bill for the construction of Liverpool Street station had only been passed in 1864! The building of the station was hampered by those same bankers who demanded huge sums of money for the compulsory purchase of their run down tenements. In 1866 the GER was in Chancery (bankrupt). That it recovered from this situation was remarkable, but due mainly to the *need* for a railway into the City. The station was opened in 1875 with ten eastward-facing platforms, and all prospect of linking with west London abandoned due to the construction of the underground. Liverpool Street would serve the poorest districts of London, and would remain poor as long as they did. Even at its opening the Board of Trade had serious misgivings about the safety of the new station, for as yet it had no roof, and this was to be constructed in between passenger movements! No wonder Captain Tyler, the Railway Inspector of his day, was concerned!

Four more platforms were added in 1893, with the east side used for suburban traffic in 1894. By 1899 seven million commuters used the station (they were referred to as 'workmen' by the GE who recognised the poverty of the area they served). The Queen even denied the station her patronage, preferring to travel to Sandringham via Kings Cross. Someone might have pointed out to her that Kings Cross lay in the middle of a notorious red light district of London!

The LNER did its best to raise the image of the GER terminus, even going to the length of streamlining two B17s, but it had been labelled a working man's station, and that remained its image throughout the days of steam right into BR days. And that is why I loved it more than all the rest. It was a real station, a working man's station. It was always smoky, slightly seedy, and overcrowded (except late at night). It was a miracle that the GER had ever afforded two million pounds to built a London termini at all. The station served the whole of East Anglia, and one only has to read this in conjunction with the comments on Norwich station to see why that terminus was of such mediocrity. War came and went, and of course Liverpool Street station caught more bombs and suffered greater destruction than any other London station. A grateful government rewarded it in the usual way, and Liverpool Street sank into an even greater depth of grime whilst carrying ever more passengers.

In 1955 the station still possessed two station pilots for shunting empty stock in and out of the terminal. The east side pilot was this delightful little engine 68619 which was variously painted black or dark GER blue, but always kept immaculate. I have tried to capture the smoky atmosphere and the lovely red brick office buildings adjacent to the Great Eastern Hotel. A B12 has brought in a train from Ipswich. The soot-begrimed roof is also covered in pigeons' droppings while little light penetrates the gloom except in odd patches and streaks, enhancing the cathedral-like atmosphere.

Today it has all been swept aside (how many times will I write this?). The east end has become the *in* place to live. Most of it has been demolished and reconstructed. So has Liverpool Street station, which is now a shopping arcade with a station buried somewhere beneath it.

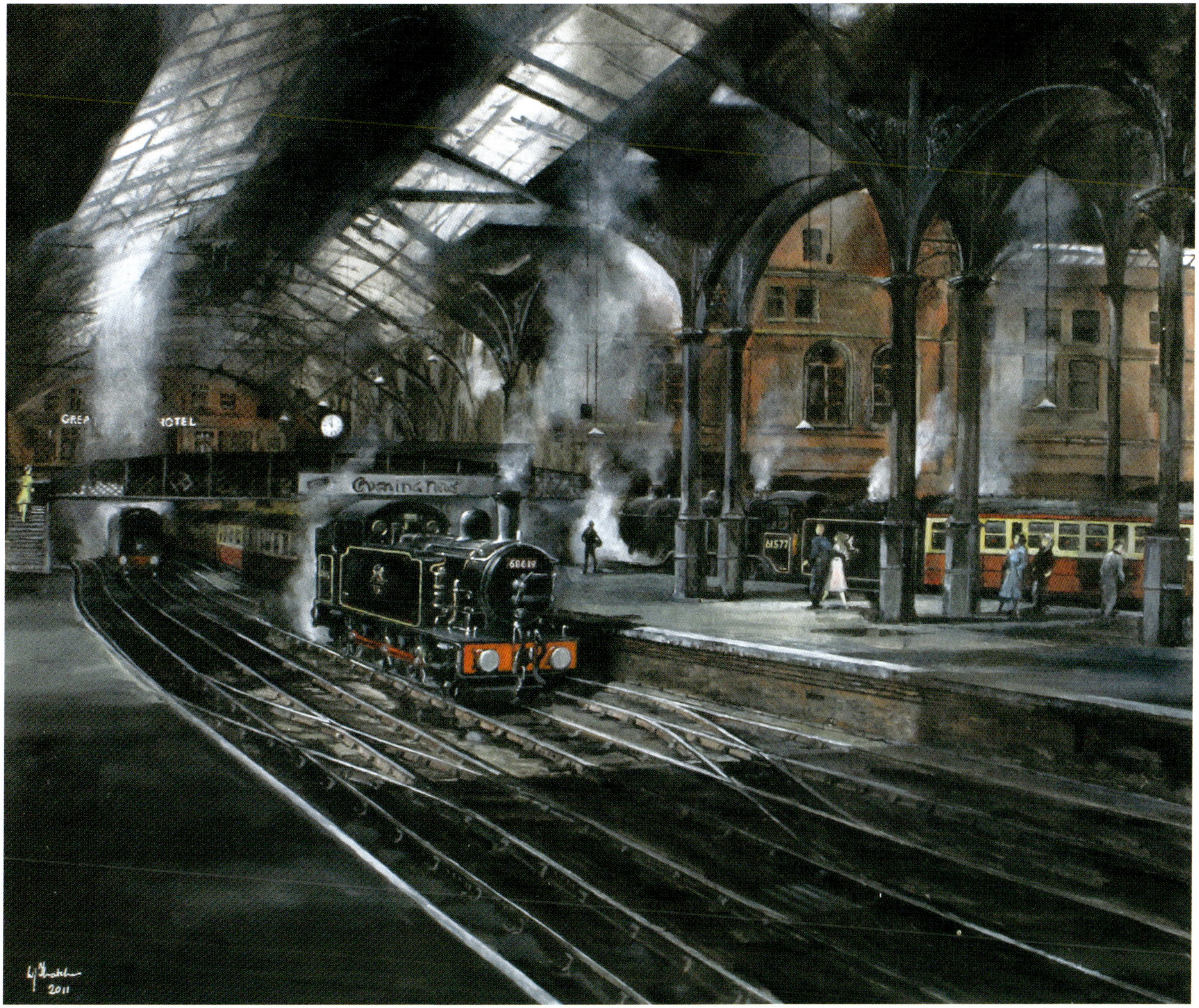
HOTEL
Evening News
68619
61577
2011

Quiet Morning in the Cathedral

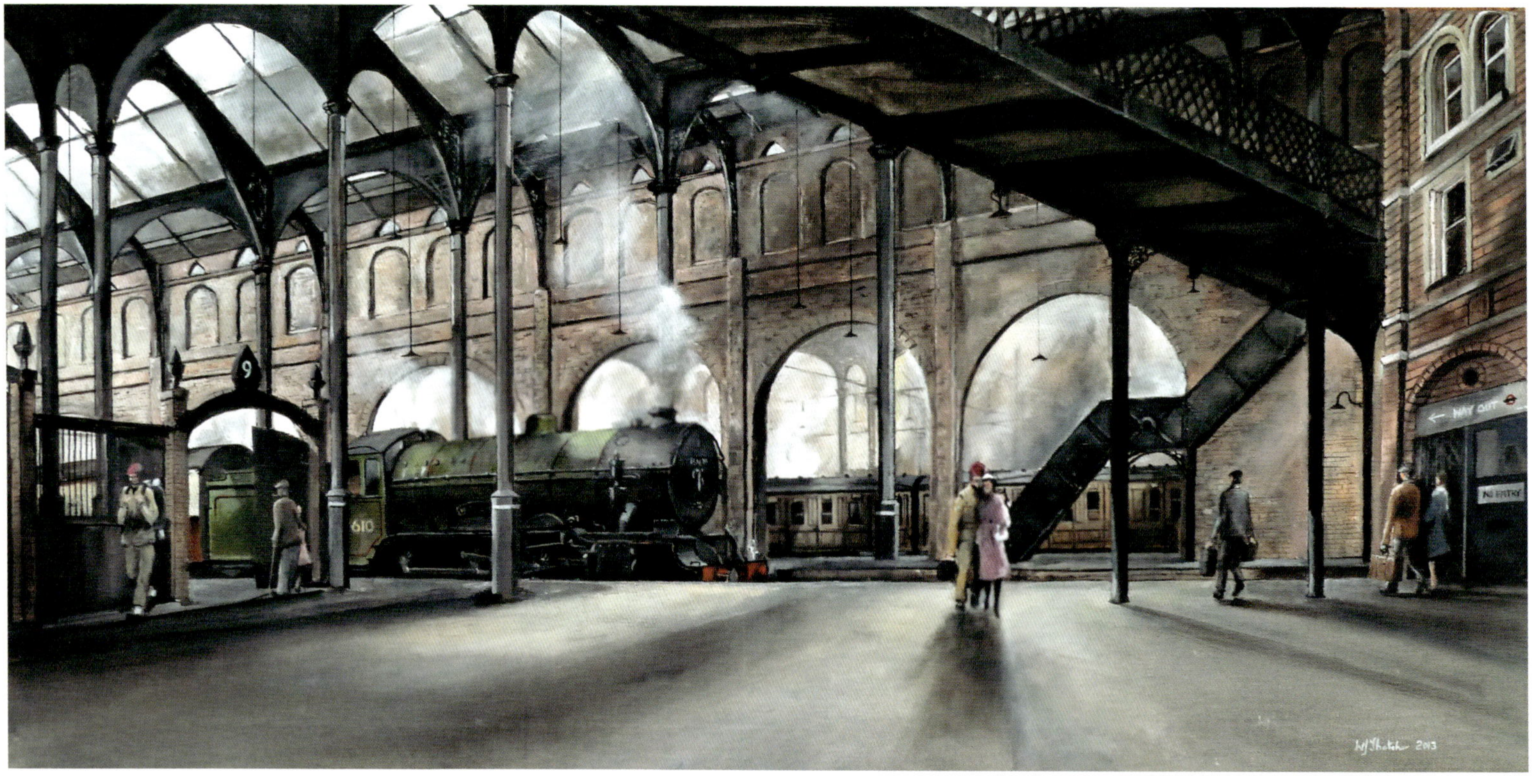

Two more paintings of Liverpool Street. In this one I experimented with backlighting to give a sense of nostalgia and emphasise the extent of the cathedral-like arches and the light and shade effect only found in this station. It is post war – the engine has a BR number, B17 61610 – 'Honingham Hall', but it is relatively unimportant compared to the people and the station. Soldiers on leave have just arrived home, while an old man and his granddaughter wait at the gate of Platform 9. Three passengers head for the east side.

The Cathedral, Liverpool Street

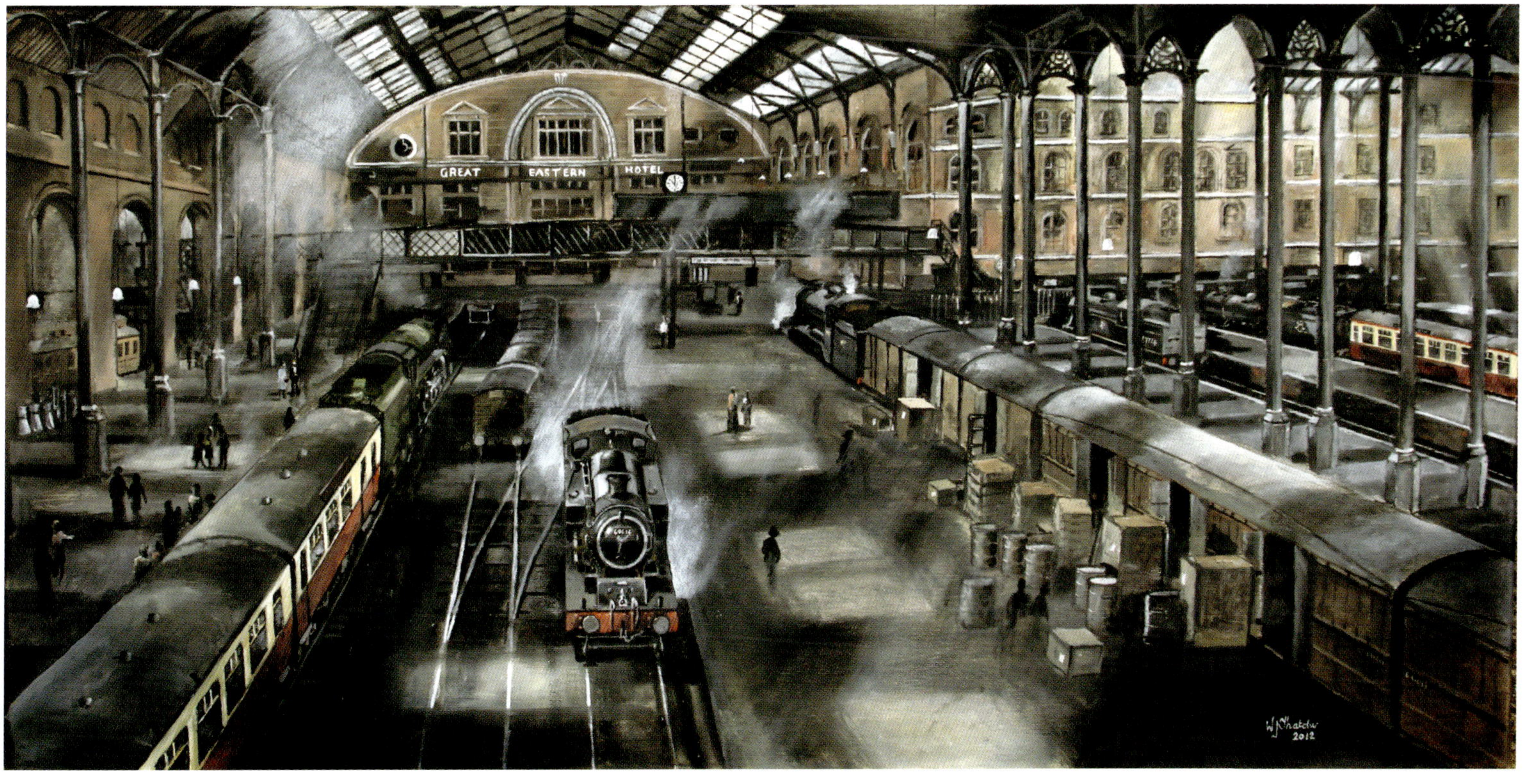

A painting intended to show the station in its usual state with goods being unloaded on to the platforms in the patches of sunlight coming in shafts from the cleaner parts of the roof. An assortment of locomotives occupy the platforms but the occupants of the trains either have not disembarked or have fled the smoke and grime! From the left, a Britannia on a Norwich train is arriving, the other pilot, an immaculate N7 awaits its next duty, a K3 has brought in the parcels train, while an L1 and a B12 wait to return to Stratford. The magnificent Great Eastern Hotel, the finest Railway Hotel in London, can be seen at the end of the main line platforms with their curious reverse curve.

County March

This painting was the result of a strange set of circumstances. Holidays during my university days were something of a luxury. My father had always had laid down very strict rules for me once I had completed my school life – if I wanted to go to university that was fine but I would have to pay my own way through it. I think that was his way of making sure that I would work hard and not waste my time, but it seems he did not know his son very well in that respect. Perhaps there were other reasons; I will never know because he died at the age of 56, by which time I was teaching in St Andrews University in Scotland, some 100 miles from this location.

While still a student in London I became good friends with a fellow student Jeffery Spickett, who was later to become a Professor in Perth University, Western Australia. Together we decided we would hitchhike up the west coast of Scotland staying in youth hostels. We had little money and nothing was pre-booked, so it was imperative that we reached shelter each evening, preferably before 4pm when the youth hostels started filling up. And so it was we found ourselves walking the long, long road from Crianlarich to Fort William which leads directly past this location, an area of the highlands known as County March. Here the railway from Fort William to Glasgow meanders along the side of these mountains at a constant elevation, making many changes in direction and in one place traversing a complete horseshoe curve.

On the day mentioned above it was raining as it can only rain in the highlands. Jeff and I had split up so as to increase our chances of getting a lift, agreeing to meet in Fort William Youth Hostel that night. I was getting quite fed up with the cold rain and heavy rucksack when I saw smoke! It must have been one of the very last steam operated services on the line , although all I could see through the rain was the smoke! The rain on my plastic hat was so loud I could not even hear it; it was like watching a silent movie! I took a photograph of the location out of a sense of desperation combined with annoyance, and wished the sun had been decent enough to break through just for that fleeting few minutes (nearly 15 actually) that it took the train to pass me on its way to Crianlarich.

Some 45 years later I saw a photograph taken by Bob Green (a master of preserved railway photography) and published in a book called *Images of Steam* compiled by another excellent photographer, Mike Tyak. I contacted him and asked permission to use his photograph as the basis for a painting which he very kindly agreed to, and here is the result. It is another painting which could be entitled 'one that got away'. The black clouds over the hills to the right are exactly as I recall them in my sodden state. That road seemed to go on for ever, so I had plenty of time to etch it on to my memory, but as this is the wettest area of the British Isles, pictures of it in the sunshine will be as rare as hens' teeth!

The line is occasionally used by preserved steam specials today. It seems to me that it would make a perfect complimentary journey to the Jacobite if Scotrail decided to risk another foray into the world of steam-hauled tourist trains, as this is the same line which crosses Rannoch Moor, an area of outstanding natural beauty – when the sun shines!

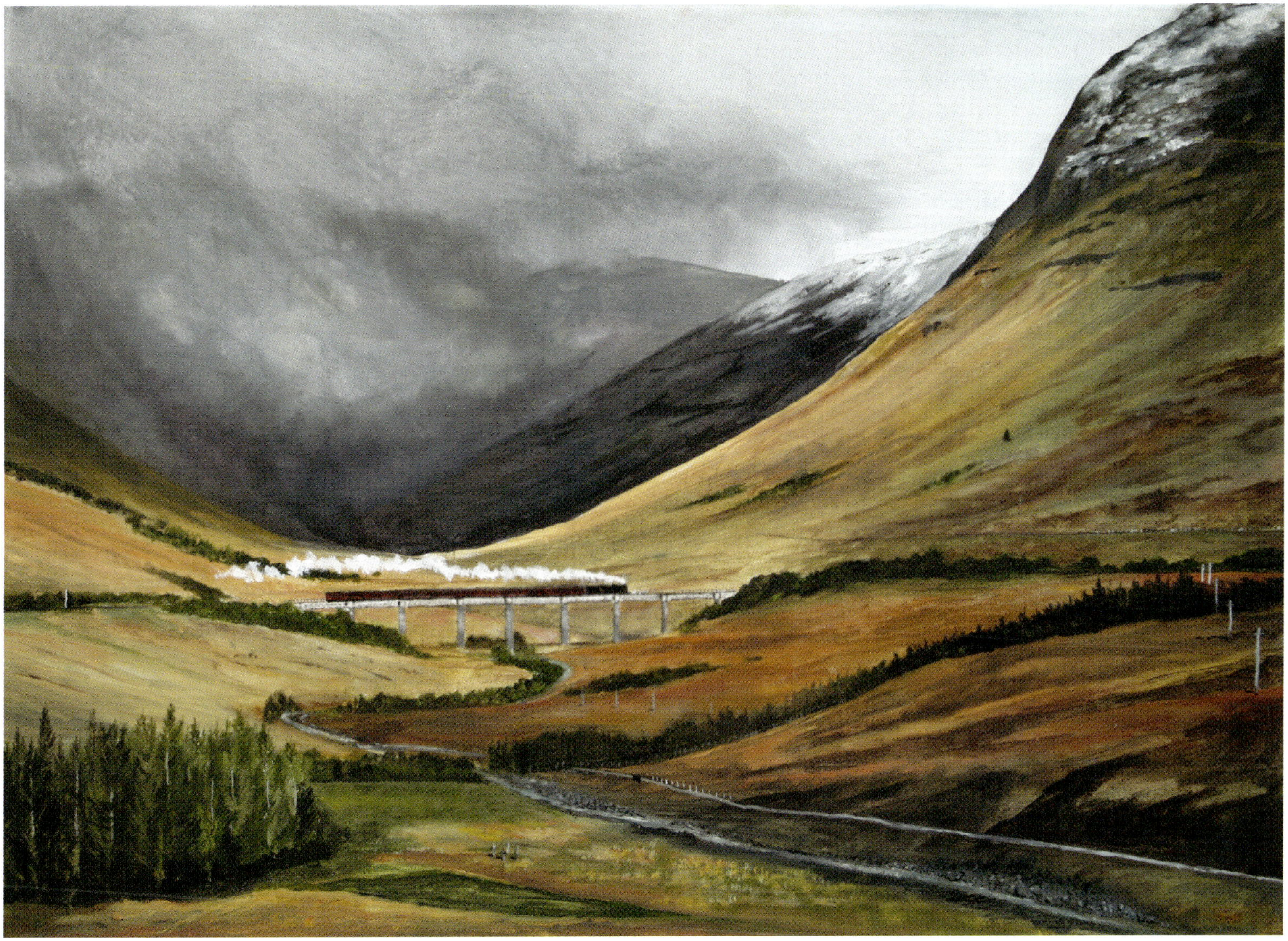

Nevada Challenger

This painting was a complete departure from my recordings of British steam and its related architecture. During my time working in industry I was privileged to be able to work in the USA and in various locations in that vast country. Part of my time was spent in Phoenix, Arizona, from where I was able to travel north to the National Parks of Utah and across Nevada, through Death Valley to California.. In 2012 I was able to make a similar journey whist on holiday, travelling from Los Angeles to the Grand Canyon. The immense distances one has to travel to 'get anywhere' in the USA are always a source of amazement when one is used to the relatively short journeys between one town and another in the UK, and it made me think on more than one occasion about the journeys made by train across that continent.

The journey between Williams in Arizona and Bakersfield in California is long , and in the summer the extreme brightness of the almost unfailing sunshine is also very tiring. Road and railway run alongside one another for mile after mile; no paranoia about health and safety here – not a fence to be seen, crossings unmanned with only a light and a bell to warn of approaching trains. And what trains! Diesel hauled maybe, with perhaps three or four units at the front, they stretch for miles, a seemingly never-ending procession of freight cars trundling past, finally backed up by another two or three diesel units at the rear.

That made me think. These were big diesels – maybe 4000 horsepower each unit. That's about 20 000 to 24 000 horsepower per train. How did steam cope with trains like that? *Did* steam cope with trains of that length? The biggest of them all, the so called Big Boys, had a total power output of around 10 000 edhp – about half that of five diesel units! And they could haul trains of 4000 tonnes unassisted. Furthermore they were designed to run at speeds up to 80mph, although film of them doing so looks decidedly odd with four sets of pistons out of synchronisation with one another. As that great Victorian railway engineer Patrick Stirling said: 'like a laddie running with his breeks doon!' 25 of these giants were built of which 8 are preserved.

The forerunners of the Big Boys were the Union Pacific Railways Challenger class locomotives. Not as powerful, they were still mighty machines, and, like the Big Boys, were articulated. The state and the curvature of the tracks across Nevada alone (one of the flatter states), makes it obvious why articulation was needed. When I asked why the curvature on apparently flat desert, a railway ganger told me that the tracks were simply laid over the firmest land – a quick build approach – rather than excavating quicksands and laying a straight track on built up foundations as we did in the UK. I have had many chances to look at the track standards over there, and they are not as high as in most of Europe, especially France, though a great deal better than some of our rural lines, and even some of our trunk routes.

So that is the basis of my painting showing the desert early in the morning, which was the coolest and most pleasant time to travel. I put a Challenger locomotive with a long train of freight cars on the track, coping with the very sharp curvature of the line, and I thought what it must have been like for the driver (engineer in the USA) and fireman as the heat of the day increased.

No wonder the demise of steam occurred much sooner in the USA than in Europe!

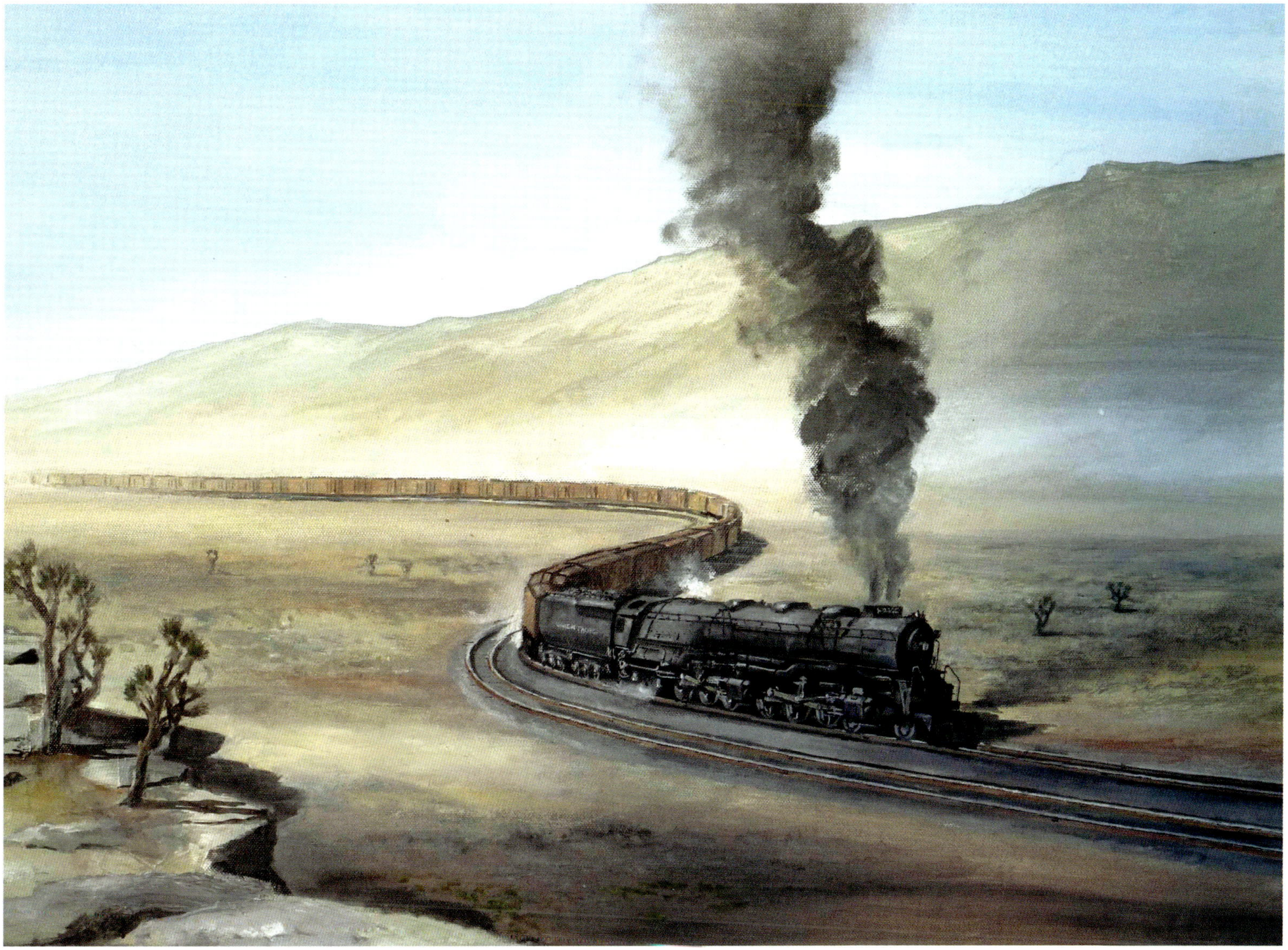

Opposites!

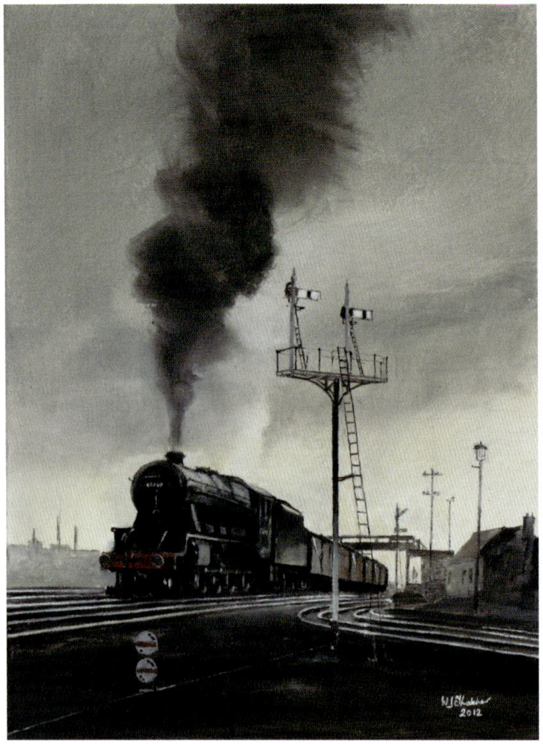

Warrington 8F

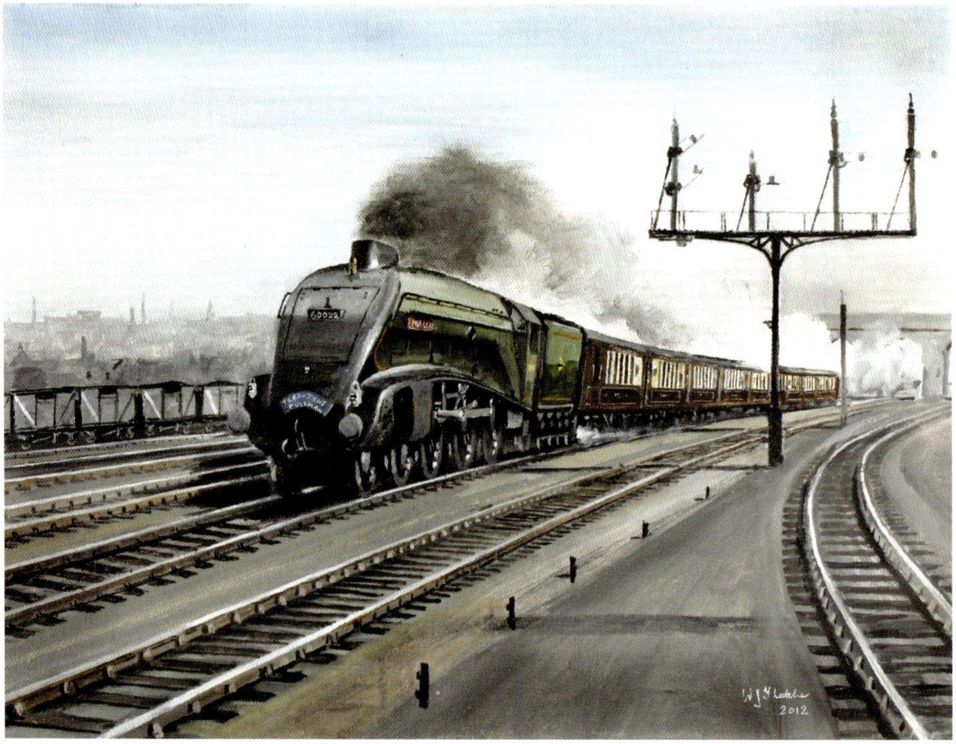

Fastest of them all

Two small paintings which illustrate the opposite ends of the steam locomotive spectrum, from the plodding reality of a Midland Region 8F slowly climbing the bank at Warrington to the glamour of A4 streamlined Pacific locomotive 60022 'Mallard' at Harringay on the Eastern Region. We tended to overlook the freight, and concentrate on collecting the 'namers', little realising that the freight trains paid for the railways whereas the passenger trains in the main, did not. In spite of which I feel sure the image of Warrington is the one most of us will associate with the steam railways of the past. How many think of diesel or electric hauled freight trains today?

Cromer High

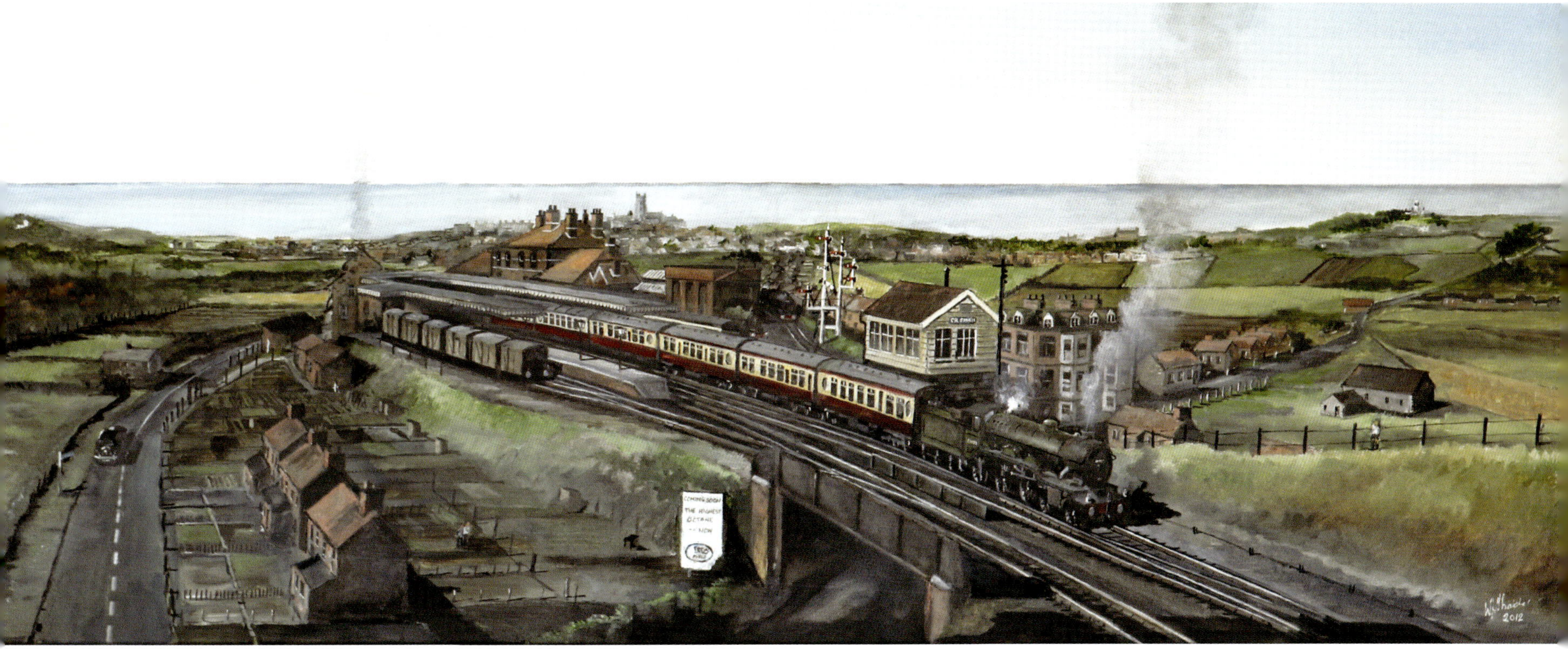

This painting really is a nostalgic trip to the past for me, as Cromer High station, built by the G E Railway, was forced by the local landowners (many of whom were shareholders in the MGNJR) to terminate their line on a little plateau a mile outside the town it served and only a matter of a few hundred yards from where my grandparents owned their smallholding. Sadly I saw it only for a few years as it was decimated in the early 1950s, although I remember carriages being left up there much longer than that. Engine 61620 'Clumber' is making her usual grinding exit from the station with a Norwich local. The small engine shed with the turntable behind it is just visible. The grand presence of the Suffield Park Hotel stands below and behind the signal box. Cromer lighthouse and church can be seen on the horizon, and also smoke from the 'competition', i.e. the Midland and Great Northern, in Cromer Beach station. The location of all the buildings and roads were established precisely from the BR plans of the station issued in 1950 viewed from an imaginary balloon over the water tower.

Today nothing remains of this scene save the bridge in the foreground. Houses cover almost the entire area seen here. It is all part of the new Suffield Park Estate, which never seems to get finished.

V2 at Hartlepool

At the same time that I visited Newcastle (see the painting entitled 'Kittiwake' on page 101), I made a diversion to the town of West Hartlepool close to where my former mother-in-law had been brought up in the Durham village of Wingate. The station was of historical importance, having been built in 1841 at the behest of the Stockton & Hartlepool railway. I had seen many photographs of the station and its environs, and so I was totally unprepared for the sight that greeted me. I still find it hard to understand how a location which once thrived on the railways and all that they brought to the community, could abandon them with such an air of indifference. Where six tracks had once snaked their way out of a station, covered with a respectable train shed, there was now just one. Platforms had been demolished and heaps of bricks and timber showed where they had once been. The single track made its way through these piles of rubble as though through a cutting, with barely any clearance either side. Of the magnificent signal box seen on stilts to the left of the painting, there was no trace except for a rectangle of foundation stones among the debris. The equally magnificent signal gantry had been allowed to collapse just where it was, and the broken pieces of steel had simply been cleared sufficiently to make room for the single track, rather like a dinosaur which had died suddenly and been picked over by predators. Collectors of railway ephemera would have had a field day (for there were hundreds of artefacts laying there) if British Railways had only shown the sense to pick them up and sell them on the open market. It seemed that no one cared.

A single car diesel unit came in, waited while nobody got off or on, and went back out again. An afternoon passed and a total of four people disembarked similar units, but I was the only other person on the platform.

So the painting was an attempt to resurrect the days when the railways served a useful purpose. I used photographs obtained from different sources to get the details about the signals and the box, researched the locomotives likely to have used the line, and settled on a moderately clean V2 and a BR Standard to convey the latter-day passengers to and from the town of West Hartlepool. The days of A1 Pacifics with trains of ten or eleven mark 1 coaches were probably well past.

This was the first painting where I used a yellow sky to accentuate the smoky atmosphere. I had experienced skies like this in London during the smog of the 1950s but they seemed an almost permanent feature of the area around Sunderland and Newcastle in the latter part of that decade, and into the sixties even when steam trains had long gone. With the disappearance of mining, steel and a lot of other heavy industry from the North East, and with only the ICI Billingham plant nearby which could be classified as heavy industry, the skies today are undoubtedly cleaner but at what cost?

Today there has been some improvement. The Durham Coast modification scheme has instituted a modified signalling system which has replaced three signal boxes near to the station. There is still only one operational platform which is bi-directional, although there are plans to re-open a second. The overall roof has been reinstated to a modern design, and a total of 533 000 people passed through the turnstiles in 2013, although many were probably going to catch the connecting buses which have replaced nearly all the local train services.

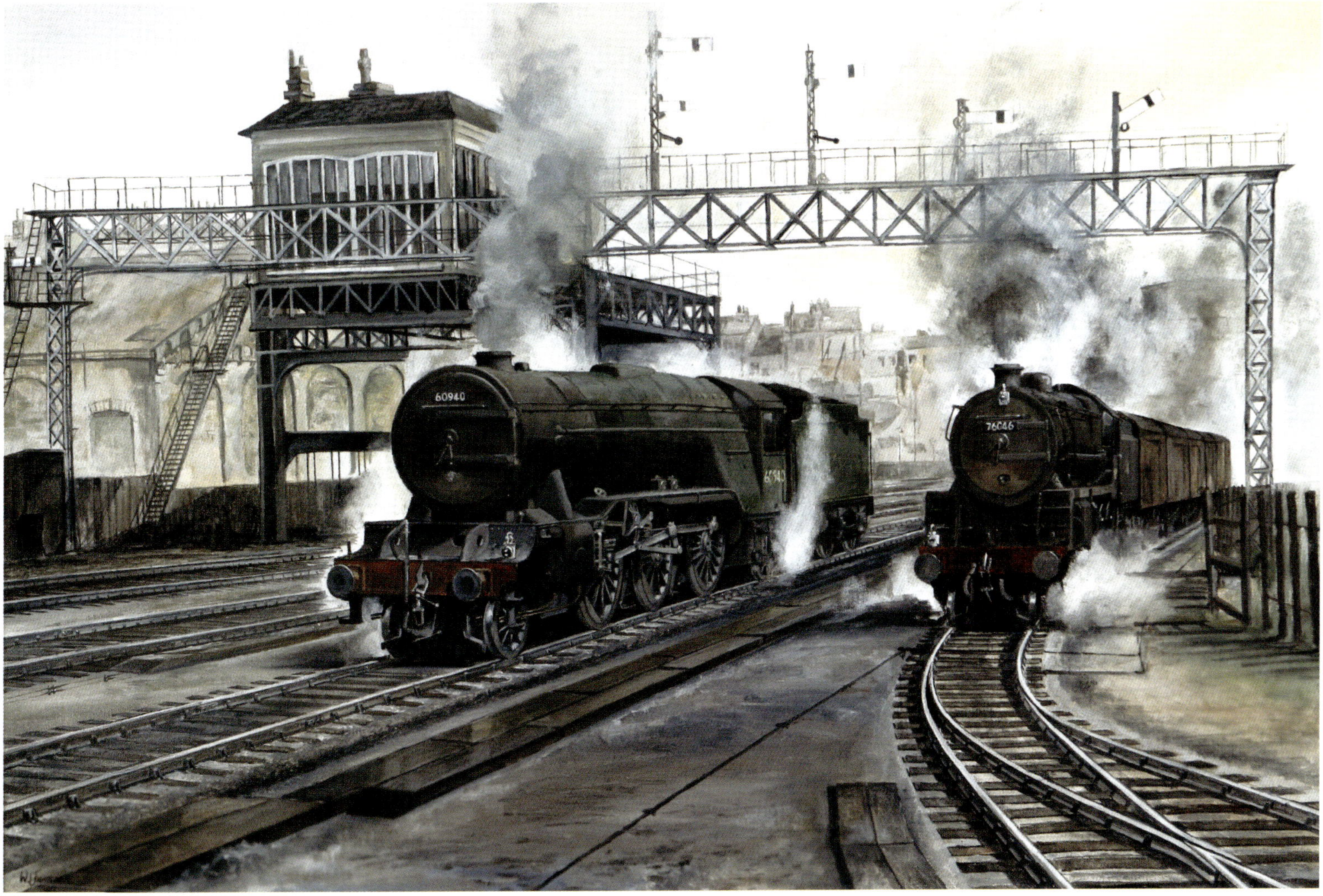

A V2 and a BR Standard at Hartlepool

City of Carlisle on Beattock

Almost due west from West Hartlepool, on the other side of the country, the West Coast main line runs through the rugged outskirts of the Lake District. It is not often recognised that Newcastle is actually north of Carlisle, as we tend to think of that town as the border city. The West Coast railway line shows no sign of easing in its difficulty as far as enginemen are concerned because the climb over Shap summit in England is immediately replaced by a longer stiffer climb over Beattock in the southern highlands of Scotland. When one compares this route with the easily graded one established by the Stephensons around Newcastle, we come to the conclusion that the ill-educated but astute George Stephenson recognised quite early what the limitations of the steam engine would be. It is ironic that his son Robert, would engineer the London to Birmingham line which was to become an essential part of the West Coast route.

Beattock Bank has become one of the best known locations for railway photographers, and for those who enjoy measuring the strength and performance of locomotives. This includes such well known figures as Cecil J Allen whose meticulous timing and calculations of engine horsepower in the steam age reveal how dubious and slipshod the efforts were of his predecessors such as Charles Rous-Marten. The records gathered by Cecil Allen were published in a series of papers entitled 'Locomotive Practice and Performance' and were published in *The Railway Magazine*.

As a boy I was a regular reader and, when I could afford it, subscriber, to this magazine, and the performance figures which it revealed. They nearly all show that the most testing location for any steam engine was on Beattock Bank. Of course we were strictly partisan in those days – whenever have railway enthusiasts not been? I wanted to see 'my' east coast locomotives emerge as the superior breed, but I now have to concede that they were not. The true master of the express steam locomotive, the most powerful of its kind, was the LMS Princess Coronation class, or Duchesses as they were more commonly known. These splendidly brutal looking machines regularly achieved power outputs of around 1700edhp in daily use over that bank while on the east coast an output of that magnitude was unusual from an A4. On test the Duchesses could give over 2500edhp, but it needed two firemen to achieve such figures! In fact the true maximum output of these engines may never be known, for their performance was always limited by the rate at which coal could be thrown into their huge fireboxes, and unlike the American machines seen in earlier paintings, there was no mechanical stoker on their British counterparts.

The painting shows a Duchess in wintry conditions. I have tried to catch on canvas the icy gully beneath the walls, and the fresh snow lying on the hills. 'City of Carlisle' repainted in Midland red, is making the climb unassisted, having refused the banker at the foot of the bank in order to save time. Different engines were used over the years for this purpose, but the best- and most short lived, was an off duty 9F! The bankers could be expected to do most of the work if the express had already climbed Shap so in this case the fireman may not be too pleased at his driver's decision because it means that for some 30 miles he will have a lot of very hard shovelling to do. At least once over the top he will have a rest while the Duchess has a fast and easy run down into Glasgow.

Today modern electric trains whistle up the bank at 130mph or more under an overhead gantry which provides all the energy that formerly came from sweat and hard labour. But the banks always have the last say. In a recent winter the snow brought the electric overhead wires down, and the winter before that the wind did the same. It took a lot more to stop a Duchess!

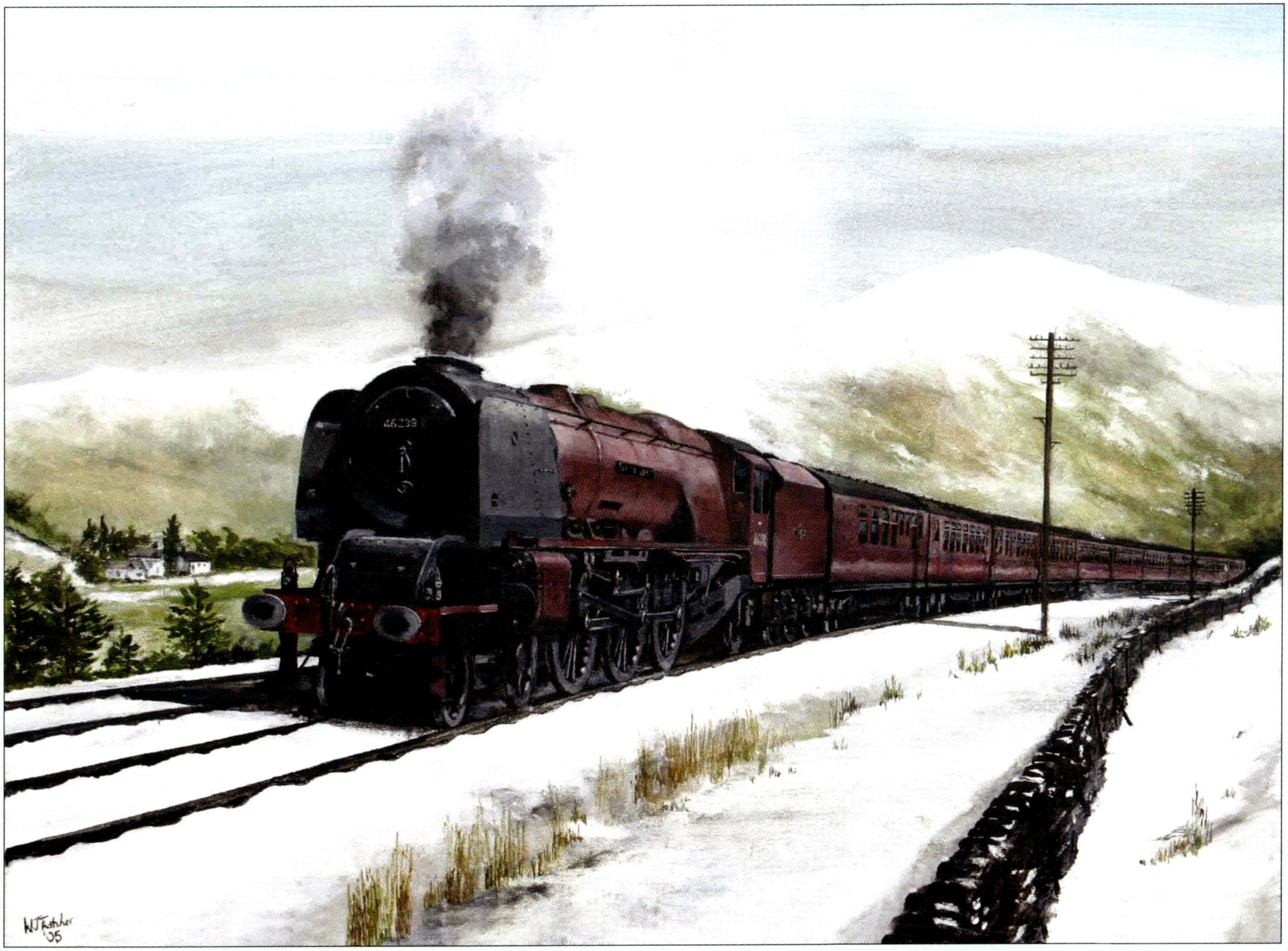

Merlin at Hatfield North

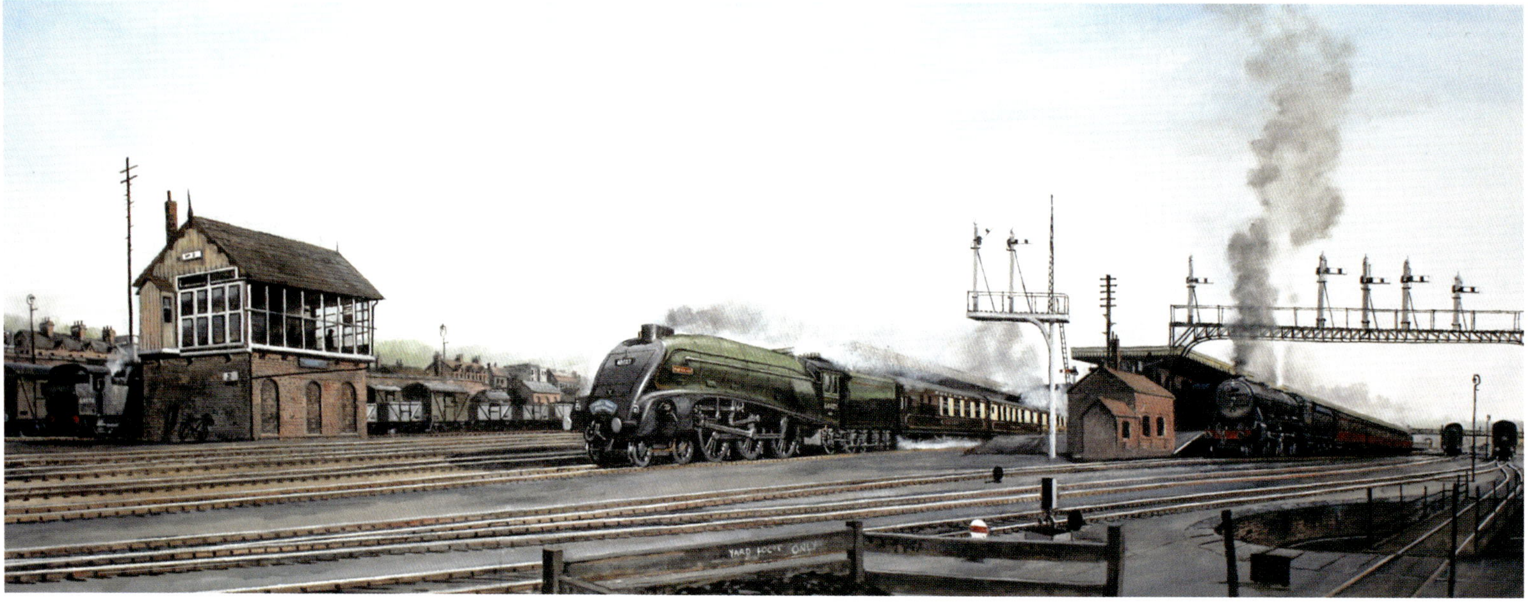

This location should be quite familiar to the reader by now. The yard to the right featured in 'The Decline of Steam' (page 75), and the A4 Merlin has just raced through in the opposite direction to its path in the snow as seen in 'Racing the Storm' (page 110). The view shown here would have been inaccessible to railway enthusiasts as well since it was right down by the old turntable – long out of use – and just below the road bridge which joined the A1000 or Great North Road that ran parallel to and behind the signal box. The large gantry which controlled traffic in and out of the yard is now in its rightful place, and a K3 is heading up a local which is being held until the Tees Tyne Pullman is well clear. Presumably this means the local will gain the main line shortly after leaving. I chose a K3 as the locomotives designed by Thomson seem out of place in the presence of Gresley's masterpiece.

A King at West Ruislip

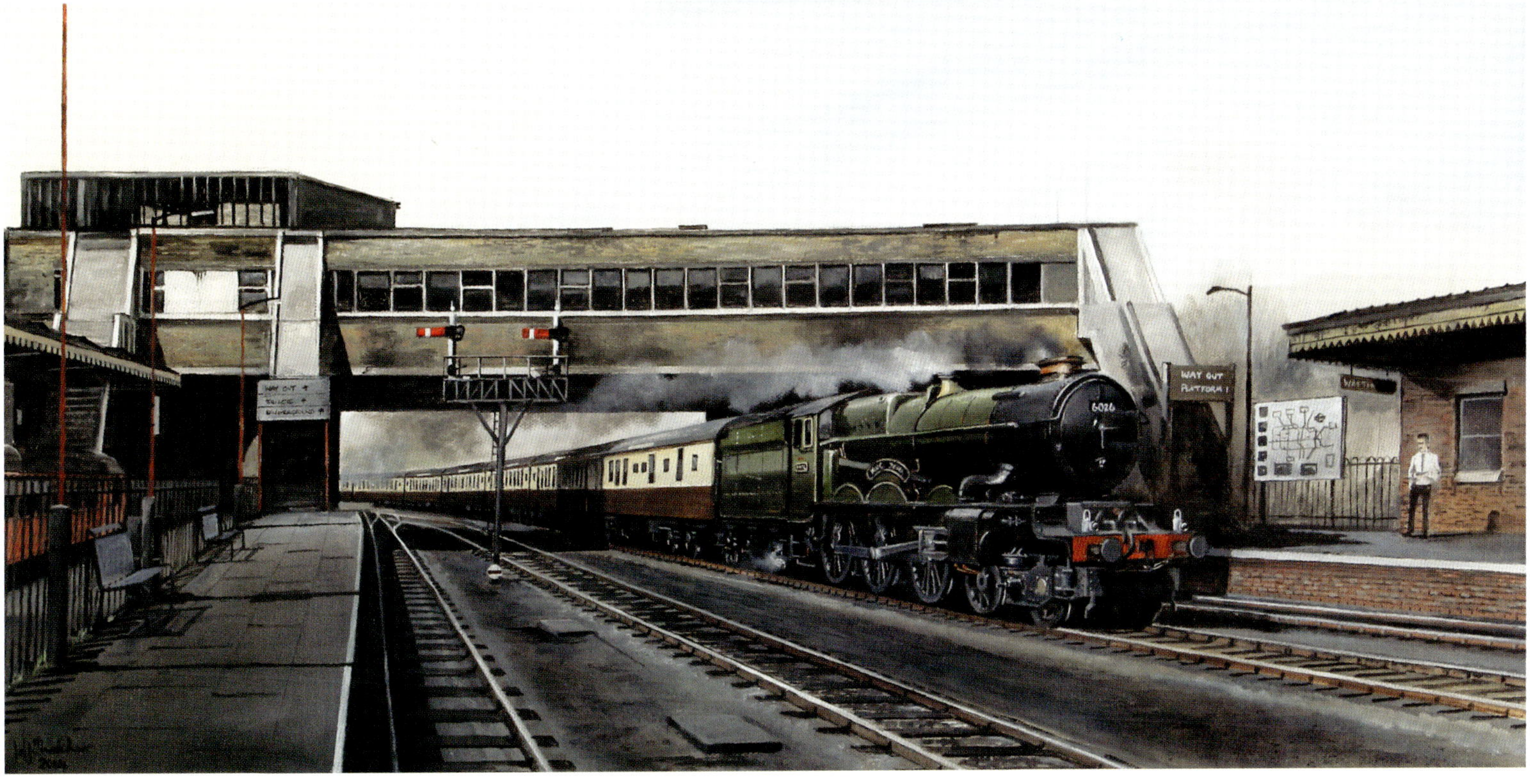

King John was one of the powerful King class locomotives designed by C B Collet for the Great Western, and intended for the very heaviest of that railway's express trains. It was also a publicity statement by the GWR . The engines were so heavy that their route availability was limited to the trunk lines only. The London to Birmingham to Snow Hill was one of these routes and here we have one of the tightly timed trains complete with chocolate and cream stock storming through West Ruislip on its final part of the journey to London.

Note the underground line separated only by a railed fence. West Ruislip was also served by the central line, and so had an excellent service into the capital. The central line was a genuine tube, i.e. not built by cut and cover, so it used the low clearance tube stock shown in the picture. The overhead bridge remains virtually unchanged to this day, although the track layout has been simplified, and the semaphore signals replaced with colour aspect lights.

Graham Elliot, who commissioned this painting, can be seen as a young man, standing on the far platform watching the progress of the King. We dressed smartly in those days. Sports jackets and ties were the fashion before anoraks! How many of us have memories like this?

'Sandwich' at Newcastle

What a name for a steam locomotive. The A3 Pacifics were named after racehorses, which they certainly were, and perhaps significantly after Derby winners. Perhaps there was an element of mischief in Sir Nigel Gresley's choice in this respect. The heritage of these locomotives which entered service just before the grouping in 1922 was plain to see. The Ivatt Atlantics were in the process of being rebuilt by Gresley with larger boilers and fireboxes. These were a preliminary and successful experiment which led directly to the design and construction of the A1s which was their classification when first built. The original Pacifics had a low level of superheat and a boiler pressure of only 180psi, identical to the new Atlantic boilers, and as such their performance was fair but not outstanding. One of the greatest attributes to Nigel Gresley was that he learnt from his own mistakes and from the experience of others. It was not until after the interchange trials with the GWR, where one of that railway's Castle class locomotives easily outperformed an A1, that the LNER locomotives were upgraded with higher boiler pressure of 250psi, higher superheat and, most crucially, long lap piston valves which gave better exhaust steam clearance.

As such these fine-looking machines, which had received much publicity, finally had a performance to match their looks. The undoubted star of the class was 'Flying Scotsman' which is arguably the best known steam locomotive in the world. I have lost count of the number of times I have been asked to paint this particular engine! Its history has been well documented, and is now owned by the National Railway Museum. The first authenticated 100mph by a steam locomotive was by another A3, named 'Papyrus'. The claims of 100mph by 'City of Truro' on Wellington Bank remains in doubt in spite of the many articles written about it in the railway press both at the time and as recently as a couple of years ago! Charles Rous-Marten, who timed that train, was known to exaggerate his observations, and my own belief is that he exaggerated that one too, but we will never know, so the Great Western supporter will always claim the record for 'City of Truro'.

Gresley always preferred the A3s to his celebrated, and faster A4s. In fact there was little difference in their performance. The physics of streamlining are quite complex, but the reduction in front end pressure by a wedge-shaped nose only becomes significant at speeds of over 100mph, but becomes very significant at 120mph when the resistance becomes proportional to the cube of the speed. This has to be offset by the additional weight a streamline casing might cause. Once again Gresley and his team got it right with the air smoothing of the rolling stock of the Silver Jubilee. It is a great shame that more attention was not paid to this until the advent of the HST125 diesel units of BR/Network Rail days.

It took quite a long time to convert the A1s to class A3. 'Sandwich' was a lesser-known member of the class, but an A3 which I saw frequently from the line side in Hatfield, so that is why I chose it for a painting at this location just outside Newcastle, with its magnificent signal gantry and great station roof visible in the background. More of the history of Newcastle can be found in the description of the painting 'Kittiwake' (page 101).

The smoke from 'Sandwich' has obscured the cathedral which looms over the railway at this point. I have chosen this deliberately because it gives the line a somewhat closed-in appearance which belies the width of the track work. The blood and custard Mark 1 coaches looked good when clean (and awful when filthy!), and complement the clean and elegant locomotive, still with its single chimney, and before the ruination of German-style smoke deflectors which we called elephants ears.

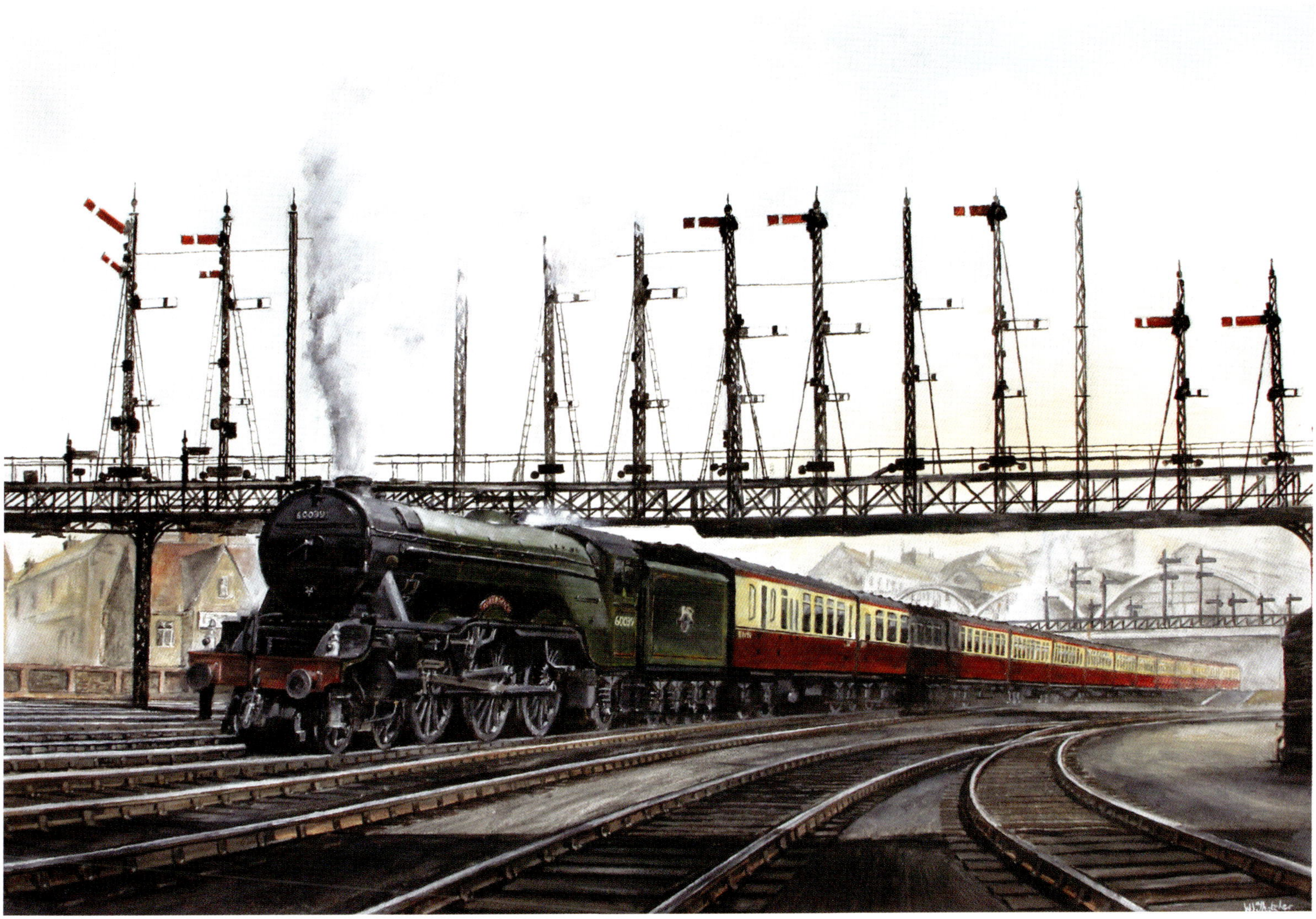

A3 Pacific 'Sandwich' at Newcastle

Redcar: Dante's Inferno

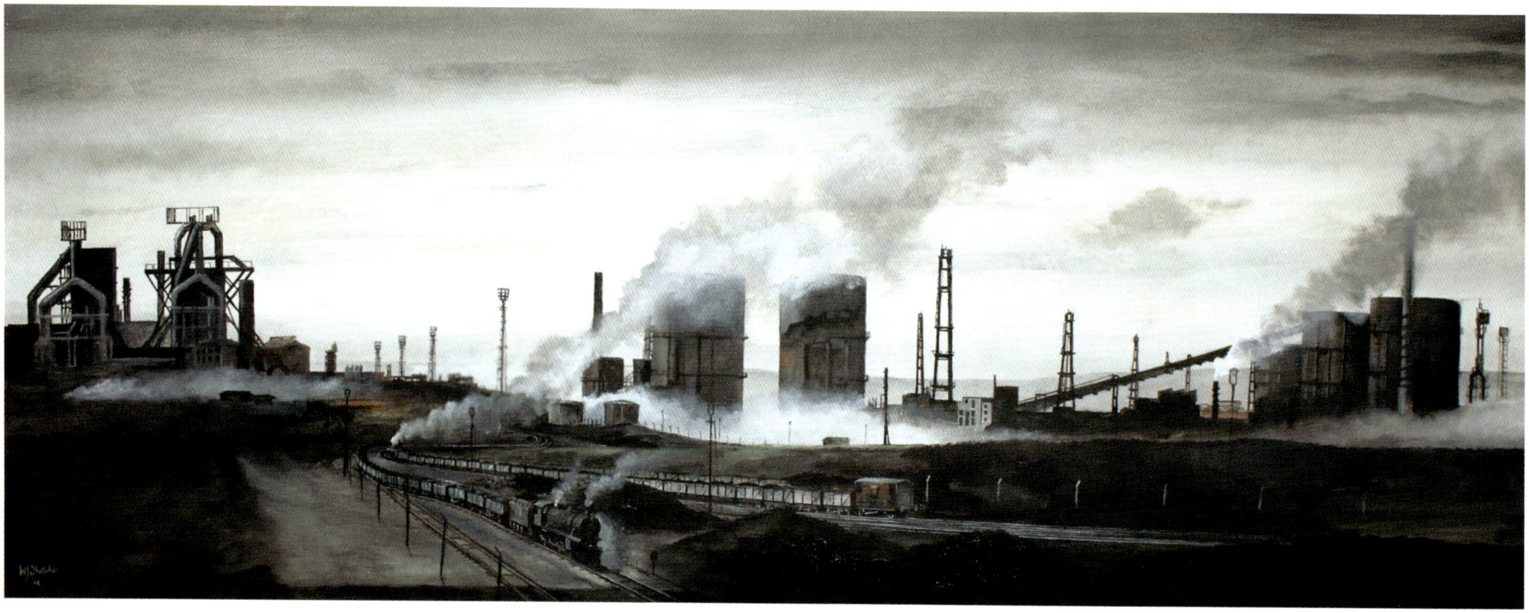

I made a special visit to Teesside in 2010 with the express aim of photographing the remains of heavy industry in the UK with the purpose of using it for a backcloth for one of my paintings. This proved very much more difficult than I had imagined. My father had worked for ICI for over 25 years and had helped design the Billingham plant, but I was refused permission to even point a camera in the direction of the plant from the gatehouse.

We retreated to Redcar on the coast; it still has a grim industrial look to it, and the wind turbines built so close to the shore do nothing to dispel this image. Then finally from the coast road to the north of the town I came across this vista. Smoke, steam and grime everywhere. It was not quite what I was looking for: heavy plant, conveyors cooling towers as in Billingham, but it simply reflected the depressingly grim aspect of a mining area combined with power generation.

So that is what I painted. I hope it captures the spirit of determination to keep the wheels of industry turning. The glimpse of the Yorkshire moors in the distance almost taunts the inhabitants of the industrial complex.

The Waverley

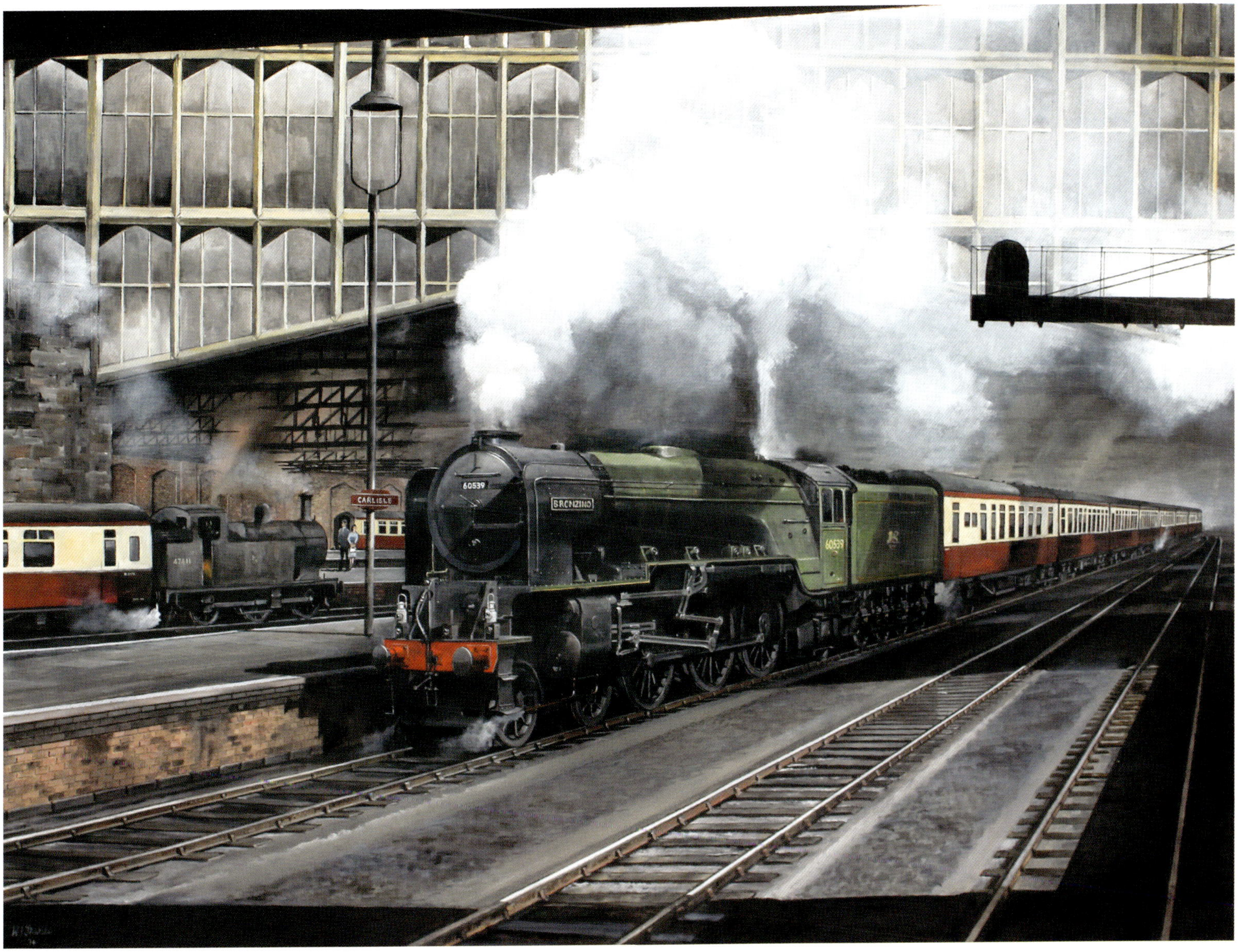

A2 pacific 'Bronzino' leaving Carlisle for Edinburgh on the old Waverley route

Victorian Splendour

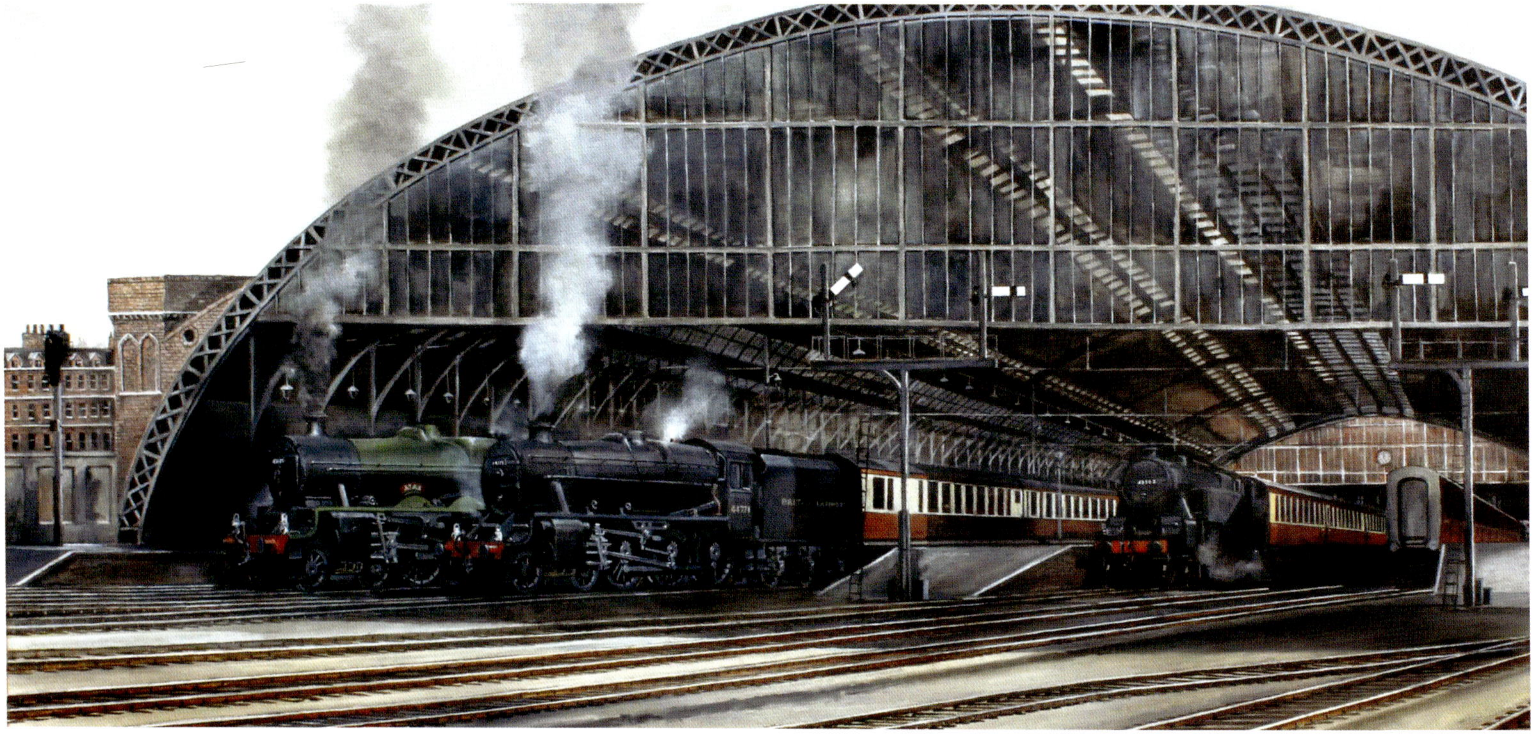

The title refers to the splendid train shed of St Pancras as it was in the early 1950s. This magnificent span was the largest of its kind anywhere in the world when it was built, by William Henry Barlow, and remained so for nearly a century. The Midland Hotel which stands in front of the station is now a listed building, one of the finest in London. The whole structure was intended to show Victorian England that the Midland Railway Company had plenty of money and would provide the most comfortable travel amenities (if the slowest!). A Jubilee, and Black 5 are about to depart while a Fowler tank waits to exit with empty stock. Today the station's appearance from this angle has been ruined by the construction of the Eurostar terminal abutting a graffiti-decorated skateboard park.

Grantham

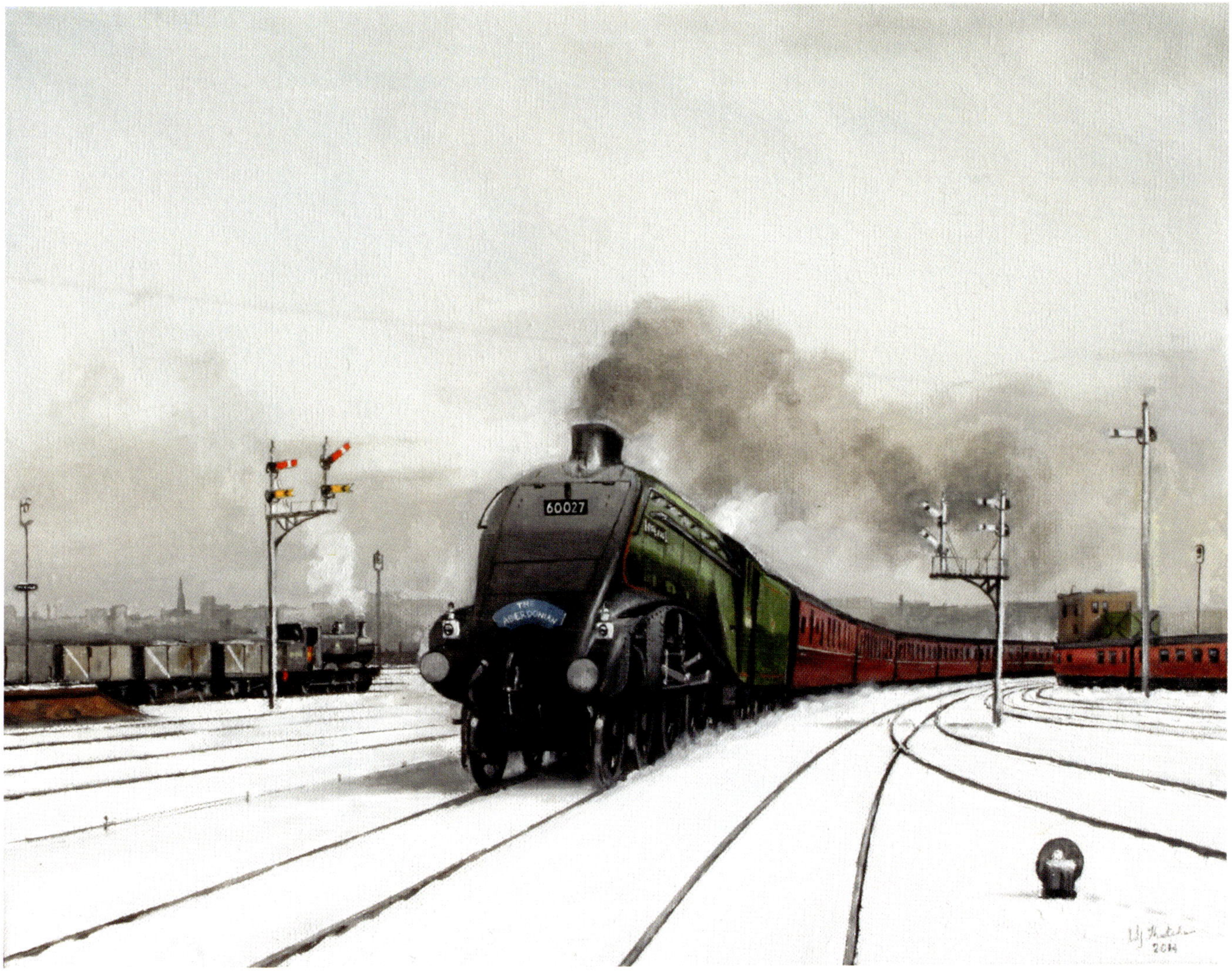

Grantham in the last days of steam was nearing the end of the racing stretch south of York. A4 60027 'Merlin' was a favourite locomotive for the task of hauling the Anglo-Scottish expresses such as the Aberdonian seen here. Some of the A4s were considered to be much more reliable than others, and at one stage 'Merlin' hauled more than twenty consecutive express trains between Edinburgh and Kings Cross – a record for any of the class, although 'Silver Link' held another record – 40 trips in one year (1961) on the Elizabethan non stop.

The Streak

This location should be thoroughly familiar to the reader by now; it is just north of Hatfield station, between the bridge which carries the St Albans Road past the bus station, and the A1000 or Great North Road, which will wind its way through the rest of the suburbs and join hands with the A1 at Jack Olding's Corner. Those who knew the town from fifty years ago will recognise those locations. Anyone born later or not familiar with Hatfield won't because they have all been demolished, along with the A4 in this picture, 60014 'Silver Link' which was the first of the class withdrawn in 1962 and cut up just two months later with almost indecent haste, as though those in authority feared that a case might be made for its reinstatement..

The loss of this engine indicated the indifference and insensitivity of the Eastern Region management based in York. It is comparable to the destruction of Sir Nigel Gresley's first Pacific engine 'Great Northern' by his successor Edward Thompson, an act which has been much vilified in the press and other publications. 'Silver Link' was the first of the A4s, a record breaker in its own right, far more worthy of preservation than, say 'Dominion of Canada', 'Dwight D Eisenhower', 'Union of South Africa', or 'Bittern' all of which are either in museums or running on the main line today. Only 'Mallard' has a greater claim to fame.

'Silver Link' was a regular performer on the titled trains, and was always one of the best performers of the A4s, for there were considerable differences in that respect. 'Empire of India' was one of the lesser lights for example, and I only ever saw it on freight trains – even then not on the prestigious '266 down'.

The layout of the northern end of Hatfield yard can be seen under the bridge to the rear of the train. The line diverging to the right was a connecting line to St Albans. It was little used, and I believe it was pulled up before the Beeching cuts. It would have been unwise in the extreme for me to have taken a photograph from this location, so I have had to assemble shots taken through both bridges and from over the parapets of the St Albans Road and A1000 bridges to compile enough data for this painting.

This has always been one of my favourite paintings; I think it captures the very essence of these fine racing machines. The title derives from the inevitable shout from the trainspotters whenever an A4 was first sighted: 'It's a streeeeak!!!' There were only 34 of them. I think it was the ambition of every boy I knew in the number collecting fraternity to 'bag' all the streaks. I am sure some of the spotters did, but I was a long way off, as most of the Scottish examples eluded me. I still envy the railway enthusiasts living between Edinburgh and Aberdeen. The early diesels were such a significant failure in that area that the General Manager of the Scottish Region had the initiative, and the courage, to acquire some of the A4s due to be scrapped, and put them to work on the Aberdeen to Edinburgh turns. It was an Indian Summer for those engines, and kept steam alive North of the border until 1966.

I have often been asked which my favourite livery was for these engines. Strangely it is British Railways Green, followed by the original silver of 'Silver Link'. Garter Blue looked better when the red wheels could be seen after the fairings were removed. I never really enjoyed the dark blue used by BR and currently displayed on the preserved 'Sir Nigel Gresley', but worst of all was wartime's unlined black...

I would like to see them all running today, even in unlined black!

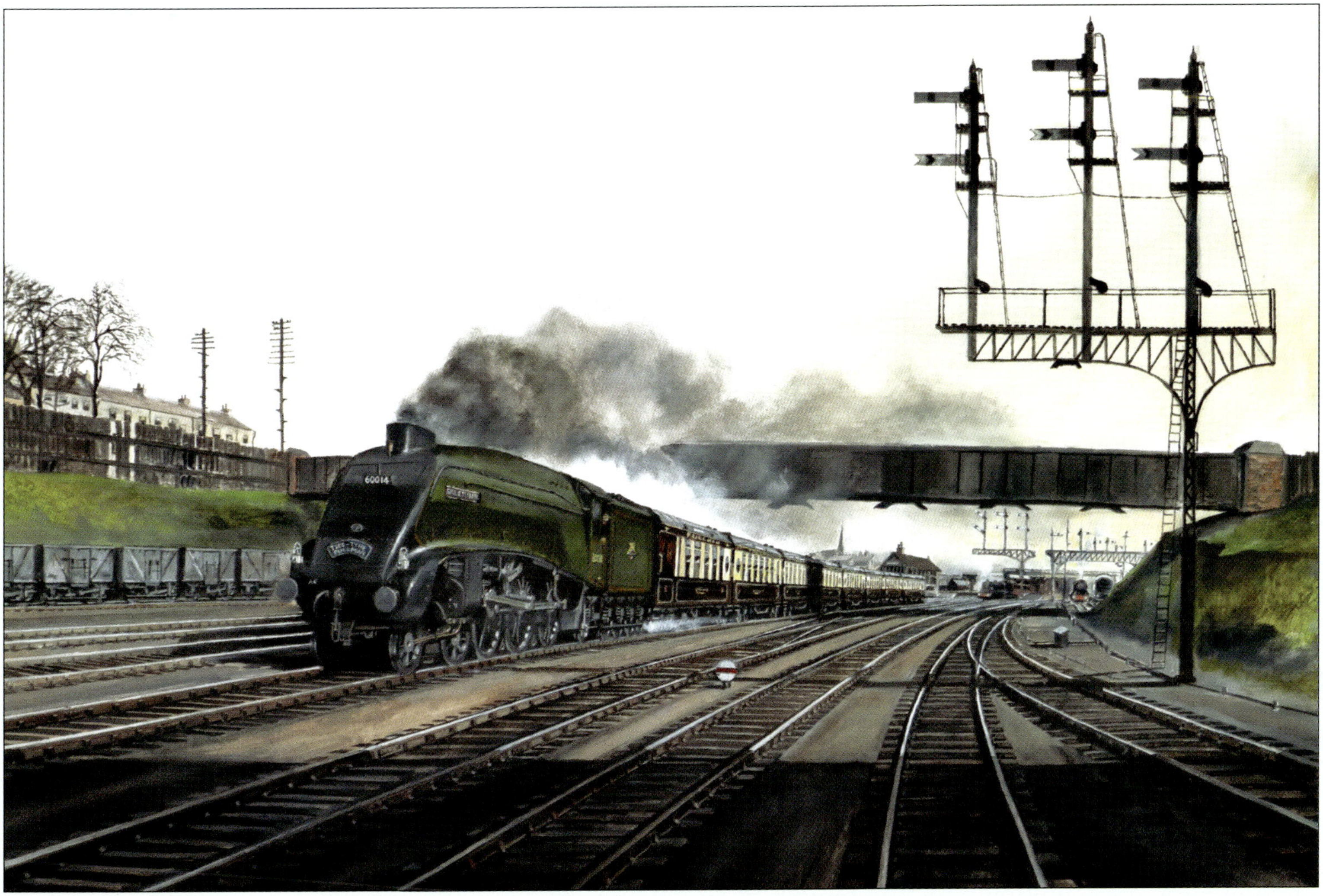
60014

Index of Locations

Beattock 30, 132
Bishops Stortford 13, 36, 114
Bristol 32, 42, 77, 104
Buxton 26

Camden Bank 34, 35, 53
Cannon Street 40, 41
Carlisle 83, 95, 132, 139
Charing Cross 40, 41, 46, 47
Chatham 46, 114, 115
Chilcompton 72, 73
Colwall 106
Cromer 18, 24, 25, 52, 68, 102, 111, 129

Derby 30, 49

Eastleigh 34, 91
Edge Hill 45, 59, 66, 84
Edinburgh 6, 30, 54, 6100, 118, 119, 139

Fort William 62, 82, 124

Grantham 141

Hatfield 7,12, 36, 72, 106, 130, 138
Harringay 128
Hartlepool 130, 131, 132
Hitchin 18, 64
Holt 76, 86
Hornsey 74, 112
Huddersfield 92, 98

Kings Cross 15, 18, 34, 38, 46, 50, 54, 55, 60, 64, 70, 71, 87, 88, 100, 102, 112, 141
Kings Lynn 111

Leeds 97, 98, 99
Liverpool Street 15, 36, 37, 46, 58, 88, 91, 102, 120, 122, 123
Lochinver 18
London 59, 85

Melton Constable 52
Monsal Dale 108,109

Newcastle 50, 99, 100, 101, 102, 130, 132, 136, 137
Newton Abbot 104
Nevada 126
Norwich 36, 52, 68, 69, 86, 102, 103, 120, 123, 129

Old Oak Common 32, 33

Paddington 15, 32, 42, 46, 63, 88, 90, 91, 96, 106

Rannoch Moor 62, 124
Redcar 138
Retford 50, 51
Ribblehead 94, 95
Roughton Road Junction 68, 69
Rugby 22, 23

St Pancras 14, 15, 26, 60, 70, 71, 79, 87, 88, 90, 140
Shap 30, 31, 132
Sheringham 19, 86
Skipton 83
Stewarts Lane 28, 29, 116, 117

Tyneside 99

Victoria 15, 40, 114

Waterloo 40, 88, 89, 102, 114
Warrington 128
West Ruislip 135
Weybourne 80, 81
Wolverhampton 48

York 7, 42, 50, 54, 64, 91, 92, 98, 141, 142